Jill Foulston, a former commissioning editor of the Virago Modern Classics, has also published *The Virago Book of the Joy of Shopping*. She lives in London and Italy.

Also by Jill Foulston

The Virago Book of the Joy of Shopping (editor)

The Virago Book of Food
THE JOY OF EATING
Edited by Jill Foulston

virago

VIRAGO

First published in Great Britain in 2006 by Virago Press
This paperback edition published in 2009 by Virago Press

This selection and introduction copyright © Jill Foulston 2006

Acknowledgements on pp. 395–405 constitute
an extension of this copyright page

The moral right of the editor has been asserted

A CIP catalogue record for this book
is available from the British Library.

ISBN 978-1-86049-905-0

Typeset in Goudy by M Rules
Printed and bound in Great Britain by
Clays Ltd, St Ives plc

Papers used by Virago are natural, renewable and
recyclable products sourced from well-managed forests and certified in
accordance with the rules of the Forest Stewardship Council.

Virago Press
An imprint of
Little, Brown Book Group
100 Victoria Embankment
London EC4Y 0DY

An Hachette UK Company
www.hachette.co.uk

www.virago.co.uk

For Jean Foulston, my mother
and Audrey Bernhard, my grandmother

Cookery means the knowledge of Medea and of Circe and of Helen and of the Queen of Sheba. It means the knowledge of all herbs and fruits and balms and spices, and all that is healing and sweet in the fields and groves and savory in meats. It means carefulness and inventiveness and willingness and readiness of appliances. It means the economy of your grandmothers and the science of the modern chemist; it means much testing and no wasting; it means English thoroughness and French art and Arabian hospitality; and, in fine, it means that you are to be perfectly and always ladies – loaf givers.

—RUSKIN

CONTENTS

INTRODUCTION

We lust after food. We savour it, spurn it, measure it, analyse it. We hoard it, waste it, dream about it. For millennia, we have told our lives through it. In letters, diaries, memoirs, recipes and fiction, we have sought to make sense of this wholly necessary, often ecstatic, sometimes fraught relationship. It is tempting to see food obsessions and anxieties as peculiarly modern, yet if we look at the oldest forms of food writing, and in particular, women's food writing, it is clear that they're not.

Historically, women have always been intimately connected to food – in the most basic sense, women *are* food for their offspring – and an awareness of it infuses all of their writing, regardless of genre. Lovers of food and good food writing all have Jane Grigson, Elizabeth David and Dorothy Hartley on their bookshelves. Yet writers as diverse as Mrs Gaskell, Isabel Allende, Emily Dickinson and Joni Mitchell also dwell on appetites and their satisfaction, in novels, poetry and songs. And who's heard of Madame Wu, Philippine Welser or Encarnación Pinedo – women responsible for some groundbreaking 'firsts' in cookbooks?

One of the richest and earliest sources of information about women's lives is the household book, a kind of hybrid cookbook-cum-diary. The earliest examples in English date from the Middle Ages, and contain recipes, accounts, remedies – even veterinary advice. They were usually handed down from mother to daughter, though often less directly to servants, distant relatives or friends, in much the same way that we exchange recipes with each other today.

The novelist and musicologist Sylvia Townsend Warner, herself a keen cook, left a seventeenth-century manuscript in her possession, 'Elizabeth Segar: Hir Book', to her friend and literary executrix, Susanna Pinney. Its recipes for Dyett Bread and Plague Water are published here for the first time. The form persisted into the nineteenth century, and the most famous example is *Mrs Beeton's Book of Household Management*.

Although Aphra Behn is often cited as the first woman to have earned her living by her pen, her contemporary, Hannah Woolley, probably beat her to it. Woolley's popular and successful cookery and conduct book, *The Gentlewomans Companion or, a Guide to the Female Sex* (1673), is similar in content to a household book, since it includes advice for servants and templates for writing letters alongside the recipes (mostly culled from her earlier books). But this was not the first cookbook, or even the first by a woman (some even question Woolley's authorship of *The Gentlewomans Companion*). Hsiang Ju Lin and Tsuifeng Lin mention one from the Sung dynasty (tenth to thirteenth centuries) by Madame Wu, and the recipes collected by Philippine Welser (1545) may well constitute the first Western European cookbook by a woman. *The Art of Cookery, Made Plain and Easy* (1747), by Hannah Glasse, was the most successful cookbook of the eighteenth century, notwithstanding Dr Johnson's spiteful declaration upon reading it that 'Women can spin very well, but they cannot make a good book on Cookery'. It was closely followed in popularity by *The Experienced English Housekeeper* (1769), the work of Elizabeth Raffald, who found time to write in between bearing fifteen daughters. Englishwoman Eliza Smith was the first to publish a cookbook in the United States, *The Compleat Housewife* of 1758, but it was Amelia Simmons, 'Orphan', who published in 1796 what is now recognised as the first cookbook by an American author. Included in this anthology are other significant early cookbooks within the varied ethnic traditions of the United States. Not a hundred years after Amelia Simmons's *American Cookery*, the former slave and plantation cook Abby Fisher published what was until recently considered the first cookbook by an African American: *What Mrs Fisher Knows about Old Southern Cooking* (Women's Cooperative Printing Office, 1881). '*Aunt Babette's*' *Cook Book* (1889) was an early Jewish collection featuring non-kosher recipes, and Encarnación Pinedo was the first Hispanic to publish a cookbook in the United States, *Encarnación's Kitchen* (*El Cocinero Español*, 1898). When we get to the nineteenth and twentieth centuries, the names become much more familiar.

Cookbooks look back to the household book, and forward to diaries, since women commonly stuff between their leaves inserts pertaining to daily life (such as invitations to birthday parties or programmes for school plays), or write notes in the margins to remind themselves of some unrelated, mundane obligation ('pick up dry-cleaning', 'phone Mum'). We have all discovered the odd second-hand book with a postcard or review clipping in it, and women's cookbooks often function something like kitchen filing cabinets for anything flat: bartered recipes, shopping lists, even unfinished letters. Cookbooks easily reveal as much of our past as photographs or history books: we eat the way we live.

But you don't have to be stirring a pot or turning a spit over an open fire to be concerned with food. You might just be visiting friends or riding your horse. Some of the intrepid early women travellers were particularly attentive to the food they ate. Dorothy Wordsworth's *Grasmere Journal* (1800–03) and her *Recollections of a Tour Made in Scotland* (1803) provide meticulous accounts of the tedious rituals associated with the provision of food at home in the Lake District, and the unusual, sometimes miserable meals she was offered on her travels with her brother William and their friend Coleridge. When she describes something new or especially delicious, Wordsworth's language becomes poetic; yet her accounts of the daily chores of housekeeping are dry and staccato. Before Wordsworth, Celia Fiennes recorded in *Through England on a Side Saddle* (1685–1712) the delights, the peculiarities, even the cost of the food she ate as she travelled through every county in England. In its comprehensiveness, her account is unequalled until the publication of Florence White's *Good Things in England* (1932). White, the first freelance journalist in England to specialise in food, documented and preserved the regional and rural traditions of English cookery, as did Dorothy Hartley, whose *Food in England* (1954) is now a classic. Clementine Paddleford, now piloting her own plane rather than riding a horse, achieved something comparable with *How America Eats* (1961). She famously claimed, in a parody of Brillat-Savarin: 'Tell me where your grandmother came from and I can tell you how many kinds of pie you serve for Thanksgiving.'

Mediaeval housewives Margaret Paston and Jayn Stonor both wrote to travelling male relatives with urgent additions to the shopping list: treacle, in Paston's case, various herbs in Stonor's. Since the ones included here were rarely written with a view to publication (with the possible exception of Lady Mary Wortley Montagu's), letters often unintentionally reveal the centrality of food in women's lives. Here, Colette rhapsodises over the lush plenty of ripe fruit and nuts in the French countryside, while Edith Sitwell despairs of her father's eccentric and inconvenient appetites. In *A Lady's Life in the Rocky Mountains*, Isabella Bird describes for her sister at home in Victorian England the local methods of breadmaking and the reliance on rotting meat and dwindling supplies during the harshest winter she has ever known.

The development of the novel provided women with a new and elastic form for the description of the domestic sphere. Jane Austen, the Brontë sisters, Susan Ferrier and Louisa May Alcott wrote what are now some of the best-known passages in the literature of food – on the horrors of institutional porridge, the delights of picnics and regional specialities. In the twentieth century, Barbara Pym used food to mirror her characters' feelings, and Barbara Comyns wrote an entire novel premised on the idea of food poisoning (*Who Was Changed and Who Was Dead*). Few novelists have described food so cosily, wickedly or erotically as Alice Thomas Ellis, Michèle Roberts and Chitra Banerjee Divakaruni.

We often search for the right book to suit our mood, discarding several before we settle on the perfect one. This anthology caters to every taste. If you are feeling greedy, you have only to turn to Unrestrained

Appetites. Curious? Read The Secrets of Good Housekeeping. If you're single, try Solitary Pleasures, in love – The Food of Love; for armchair travelling, you'll probably enjoy On the Hoof. The scope of most of the categories will, I hope, be obvious.

But what is 'exotic' food? Exoticism lies, like beauty, in the eyes of the beholder, and depends largely on where you stand in time and space. So, for example, the olive oil integral to the preparation of Mediterranean food was, until the Gospel of St Elizabeth (David), unknown or unpalatable to the British, however unthinkable this may be from our current vantage point. Similarly, in Washington, D.C. in early 1942, the anthropologist, Margaret Mead, then Executive Secretary of the National Research Council's Committee on Food Habits, was asked to draw up a list of unusual foods essential to the cultural habits of people from varying ethnic backgrounds. Access to these special foods was considered important to maintaining morale during wartime. And yet most of those foods – bean sprouts (for the Chinese), chili peppers (for Mexicans), dill (Czechs and Poles) and olive oil (Greeks and Italians) – are nowadays widespread in America and Britain; the passage of time has rendered them common rather than exotic. What was deliriously glamorous and exotic to the Fanny Cradock generation of the fifties now seems hopelessly tacky – and in many cases inedible. The exotica in this collection may seem quite ordinary to readers in other times and places.

Far removed from the exotic, or even the ordinary, the selections in Meagre Rations concentrate on opportunities not taken and, in many cases, unavailable. The most disturbing extracts in the book are to be found in this section, which deals with wartime privation and eating disorders. While Joan Wyndham managed to be reasonably jolly, huddling with her neighbours in the bomb shelter and working herself into a kind of 'gastric frenzy' thinking of cheese omelettes and *entrecôte* steak, *In Memory's Kitchen* is a heart-wrenching compilation of recipes longingly recalled by the women incarcerated in the concentration camp at Terezin, in the former Czechoslovakia. The recipes are notable for their contrasts: some are practical, and others completely given over to the fantasy associated with deprivation: 'Rich Chocolate Cake'. At the other end of the spectrum, magic has inspired a section containing not only the literature of make-believe – by E. Nesbit, Frances Hodgson Burnett and J.K. Rowling and others – but also passages expressing astonishment at the transformative power of taste, such as those by Emily Dickinson and Opal Whiteley.

The preparation of food is often considered an art form, and artists themselves often turn out to be foodies. Frida Kahlo's step-daughter describes the meals Kahlo used to prepare for Diego Rivera when he was working in his studio, while the spirited Elisabeth Vigée-Le Brun regales us with tales of her extravagant dinner parties. An American artist in Paris, Cecilia Beaux, examines the dinner she is served in a hotel with a painter's eye for composition. And if Matisse was snubbed by one of Gertrude Stein's cooks, Picasso ate well when Alice B. Toklas was in the kitchen.

Every anthologist has to face the fact that her book cannot be all-inclusive. If I have left out some of the more famous examples of women's food writing – Virginia Woolf's tantalising *boeuf en daube* or Isak Dinesen's sumptuous 'Babette's Feast', to name but two – it is only to offer a taste of other writers less frequently sampled. Selections range from the twelfth-century writings of Hildegard of Bingen to the Pulitzer Prize-winning short stories of Jhumpa Lahiri. Sandwiched in between are references to food from some unexpected sources: Sue Grafton's detective fiction, a letter from the seventeenth-century Mexican nun Sor Juana Inés de la Cruz to the Bishop of Puebla, a health food book by the romantic novelist Barbara Cartland and the diary of Anne Frank.

Yet if I have removed some dishes from the table, I have also tried to serve the freshest, most unusual and delectable fare I could find.

Tuck in.

NOTE: Dates are provided only for authors who are not contemporary.

KITCHENS

BANANA YOSHIMOTO

The place I like best in this world is the kitchen. No matter where it is, no matter what kind, if it's a kitchen, if it's a place where they make food, it's fine with me. Ideally it should be well broken in. Lots of tea towels, dry and immaculate. White tile catching the light (ting! ting!).

I love even incredibly dirty kitchens to distraction – vegetable droppings all over the floor, so dirty your slippers turn black on the bottom. Strangely, it's better if this kind of kitchen is large. I lean up against the silver door of a towering, giant refrigerator stocked with enough food to get through a winter. When I raise my eyes from the oil-spattered gas burner and the rusty kitchen knife, outside the window stars are glittering, lonely.

Kitchen
trans. by Megan Backus

ANGELA CARTER
1940–92

The house was entirely quiet. Melanie decided to adventure downstairs to the kitchen, where she had not been. She wanted to learn the new domestic geography as soon as she could, to find out what lay behind all the doors and how to light the stove and whereabouts the dog slept. To make herself at home. She had to make herself at home, somehow. She could not bear to feel such a stranger, so alien, and somehow so insecure in her own personality, as if she found herself hard to recognise in these new surroundings. She crept down the lino-covered stairs.

The kitchen was quite dark because the blinds were drawn. There was a smell of stale cigarette smoke and some unwashed cups were stacked neatly in the sink, but the room was ferociously clean. It was quite a big room. There was a built-in dresser, painted dark brown, loaded with crockery, a flour jar, a bread-bin. There was a larder you could walk into. Melanie experimentally walked into it and pulled the door to on herself in a cool smell of cheese and mildew. What did they eat? Tins of things; they seemed particularly fond of tinned peaches, there was a whole stack of tins of peaches. Tinned beans, tinned sardines. Aunt Margaret must buy tins in bulk. There were a number of cake tins and Melanie opened one and found last night's currant cake. She took a ready-cut slice of it and ate it. It made her feel more at home, already, to steal something from the larder. She went back into the kitchen, scattering crumbs.

The Magic Toyshop

EMILY BRONTË
1818–48

One step brought us into the family sitting-room, without any introductory lobby or passage: they call it here 'the house' pre-eminently. It includes kitchen and parlor, generally, but I believe at Wuthering Heights the kitchen is forced to retreat altogether into another quarter: at least I distinguished a chatter of tongues, and a clatter of culinary utensils, deep within; and I observed no signs of roasting, boiling, or baking, about the huge fire-place; nor any glitter of copper saucepans and tin cullenders on the walls. One end, indeed, reflected splendidly both light and heat from ranks of immense pewter dishes, interspersed with silver jugs and tankards, towering row after row, in a vast oak dresser, to the very roof. The latter had never been underdrawn: its entire anatomy lay bare to an inquiring eye, except where a frame of wood laden with oatcakes, and clusters of legs of beef, mutton and ham, concealed it. Above the chimney were sundry villanous old guns, and a couple of horse pistols, and, by way of ornament, three gaudily painted canisters disposed along its ledge. The floor was of smooth, white stone: the chairs, high-backed, primitive structures, painted green: one or two heavy black ones lurking in the shade. In an arch under the dresser, reposed a huge, liver-coloured bitch pointer, surrounded by a swarm of squealing puppies, and other dogs haunted other recesses.

Wuthering Heights

BARBARA COMYNS
1909–92

During the Second World War, Comyns moved to the country to escape the Blitz. There she wrote her first book, Sisters by a River, *based on her Warwickshire childhood. Her publisher chose not to correct her spelling and punctuation and even added to her eccentric mistakes.*

Our kitchen had a dusty hot cross bun hanging from the ceiling, every good Friday they put up a new one, the old one turned into a kind of mummy, there were hams hanging up too and a side of bacon, Palmer cured the pigs in the saddle room in a large zinc trough, the maids said you mustn't watch him if you had a period or the hams would get bewitched and go all wrong, Mammy said this too. There were three kitchens altogether, all leading out of each other, they had stone floors with wells in the middle, they used to have their meals in the hot cross bun kitchen because there was a huge Eagle range there which heated the water and did the cooking, once a rat fell down the chimney right into the porrage, I've never eaten any since because it always seems to smell ratty.

We liked having tea with the maids, they gave us biscuits floating in our cups of tea and they always eat heaps of vinager, after tea they used to sing, songs about dark eyed lovers, they always sounded like hymns.

Sisters by a River

DOROTHY WORDSWORTH
1771–1855

Friday, August 19th

The servant at Brownhill was a coarse-looking wench, barefoot and bare-legged. I examined the kitchen round about; it was crowded with furniture, drawers, cupboards, dish-covers, pictures, pans, and pots, arranged without order, except that the plates were on shelves, and the dish-covers hung in rows; these were very clean, but floors, passages, staircase, everything else dirty. There were two beds in recesses in the wall; above one of them I noticed a shelf with some books: – it made me think of Chaucer's Clerke of Oxenforde:—

> 'Liever had he at his bed's head
> Twenty books clothed in black and red.'

They were baking oat-bread, which they cut into quarters, and half-baked over the fire, and half-toasted before it. There was a suspiciousness about Mrs. Otto, almost like ill-nature; she was very jealous of any inquiries that might appear to be made with the faintest idea of a comparison between Leadhills and any other place, except the advantage was evidently on the side of Leadhills. We had nice honey to breakfast.

Recollections of a Tour Made in Scotland

LUCY LARCOM
1824–93

*Though known mainly for her hymns, the American writer
Lucy Larcom also published a childhood memoir which has become
a classic of its kind.*

Primitive ways of doing things had not wholly ceased during my childhood; they were kept up in these old towns longer than elsewhere. We
used tallow candles and oil lamps, and sat by open fireplaces. There was
always a tinder-box in some safe corner or other, and fire was kindled by
striking flint and steel upon the tinder. What magic it seemed to me,
when I was first allowed to strike that wonderful spark, and light the
kitchen fire!

The fireplace was deep, and there was a 'settle' in the chimney
corner, where three of us youngest girls could sit together and toast our
toes on the andirons (two Continental soldiers in full uniform, march-
ing one after the other), while we looked up the chimney into a square
of blue sky, and sometimes caught a snow-flake on our foreheads; or
sometimes smirched our clean aprons (high-necked and long-sleeved
ones, known as 'tiers') against the swinging crane with its sooty pot-
hooks and trammels.

The coffee-pot was set for breakfast over hot coals, on a three-legged
bit of iron called a 'trivet.' Potatoes were roasted in the ashes, and the
Thanksgiving turkey in a 'tin-kitchen,' the business of turning the spit
being usually delegated to some of us small folk, who were only too willing to burn our faces in honor of the annual festival.

There were brick ovens in the chimney corner, where the great bak-
ings were done; but there was also an iron article called a 'Dutch oven,'
in which delicious bread could be baked over the coals at short notice.
And there never was anything that tasted better than my mother's 'fire-
cake,' – a short-cake spread on a smooth piece of board, and set up with
a flat-iron before the blaze, browned on one side, and then turned over
to be browned on the other. (It required some sleight of hand to do
that.) If I could only be allowed to blow the bellows – the very old

people called them 'belluses' – when the fire began to get low, I was a happy girl.

Cooking-stoves were coming into fashion, but they were clumsy affairs, and our elders thought that no cooking could be quite so nice as that which was done by an open fire. We younger ones reveled in the warm, beautiful glow, that we look back to as to a remembered sunset. There is no such home-splendor now.

When supper was finished, and the tea-kettle was pushed back on the crane, and the backlog had been reduced to a heap of fiery embers, then was the time for listening to sailor yarns and ghost and witch legends. The wonder seems somehow to have faded out of those tales of eld since the gleam of red-hot coals died away from the hearthstone. The shutting up of the great fireplaces and the introduction of stoves marks an era; the abdication of shaggy Romance and the enthronement of elegant Commonplace – sometimes, alas! the opposite of elegant – at the New England fireside.

A New England Girlhood

ANNE HUGHES
18th century

Original documents recording the lives of early modern women are extremely rare, so there is some doubt about the authenticity of the diary from which this extract is taken. Real or fake, it is an entertaining account of country life.

She didde tell mee off a cooken grate that does hav an oven toe bake att its side, wyke doe open wyth a lidde were thee cakes and mete can be cooked, but I doute mee iff it bee off any use. I doe not thynk itt woulde doe soe well as mye bigge oven were I doe make my bredde, so shall nott worritt John to get me one.

The Diary of a Farmer's Wife, 1796–97

KINTA BEEVOR
1911–95

Kinta grew up in a castle in a remote part of Tuscany. Her memoir lovingly recalls the local foods she enjoyed.

Agostino's kitchen, with all its subsidiary rooms such as the cold-store and larder, was on the first floor. A service lift to a pantry below formed the key link to the dining-room. The kitchen took up most of the north side of the house, with the square tower above used mainly as a store-room. Kitchens were traditionally installed upstairs in Florentine villas so that the smell of cooking did not enter the reception rooms and main bedrooms on the ground floor. I often used to climb the stone staircase to Agostino's domain. On one occasion, I heard curious slithering and clattering noises coming down towards me: I looked up and saw an escaped lobster. It made me feel a little like Alice in Wonderland . . .

The *dispensa*, or larder, was a gastronomic Aladdin's cave. Rows of jars contained preserves in every form: dried tomatoes, tomatoes in oil and artichokes in oil (*sott' olio*), pickled vegetables, capers, pine nuts, breadcrumbs, juniper berries for ground game and saffron for risotto. There was also a large terracotta jar full of olives . . .

I particularly remember Agostino's *involtini di vitello* – little rolls of veal with thin slices of *prosciutto* or *mortadella* inside, speared with toothpicks. (My greatest cooking disaster in later life was to replicate this in England using toothpicks purchased from the chemist. They turned out to have been medicated.) Trout, basted with oil and herbs, were grilled over a very low woodfire, and chicken or rabbit on the mechanical rotisserie. Simplicity of this order was no hardship. Agostino's greatness as a chef lay in dishes that managed to be both simple and exquisite.

His antipasti, mainly vegetables fried in Poggio's purest olive oil, were so delicate and delicious that you wanted to go on eating them throughout the meal. These included the flowers of zucchini fried in a batter so light that you were hardly aware of its existence; slices of

fennel in batter served with pesto or lemon; *frittate* of cardoons or artichoke; asparagus served in half a dozen ways, such as *alla Parmigiana*,
grilled with cheese; *alla'Italiana*, with coddled eggs and cream; and *ai
gamberi*, with prawns and a lemon mayonnaise. Sometimes he served
crostini di fegatini – minced chicken livers with herbs on fried bread, or
a *risotto ai carciofi* (with artichokes), or a *risotto toscana* (with mushrooms), or a *soufflé ai piselli* made with the freshest peas from the garden.

Agostino's *dolci* reduced everyone to silent ecstasy. They included
nocciola, pounded hazelnuts with egg and cream; *biscuit* made with
amaretti, eggs and cream; chocolate mousses surrounded by boudoir
biscuits dipped in brandy; and curled wafer biscuits filled with cream.

A Tuscan Childhood

DOROTHY HARTLEY
1892–1985

Hartley's magnificent Food in England *documents and preserves
rural customs and the traditional recipes associated with the cooking
of previous generations. First published in* 1954, *it is still in print.*

My first kitchen was a stone-floored cottage in the Yorkshire dales. It
had a thick rag rug on the hearth and a ceiling rack that held thin
brown oatcake. When soft and newly made, the oatcake hung in loops,
which later dried out stiff and brittle. The stone slab where it was baked
made a little separate hearth at one side of the fireplace. The high
mantelpiece had a polished gun over it, and on it two china dogs and
brass ornaments. The window, almost blocked by red geraniums in
flower-pots, was set deep in the thick stone wall; and most of the light
came through an open door that gave onto the moor. Fresh mountain
air and the smell of cooking always filled this brightly polished kitchen.
I can remember a basin of mutton broth with a long-boned chop in it.
A man reached up to lift down a flap of oatcake to crumble into the
broth, and I remember the warm, safe feel of the big sheepdog I leant
against. I remember, too, being carried high on the farmhand's shoulder,

and feeling him drop down and rise up as he picked white mushrooms out of the wet grass. Once a week a wagonette ran to Skipton to take people to market.

My next kitchen was in a convent of French nuns at Skipton. It had a high ceiling and a sense of space and peace. The wooden tables were scoured white as bone, scrubbed along the grain with sharp river sand and whitening. The wide range shone like satin; the steel fender and stands were rubbed bright with emery cloth. In the wintry sunshine brass pans and silver dishcovers glittered on the cream plaster walls. To prevent clogs slipping the flags were lightly sanded, and the hearthstone was white as drifted snow. At one side of the fireplace stood an iron coffee-grinder; at the other sat a black-gowned little Sister, with white coif and blue apron, slicing vegetables, her clogs laid beside her and her white-stockinged feet on the rolled-back hearthrug . . .

My largest kitchen, masculine and enterprising, was at a boys' school. Being 'northern' the bread was homemade, rising each week in a huge tub set before the fire. Piles of Yorkshire teacakes came daily from the baker, and a new gas-stove supplemented the oven range. It was here I first realised the specialities of England, for my enterprising mother sent away to her Welsh home for small Welsh mutton, as she thought the large Yorkshire sheep very coarse. We had bilberries from the mountains in leaking purple crates. From the east coast came barrels of herrings and boxes of bloaters, and cream cakes in wooden shelved hampers from 'Buzzards of London'. Apples came from Gloucestershire, and cream, in hygienic containers that weighed a ton, from Devon. From the north came sacks of oatmeal. Oxfordshire sent crates of wonderful fruit, Moorpark apricots, and apricot hams. The beef was local: all the pressed beef and brawn moulds were learned in that kitchen and are genuine Yorkshire recipes from the dale farms.

Food in England

ELIZABETH EHRLICH

My immigrants, the grandmothers, kept kosher kitchens. They had dairy spatulas and meat spatulas, and they always knew which were which. They had enamel pots, *milikhdike*, for creamy fish soup, and wooden bowls to chop liver, and glasses for tea. They rendered chicken fat in one pan and fried cheese blintzes in another. They had dishtowels trimmed in blue to dry plates after blintzes, and red-bordered towels to dry after meat.

My father's mother had six sets of dishes. Behind the glass breakfront she stored the yellow scallop-edged crockery, with its frieze of burnt-orange blossoms, dishes that cried out for oatmeal with whole milk, potatoes with butter, and coffee ice-cream. She had everyday meat things and the good meat dishes, for Sabbath and holidays during the year.

She had Passover dishes, *milkhik* and *fleyshik*, and also the grand Passover dinner set. These were white bone china edged with a thick band of gold. The platters, gravy boat, soup tureen, and covered vegetable dishes had dressy gold handles. They never held dairy, but were dedicated to meat. Nor had one crumb of bread ever touched them, only the Passover matzo of her Seder meals.

The dairy silverware lived in a red-handled drawer in the tin-topped kitchen table. The Passover dishes were stored in the basement fifty-one weeks of the year. She had blue glass bowls in the shape of fish, in which nothing but freshly cooked, pink, lemony applesauce was served. So expertly was that applesauce heaped that it rose in a convex meniscus above the bowls' edges, and yet not a drop ever spilled.

Glass can be used for meat or dairy. Glass is *pareve*. You'll want a few glass things in a kosher kitchen.

There is a heightened sense of reality in a kosher kitchen. You have to think about where your food comes from, at least somewhat, at least slightly. You need awareness in a kosher kitchen. You draw lines, and say, Some things I will not eat. You set limits on appetite. That seems to me not a bad thing, but of value in a society bloated with excess.

You don't keep kosher for heightened awareness. Keeping kosher is in the Torah. It's an obligation. It's not an opinion.

It's discipline, a kosher kitchen. It is an encompassing way of life, in which discipline and meaning, the mundane and the spiritual, are inextricably tied. You are only washing your dishes, but you are doing something more. You are tending something ancient, and it matters. That meat knife matters. Your work matters.

Zen tea-making must be something like this.

I think my grandmothers knew their work mattered. They knew they were bringing forth more food from their kitchens. They cooked twenty-one meals a week, fifty-two weeks a year, all their adult lives. On the menu, however, were other things too: history, tradition, community connection, anger, humor, and just about anything else worth conveying. I sat there fiddling with the silverware drawer in the kitchen table. They served me emotion and substance on a dairy plate.

You don't keep kosher to honor emotion, or even for history's sake. You do it to keep a commandment. You shouldn't romanticize. Do you even believe in commandments?

It's a lot of work. It's a real pain. Who wants a kosher kitchen?

I do. I mean I might. I'm thinking maybe I'll try.

Miriam's Kitchen

LILY PRIOR

La cucina is the heart of the *fattoria*, and has formed the backdrop to the lives of our family, the Fiores, as far back as, and further than, anyone can remember. This kitchen has witnessed our joys, griefs, births, deaths, nuptials, and fornications for hundreds of years.

Even now the ghosts of our forebears gather in the kitchen, sitting around like old friends, participating in discussions and passing judgment on the activities of the living.

La cucina bears the scents of its past, and every event in its history is recorded with an olfactory memorandum. Here vanilla, coffee, nutmeg, and confidences; there the milky-sweet smell of babies, old leather, sheep's cheese, and violets. In the corner by the larder hangs the stale tobacco smell of old age and death, while the salty scent of lust and satiation clings to the air by the cellar steps along with the aroma of soap, garlic, beeswax, lavender, jealousy, and disappointment.

La Cucina

COLETTE ROSSANT

I spent a lot of time with Ahmet in the kitchen despite my grandmother's admonition that this was not the place for *une jeune fille de bonne famille*. The kitchen was very large, with two windows overlooking the back garden. There was a wide, deep stone sink with a copper faucet, and a large counter with bowls of limes and lemons and jars of spices. On the floor near the window were 'primus' kerosene burners on which most of the cooking was done. A large refrigerator dominated the corner of the kitchen, and on the opposite corner was a large gas oven for baking. Near the counter were a couple of high stools where I would often sit watching Ahmet prepare lunch or dinner, or just put up pickles for the family . . .

Every year around April, a drama would unfold in our household: Ahmet would announce that it was time for him to go to Upper Egypt and visit his wife. Life in our house would be turned upside down. I can still hear my grandmother's high-pitched voice trying to convince Ahmet that he should try not to have any more children. Ahmet would smile at her mockingly and say, *'Insha Allah!'* ('God bless!'). After all, she had had nine children of her own! My grandmother would take over the kitchen with Aishe and the chauffeur, Hassan, as her helpers . . .

I was allowed in the kitchen to watch Grandmaman prepare her delicious *sambusaks*, and I was also allowed to knead the dough. The mixture was warm, and I loved putting my hands in the middle of it. She would roll the dough thin, cut it into rounds with a Turkish coffee cup, and create half-moons filled with the cheese stuffing. While the *sambusaks* were baking, my cousins would slowly drift into the kitchen, but if Grandmaman called upon them to help, they would all disappear until the *sambusaks* were brought to the terrace. I also helped her make stuffed cabbage, learning to stuff the blanched leaves with the ground beef and rice and transform them into a large cabbage. When Ahmet returned from his trip, Grandmaman could not hide her pleasure at seeing him again. She would greet him like an old friend, ask about his wife and children, and then immediately order dinner . . .

Almost thirty years after leaving Egypt, I finally returned to Cairo with my husband and son. Our first stop was the house in Garden City. My grandparents had long since died, and my uncles and aunts had moved away – but the house was still there. I peered through the black gate into a mostly decrepit garden and spied the flourishing mango tree. My heart beat furiously as I rang the bell. A tall, handsome Arab, wearing a long robe and a white turban around his head, appeared. In faltering Arabic I told him that I had once lived in the house with my grandparents. He suddenly tapped his fingers over his lips and made a high-pitched cry. 'I am Abdullah, Ahmet's son,' he explained. 'You came back! I knew you would! *Al-hamd-lil-lah!* (Praise Allah!)' The next morning we met in a café, and Abdullah told me that his father had returned to his village in Upper Egypt when my grandparents died and that the house had been sold by my uncles. Abdullah had married, had two grown sons, and was now the guardian of the property. We lingered over strong coffee and shared memories of the tastes and smells of his father's kitchen.

Apricots on the Nile: A Memoir with Recipes

CAROLINE B. KING
1871–1947

Sometimes, on my very busiest days, my bandbox kitchen all set for a morning of intensive baking, scientifically correct beaters and mixers and regulators just awaiting the flick of my finger to be at their whirling and whizzing, and time altogether too precious to be spent daydreaming – sometimes, on just such a morning, a whiff of heliotrope sweetness from the vanilla bottle or a breath of oriental fragrance from a spice can will send me far, far away. In a trice I'm back in the familiar casual old kitchen of my childhood, beating eggs on a huge cracked turkey platter, or measuring sugar or flour in a gigantic coffee cup which, having lost its handle, is no longer fit to appear in the polite society of the breakfast table.

It's a bustling place, that shabby, cozy old kitchen of ours, on a morning like this, and a fascinating place, too, even for a girl of twelve or thereabouts. There in the place of honor stands the chief actor in the morning's affairs, the heavy iron stove beaming under its coat of fresh polish which Anna, our hired girl, has applied by dint of elbow grease. Anna's strong hands have also brought the sheaf of nickel-plated calla lilies which decorates the oven door to a state of dazzling splendor, raked the ashes from the grate, and coaxed the fire to that glowing complexion which to Mother means a 'steady oven,' just right for the generous cakes and loaves that will shortly be entrusted to its keeping.

Anna at the kitchen sink, washing endless pans and bowls, spoons and forks, is sturdy, red-armed, and pleasant of countenance. She is at peace with the whole world, as well she may be, having finished a bountiful breakfast that ended with twelve whacking pancakes steeped in fresh butter and brown-sugar sirup. Furthermore, she is already enjoying in anticipation the surreptitious tastes and occasional licking of bowls and mixing spoons when the cakemaking begins in good earnest. No matter how many times she may have to empty and refill her dishpan, or how many times she will have to scour with soap and sand, the old black iron sink and the pine drainboards that flank it, Anna is happy. Saturday is her big day, beginning with her early morning struggle with kindling wood and coal hod, and ending only when the mountains of supper dishes, washed, rinsed and polished with snowy, sweet-smelling towels, are set away in their own special cupboards, and she and Henry, or whatever the current hired man's name may be, take the old Democrat wagon and set out for Anna's home on Clybourne Avenue. It is usually Sunday morning before they return, for the evening is bound to close with a dance and Anna arrives home, worn but jubilant, her shoes dangling over her arms from their long laces, to rake ashes, polish the stove, and begin breakfast preparations.

I can't picture the old kitchen without seeing Anna, perennially young and blossomy, washing dishes at the kitchen sink, or scrubbing the immaculate white pine table, Mother's pride and our vexation, for never a drop of any soilful thing must mar its dazzling purity. Candy pulls, Halloween frolics, even the spreading of jelly on slices of bread, were taboo, if in any way the cherished table must be involved. But Anna often washed the supper dishes on its spotless surface, especially if we youngsters could be coaxed by promises of fairy tales to help dry them, for the table, being of noble proportions, afforded space for several helpers to set cups and plates as they were finished. To us Anna was Grimm Brothers, Hans Christian Andersen, and half a dozen other famous storytellers rolled into one. Her glowing descriptions of kings' palaces and queens' gowns make me realize now what a marvelous decorator or *couturière* was lost to the world when Anna decided to go to work in Mother's kitchen.

Victorian Cakes: A Reminiscence with Recipes

CLEMENTINE PADDLEFORD
1900–67

Known in 1960 as 'America's Number One Food Editor', Clementine Haskin Paddleford travelled thousands of miles in order to document the regional culinary habits of her country. In her masterpiece she asks: 'How does America eat? She eats on the fat of the land. She eats in every language.' Paddleford learned to pilot her own plane in order to speed up her research, criss-crossing the United States and the Atlantic.

One can't talk about cooking in Florida and overlook our modern gypsy queens who cook in trailer kitchens. Trailer parks cover hundreds of acres and each park is a model town in itself with a manager-mayor, recreation hall, garden club, swimming pool.

How do these trailer cooks cook? With a bit of conniving, it was arranged for me to visit with the women in the Bell Haven Park in north-western Miami.

I couldn't believe my eyes! No wonder two million Americans have adopted the mobile way of life. I don't know what I expected to see, certainly not three-legged gypsy pots over open fires. Yet not what I saw – efficient, compact little kitchens designed for easy cooking, for effortless work. Most of the trailers I looked into, half a hundred at least, have automatic dishwashers, garbage disposers, eye-level ovens, double sinks, huge refrigerators, automatic washing machines. Trailer cooks have it better than kitchenette cooks. But like the gypsies of old, one-dish meals are preferred, done top-stove or in the oven depending on the weather.

First stop was to visit park manager Frederick J. Bird and his wife Selma. They lived in a thirty-six foot cruiser – three rooms, over seven feet wide, wall to wall; two porch enclosures, north side, south side. Spaciousness is the first impression on entering the living room, efficiency next, then the luxuriousness of the furnishings. There were wall-to-wall carpet, built-in television, radio, foldaway tables, comfortable sofa, easy chairs, complete electrical equipment including air conditioner.

But I came to see the kitchen. Mrs. Bird stood in the center of her workroom and pivoted a half turn in each direction to show me that she could reach sink, range, refrigerator, work counter and cupboards and never take a step. 'No bend, no stoop, no squat,' she said. Mrs. Bird had a job in the city, so like any career woman, she planned supper menus that get together in a jiffy. Her Sunday dinners are more elaborate. A favorite is a three-dish meal: fried chicken, scalloped potatoes, this from her Norwegian mother, and a green vegetable salad. Fresh fruit for dessert; add a beverage and dinner is served.

How America Eats

THE SECRETS OF GOOD
HOUSEKEEPING

SOR JUANA INÉS DE LA CRUZ
1648–95

Sor Juana was a seventeenth-century Mexican nun and poet. This extract is taken from a reply she made to the Bishop of Puebla after he tricked her into publishing a theological dispute – he prefaced her writings with a letter in which he posed as a 'Sor Philothea', and printed them. In addition to unchaste love poetry, Sor Juana compiled a book of recipes, Libro de Cocina, *while she was at the Convent of San Jerónimo. She died of the plague in 1695 after nursing her fellow nuns.*

What could I not tell you, my Lady, of the secrets of Nature which I have discovered in cooking! That an egg hangs together and fries in fat or oil, and that, on the contrary, it disintegrates in syrup. That, to keep sugar liquid, it suffices to add the tiniest part of water in which a quince or some other tart fruit has been. That the yolk and white of the same egg are so different in nature, that when eggs are used with sugar, the yolks must be used separately from the whites, never together with them. I do not wish to tire you with such trivia, which I relate only to give you a full picture of my native turn of mind, which will, no doubt, make you laugh. But, Madam, what is there for us women to know, if not bits of kitchen philosophy? As Lupercio Leonardo said: One can perfectly well philosophize while cooking supper. And I am always saying, when I observe these small details: If Aristotle had been a cook, he would have written much more.

A Sor Juana Anthology
trans. by Alan S. Trueblood

ELIZA SMITH
18th century

Though it wasn't written there, the 1742 Williamsburg edition of
The Compleat Housewife *is nevertheless the first cookbook to have
been printed in the United States. An earlier London edition of 1739
was the first book to use the word 'Applesauce' in print.*

That Esau was the first Cook, I shall not presume to assert; for Abraham
gave Orders to dress a fatted Calf; but Esau is the first Person mentioned
that made any Advances beyond plain Dressing, as Boiling, Roasting,
&c. For tho' we find, indeed, that Rebecca, his Mother, was accomplished with the Skill of making savoury Meat as well as he, yet whether
he learned it from her, or she from him, is a question too knotty for me
to determine.

But Cookery did not long remain a bare Piece of Housewifery, or
Family Oeconomy; but in Process of Time, when Luxury entered the
World, it grew to an Art, nay a Trade: For in 1 Sam viii. 13. when the
Israelites grew Fashionists, and would have a King, that they might be
like the rest of their neighbours, we read of Cooks, Confectioners, &c.

This Art being of universal Use, and in constant Practice, has been
ever since upon the Improvement; and we may, I think, with good
Reason believe it is arrived at its greatest height and Perfection, if it is
not got beyond it, even to its Declension; for whatsoever new, upstart,
out-of-the-way Messes some Humourists have invented, such as stuffing
a roasted Leg of Mutton with pickled Herring, and the like, are only the
Sallies of a capricious Appetite, and debauching rather than improving
the Art itself.

The Compleat Housewife

HANNAH GLASSE
1708–70

A dressmaker to the Princess of Wales, Glasse authored what was probably the bestselling cookery book of the eighteenth century, The Art of Cookery, Made Plain and Easy *(1747), shamelessly borrowing most of her recipes from other sources.* The Art of Cookery *contains one of the first references to Indian curry in an English cookbook. Fanny Cradock introduced a 1971 facsimile edition.*

If I have not wrote in the high polite style, I hope I shall be forgiven; for my intention is to instruct the lower sort, and therefore must treat them in their own way. For example, when I bid them lard a fowl, if I should bid them lard with large lardoons, they would not know what I meant; but when I say they must lard with little pieces of bacon, they know what I mean. So in many other things in Cookery, the great cooks have such a high way of expressing themselves, that the *poor girls* are at a loss to know what they mean: and in all *Receipt Books* yet printed, there are such an odd jumble of things as would quite spoil a *good dish*; and indeed some things so extravagant, that it would be almost a shame to make use of them, when a *dish* can be made full as good, or better, without them. For example: when you entertain ten or twelve people, you shall use for a cullis, a leg of veal and a ham; which, with the other ingredients, makes it very expensive, and all this only to mix with other sauce. And again, the essence of ham for sauce to *one dish*; when I will prove it, for about three shillings I will make as rich and high a sauce as all that will be, when done.

The Art of Cookery, Made Plain and Easy

ISABELLA BEETON
1836–65

NAMES OF ANIMALS SAXON, AND OF THEIR FLESH NORMAN

The names of all our domestic animals are of Saxon origin; but it is curious to observe that Norman names have been given to the different sorts of flesh which these animals yield. How beautifully this illustrates the relative position of Saxon and Norman after the Conquest. The Saxon hind had the charge of tending and feeding the domestic animals, but only that they might appear on the table of his Norman lord. Thus 'ox,' 'steer,' 'cow,' are Saxon, but 'beef' is Norman; 'calf' is Saxon, but 'veal' Norman; 'sheep' is Saxon, but 'mutton' Norman; so it is severally with 'deer' and 'venison,' 'swine' and 'pork,' 'fowl' and 'pullet.' 'Bacon,' the only flesh which, perhaps, ever came within his reach, is the single exception.

Mrs Beeton's Book of Household Management

JULIANNE BELOTE

This faux-colonial cookbook, an amusing compendium of remedies, food lore, recipes and tips on household management, was published two years before the American bicentennial.

How we all must regret to hear some Persons, even of Quality say, 'pray carve up that Hen,' or 'halve that Plover' not considering how indiscreetly they talk. These are the proper Terms:

cut up a turky
rear a goose
unbrace a Mallard or duck
unlace a coney
wing a partridge or quail
allay a pheasant
dismember a hern

thigh a woodcock
display a crane
lift a swan

The Compleat American Housewife 1776

CHITRITA BANERJI

HOW BIG IS THE DIFFERENCE BETWEEN SITTING AND STANDING?
A cultural universe, when you examine posture in the context of food preparation. In the kitchens of the West, the cook stands at a table or counter and uses a knife. But mention a kitchen to a Bengali, or evoke a favorite dish, and more often than not an image will surface of a woman seated on the floor, cutting, chopping, or cooking. In the Indian subcontinent, especially in its eastern region of Bengal (comprising the Indian state of West Bengal and the country of Bangladesh), this is the typical posture. For centuries, the Bengali cook and her assistant have remained firmly grounded on the kitchen floor, a tradition reflecting the paucity of furniture inside the house. A bed for both sleeping and sitting was usually the most important piece of furniture, but outside the bedroom people sat or rested on mats spread out on the floor, or on squares of carpet called *asans*. In the kitchen they often sat on small rectangular or square wooden platforms called *pinris* or *jalchoukis*, which raised them an inch or so above the floor.

From this closeness to the earth evolved the practice of sitting down both to prepare and to cook food. Enter the *bonti*, a protean cutting instrument on which generations of Bengali women have learned to peel, chop, dice, and shred. Despite the recent incursion of knives, peelers, graters, and other modern, Western-style kitchen utensils, the *bonti* is still alive and well in the rural and urban kitchens of Bengal . . .

As with any implement with a long history, this tool is endowed with a wealth of associations reaching far beyond the mundane. Although professional male chefs use the bonti, it is inextricably associated with Bengali women, and the image of a woman seated at her bonti, surrounded by baskets of vegetables, is a cultural icon. Holding the vegetable or fish or meat in both hands and running it into the blade makes the act of cutting a relatively softer, gentler motion than the more masculine gesture of bringing a knife down with force on a hard surface: The food is embraced even as it is dismembered . . .

Bengali literature contains many references to another, less domestic aspect of the woman at the bonti. Recurring images portray her as young and demure, sitting with her head bent, concentrating on her hands as she moves the vegetable or fish toward the lethal blade. Often a married woman is pictured, her head modestly covered with the shoulder end of her sari, whose colorful border frames her face and hair. But the discreet posture and modest covering are a foil for a flirtatious element in extended family life, which offers virtually no privacy. Men – whether a husband or a romantic interest – can expect many eloquent, sidelong glances cast with surreptitious turns of the head as the woman goes about her domestic tasks with the bonti . . .

Despite its long history, it is probably inevitable that in the new global century the bonti will eventually vanish. The kitchens of Bengal are rapidly changing. Knives rather than bontis are becoming the cutting implements of choice. Tables and countertops are triumphing over the floor; chairs, tables, and couches are becoming as integral to the home as its doors and windows. Women no longer live in extended families, nor do their mornings consist of the leisurely ritual of *kutno kota*, when several women worked together, forming a sisterhood of the bonti. Now women are likely to work outside the home, which leaves little time for that kind of domestic fellowship. But for those of us who remember, the bonti will continue to be a potent symbol of multi-faceted femininity.

'The Bengali Bonti'

POPPY CANNON
1907–75

Poppy was born in Cape Town, South Africa, her parents Jews from Lithuania. A copywriter and a food journalist for Mademoiselle and House Beautiful, Ladies' Home Journal and other magazines, she sometimes signed her magazine articles 'Snack'. In 1949, when mixed marriage was still illegal in twenty states, she hooked up with one of the founders of the National Association for the Advancement of Colored People, and together the two planned a study of how African-American cooking had influenced American cuisine. Poppy met Alice B. Toklas in Venice in 1954; they became firm friends and even published a cookbook together. Her trademark was an unashamed amalgamation of high-end and regrettable food: two of her books are Poppy Cannon's Eating European Abroad and at Home and The New New Can-opener Cookbook. Poppy was immensely tall, her height accentuated by the turbans she wore. In the end, she followed Amy Vanderbilt, a contemporary editor at Ladies' Home Journal, in throwing herself out of a window onto Fifth Avenue.

Something new has been added to the age-old saga of good eating. America, never before gastronomically renowned despite its wealth of excellent ingredients, burgeoning larders, fertile farm lands, herds and flocks, has developed epicurean interests – but with a difference. Our cooking ideas and ideals have their roots in many lands and cultures, but our new way of achieving gourmet food can happen only here – in the land of the mix, the jar, the frozen-food package, and the ubiquitous can opener.

At one time a badge of shame, hallmark of the lazy lady and the care-less wife, today the can opener is fast becoming a magic wand, especially in the hands of those brave young women, nine million of them (give or take a few thousand here and there), who are engaged in frying as well as bringing home the bacon.

There has developed among them a pride in preparing and serving interesting meals. It is no longer considered chic, charming, or 'intellectual' to be ignorant in the kitchen, but always there is the problem of time, the crowding of many varied interests.

To the rescue comes the manufacturer of so-called ready-to-serve foods. Actually, at least in gourmet terms, they are not *quite* ready to serve, but they do provide the basis for any number of prideful, even complicated, specialties. The modern cook looks at it this way: other people have the responsibility for the selection of my raw materials, the cleaning and preliminary preparation. When I ply my busy little can opener, I move onto the scene the way a chef comes in after a corps of kitchen helpers has done the scullery chores – the drudgery of cooking. Armed with a can opener, I become the artist-cook, the master, the creative chef.

The New New Can-opener Cookbook

CAROLYN KEENE
20th century

Under the pseudonym of Carolyn Keene, Mildred Wirt Benson wrote twenty-three of the first twenty-five books in this ever popular girl-detective series devised by Edward Stratemeyer, but the fact was kept from public knowledge for over fifty years, coming to light only when Benson testified in a 1980s' court case. The Nancy Drew Cookbook postdates Benson's influence, but reflects the style of the books she wrote.

Late one afternoon Nancy was hurriedly called to the home of Mrs. Russo, a neighbor, to help her find a valuable heirloom ring. The piece was strangely missing just before she was to give it to her niece at a birthday dinner party. No one else had been in the house all day. Mrs. Russo, who had selected the ring from her jewel box that morning, was positive she had not worn it in the kitchen while preparing dinner.

Nancy, however, refused to overlook a single possibility. After Mrs. Russo had gone upstairs to dress, Nancy began a search. She figured that if the woman had unknowingly dropped the ring into some food she was preparing, it would have sunk to the bottom. First Nancy examined the aspic salad, then the cream of mushroom soup. No ring! Next she looked at the blueberry muffins, still in their twelve-cup pan.

'If the ring's in a muffin,' she thought, 'it would have been spooned up last, so the jewelry would be in one of the end cups.'

Nancy began to break open the muffins. No luck on one, two, three. Then she halved the fourth.

The next moment she cried out, and raced up the stairs. 'Mrs. Russo, the ring was in a muffin! Your gift is safe!' As the woman thanked Nancy profusely, the girl added with a smile, 'How about my whipping up another batch of muffins for your party?'

The Nancy Drew Cookbook: Clues to Good Cooking

VICTORIA GRANOF

Un pizzico qua, un pizzico là. A pinch here, a dash there. Sicilians cook by instinct. No one is chained to a measuring cup. Yes, grams and liters are used in recipes, but these are the tools of the novice. One is expected to develop a feel for the ingredients, thereafter measuring them in handfuls and heaps. A *manciata* (handful) is larger than a *pugnietta* (fistful), but the actual amount, of course, varies depending on whose hands are doing the measuring.

When I traveled through Sicily to research this book, I was rarely given a written recipe. 'You must watch me do this,' I was always told. When a recipe was written down, it was sometimes so vague as to be comical. At one pastry shop in Messina, the baker thoughtfully presented me with handwritten instructions for baking *n'zuddi*, crunchy almond cookies flavored with orange. Neither almonds nor oranges were listed in the ingredients! When I asked him about this, the bemused baker replied, 'Well, *of course* there are almonds and orange in the recipe – can't you taste them?' He went on to detail the amounts:

'*Una mucchietta* (a little heap) of almonds.' And the orange? '*Quanto basta.*' The ubiquitous *quanto basta* is my favorite measurement of all – *as much as is enough.* Enough for what? Enough for the dough to feel the way it should. And this, I was told, I would learn to judge accurately as I developed *mani sapienti* – knowledgeable hands.

There is so much talk in America of standardizing recipes, of being *accurate.* Sicilians are amused by the concept of accuracy. 'On a dry day, your flour may want more water, and then what good are those measuring cups, *signorina*? They are made of metal and are not *sensitive.*'

Something to bear in mind is that unlike Americans, who are always trying new recipes, Sicilian cooks may make a handful of recipes in their lifetime – over and over and over. Passed hand-to-hand and rarely written down, these recipes live on in the minds of the recipient, whose job it is to keep the tradition alive.

No wonder the *manciata* is more important than the gram.

Sweet Sicily: The Story of an Island and Her Pastries

FANNIE MERRITT FARMER
1857–1915

From promising student to director of the Boston Cooking School, Fannie Farmer guaranteed her followers reliable results if they followed the precise instructions in her recipes. Because she heralded the move away from a more descriptive type of recipe-writing ('a dash of salt' became a specified quantity) she has been called 'the mother of level measurements'.

Correct measurements are absolutely necessary to insure the best results. Good judgment, with experience, has taught some to measure by sight; but the majority need definite guides.

Tin measuring-cups, divided in quarters or thirds, holding one half-pint, and tea and table spoons of regulation sizes, – which may be bought at any store where kitchen furnishings are sold, – and a case knife, are essentials for correct measurement. Mixing-spoons, which are little larger than tablespoons, should not be confounded with the latter.

MEASURING INGREDIENTS. Flour, meal, powdered and confectioners' sugar, and soda should be sifted before measuring. Mustard and baking-powder, from standing in boxes, settle, therefore should be stirred to lighten; salt frequently lumps, and these lumps should be broken. A *cupful* is measured level. To measure a cupful, put in the ingredient by spoonfuls or from a scoop, round slightly, and level with a case knife, care being taken not to shake the cup. A *tablespoonful is measured level. A teaspoonful is measured level.*

To measure tea or table spoonfuls, dip the spoon in the ingredient, fill, lift, and level with a knife, the sharp edge of knife being toward tip of spoon. Divide with knife lengthwise of spoon, for a half-spoonful; divide halves crosswise for quarters, and quarters crosswise for eighths. Less than one-eighth of a teaspoonful is considered a few grains.

MEASURING LIQUIDS. A cupful of liquid is all the cup will hold.

A tea or table spoonful is all the spoon will hold.

MEASURING BUTTER, LARD, ETC. To measure butter, lard, and other solid fats, pack solidly into cup or spoon, and level with a knife.

When dry ingredients, liquids, and fats are called for in the same recipe, measure in the order given, thereby using but one cup.

The Boston Cooking-School Cook Book

ELIZABETH BISHOP
1911–79

Lines Written in the Fannie Farmer Cookbook
[*Given to Frank Bidart*]
You won't become a *gourmet** cook
By studying our Fannie's book—
Her thoughts on Food & Keeping House
Are scarcely those of Lévi-Strauss.
Nevertheless, you'll find, Frank dear,
The *basic elements*** are here.
And if a problem should arise:
The Soufflé fall before your eyes,
Or strange things happen to the Rice
—You know I *love* to give advice.

Elizabeth
Christmas, 1971

* Forbidden word.
** Forbidden phrase.

P.S. Fannie should not be underrated;
She has become sophisticated.
She's picked up many *gourmet** tricks
Since the edition of '96.
The Complete Poems 1927–1979

JESSIE CONRAD
1873–1936

Her novelist husband introduced Jessie Conrad's rather prim cookbook with the words: 'Good cooking is a moral agent'.

Great care should be taken in the use of an onion. One often finds that if by accident a knife used for cutting an onion has been overlooked and it comes in contact with any article of food the flavour of the onion will spoil everything. It is also a fact that if an onion is cut before it is put into soup or sauce, the soup at once becomes cloudy, while on the other hand if it is merely peeled and put in whole, soup or sauce will remain perfectly clear. Then again for onion sauce or soup which would be made with milk, you must never put in any salt or any other ingredient till *after* the milk has boiled. If the onion is added before, the milk will curdle and be spoilt.

A Handbook of Cookery for a Small House

AMELIA SIMMONS
18th century

Before 1796, all cookbooks published in America were European reprints. Amelia Simmons, who calls herself 'an American orphan' in her preface, was the first to write a distinctly New World cookbook. It sold out almost immediately.

Hares, are white flesh'd and flexible when new and fresh kill'd; if stale, their flesh will have a blackish hue, like old pigeons, if the cleft in her lip spread much, is wide and ragged, she is old; the contrary when young.

Rabbits, the wild are the best, either are good and tender; if old, there will be much yellowish fat about the kidneys, the claws long, wool rough, and mixed with grey hairs; if young the reverse. As to their being fresh, judge by the scent, they soon perish, if trapped or shot, and left in pelt or undress'd; their taint is quicker than veal, and the most sickish in nature; and will not, like beaf or veal, be purged by fire . . .

Cheese—The red smooth moist coated, and tight pressed, square edged Cheese, are better than white coat, hard rinded, or bilged; the inside should be yellow, and flavored to your taste. Old shelves which have only been wiped down for years, are preferable to scoured and washed shelves. Deceits are used by salt-petering the outside, or colouring with hemlock, cocumberries, or safron, infused into the milk; the taste of either supercedes every possible evasion.

Eggs—Clear, thin shelled, longest oval and sharp ends are best; to ascertain whether new or stale—hold to the light, if the white is clear, the yolk regularly in the centre, they are good—but if otherwise, they are stale. The best possible method of ascertaining, is to put them into water, if they lye on their bilge, they are *good* and *fresh*—if they bob up an end they are stale, and if they rise they are addled, proved, and of no use.

Onions—the Medeira white is best in market, esteemed softer flavored, and not so fiery, but the high red, round hard onions are the best; if you consult cheapness, the largest are best; if you consult taste and softness, the very smallest are the most delicate.

American Cookery

S.H. EVARTS
19th century

TO PRESERVE SMOKED MEATS FOR YEARS

How often are we disappointed in our hopes of having sweet hams during the summer? After carefully curing and smoking, and sewing them up in bags, and whitewashing them, we often find that either the fly has commenced a family in our hams, or that the choice parts around the bone are tainted, and the whole spoiled.

Now this can be easily avoided, by packing them in pulverized charcoal. No matter how hot the weather, or how thick the flies, hams will keep as sweet as when packed, for years. The preservative quality of charcoal will keep them till charcoal decays; or sufficiently long to have accompanied Cook three times around the world.

The Economy Cook Book

DELLA LUTES
1872–1942

October days ushered in the cider season and the making of apple butter. Gathering windfalls and seconds into the wagon to be taken to the mill was another of those homely tasks that gave zest to the lives of country folk, for here again you reaped the fruits of your own labor, as when, for instance, you carried your own corn to mill, and took your own meal home for your own johnny-cake. When you ate buckwheat cakes in winter you thought of that hot July Fourth when it had been sown, 'wet or dry.' You smelled the bee-sweet odor of small white orchid-like flowers upheld on their stout, wine-colored stems and heard the hum of a million wings. Like God, you looked back upon your work and called it good. With your pancakes you ate sausage ground from the meat of your own hogs, and on your potatoes milk gravy made after frying salt pork out of your own pork barrel.

When you took apples to the mill you drank what special juice you preferred. My father liked the amber liquid pressed from golden russets, and when he took russet apples to the mill he got russet cider – or he knew the reason why . . .

Apple butter was made, in our house, in a big copper (or brass – I do not remember which) kettle on the back of the stove. Some of our neighbor women made it in a huge iron cauldron in the yard. Not the largest size, in which hogs were scalded at butchering time, but a squat black wench of smaller proportions.

My mother did not make apple butter in large quantity, for my father could not abide it. 'Butter!' he snorted. 'Might 's well call bran mash "butter." If I'm goin' to have butter, I want *butter!*' (And he wanted plenty of it.) 'Don't try to give me no messed-up apple sass and call it *butter!*'

Neither was I enamored of the concoction, so my mother made up but one kettleful, which was preserved in small-sized stone jars with a film of brandy over the top to keep it from spoiling. And she made even this, I think, in order to miss nothing of the continuity in 'pickin' and preservin' ' which ran its course in all good farmhouse kitchens from the time when strawberries ripened straight through to apples.

The Covells, however, made it by gallons and ate it, spread offensively thick, on bread, biscuits, and pancakes.

It was a tedious job, making apple butter, but less so, it seems to me, when brewed out of doors, especially on an October day with the sun beating warmly down upon your neck, and crimson leaves drip, dripping from the maple trees – sometimes straight into the huge pot itself, like some jocose gamester flipping cards into a hat.

But it took time. For instance, you put ten gallons of sweet cider into the cauldron and let it boil away to half. Then you added – a quart or so at a time – three pecks of pared, cored, and quartered apples. This you let cook over a slow fire for four or five hours. Then you added (stirring all the while with a long wooden paddle) ten pounds of sugar and five ounces of cinnamon and boiled it until it thickened, never forgetting to stir, lest it stick to the kettle.

And there you are with your apple butter, and welcome. To be out of doors on an October day with a blue sky overhead, sun on your back, and only the gentle *llp!* with which an autumn leaf breaks its loose hold upon a parent stem to mar the silence, would be a joy under any circumstances – almost. To have to stand and stir, stir, stir, for five, six, or more hours – well, I do not like apple butter anyway.

The Country Kitchen

LADY WINIFRED FORTESCUE
1888–1951

In the 1930s Winifred Fortescue and her husband left England to live amidst the olive groves in Provence. During and after the Second World War, Lady Fortescue's habit of distributing provisions to the poor in her neighbourhood led to her being dubbed 'Maman Noël'.

When the harvest of orange-blossom is plucked and the wild oranges turn golden, everyone picks them for *confiture d'oranges*, a delicious bitter marmalade.

Neighbours this year vied with each other in showering these wild oranges upon us until Emilia, grown desperate, announced her intention of making marmalade at once. From that moment everything in the house became sticky. Emilia and Lucienne were up to the eyes in marmalade. The kitchen table and all that was laid thereon became coated with it. Forks, spoons, and knives stuck to our hands; plates clung to the table-cloth. The smell of cooking oranges pervaded the whole house; every casserole and kitchen vessel was filled with soaking oranges; the stove completely covered with preserving pans, some of them borrowed from an obliging American neighbour. Even our *lingerie* was stiffened with marmalade after the sticky hands of Lucienne had ironed and folded it; for in Provence the maids do all the household ironing as part of their job.

When a mass of pots were filled and I had soaked papers in brandy to preserve the marmalade, and we had tied on the covers and labelled the jars, Emilia proudly invited *Monsieur* to enter her 'jam-shop.' When he made his enthusiastic exit, his feet stuck to the parquet in his study. He had been paddling in marmalade.

The cherry season is even funnier; for when the stones are all taken out of the fruit preparatory to making jam, our two maidens are stained crimson all over. Emilia dramatically informs me that she and Lucienne are murderers, and that their victim is stewing in the preserving pan.

Perfume from Provence

EDNA LEWIS
1916–2006

Edna Lewis grew up in Freetown, Virginia, a community of freed slaves. Early on she learned that cooking was a celebration of 'the good things of each season'. She is the founder of the Society for the Revival and Preservation of Southern Food and has been named a Grande Dame of Les Dames d'Escoffier International.

Raspberries grew wild along the streams and edges of the nearby woodland and they ripened later in the season than strawberries. The black raspberries were particularly good for preserving because they remained firm, so we could have them as a treat, served with cream, throughout the winter and on into the spring. We preserved them in what seemed to me a most intriguing way. We would mix the berries with equal amounts of sugar and place them in glass bottles. Then we would cork the necks with a piece of cotton and pour melted wax over the tops. We would keep the filled bottles in an opening in the ground under a board in the kitchen floor and bring them out on special occasions like hog-butchering day because the flavor was so exotic. I have never forgotten the taste of them.

The Taste of Country Cooking

ANNA McNEILL WHISTLER
1804–81

Mrs Whistler was the mother of the American painter James Abbot McNeill Whistler.

26 FEBRUARY. We all arose before the sun this bright & mild day . . . I felt the benefit of a long day – walked after having made plenty of apple pie . . .

23 MARCH. I arose at 6 o'clock . . . I assisted in the kitchen at the baking cakes to send to Debo – but felt by afternoon nearly worn out.

13 MAY. I went at sunset a walk with my dear boys & called to take Mrs Park guava jelly for Mary who is ill with Mumps.

22 JUNE. . . . made a canister of cake . . .

30 JULY. Weather exceedingly close – I had to be in the kitchen – making currant jelly until late in the afternoon.

Whistler's Mother's Cook Book

ISABELLA BIRD
1831–1904

Isabella Bird suffered from chronic ill health, but when her doctor recommended travel as a panacea, she began a series of remarkable journeys. The letters she wrote from the western United States to her sister in England resulted in A Lady's Life in the Rocky Mountains, *in which she describes riding through a blizzard with her eyes frozen shut and being wooed by a lonely outlaw.*

When the men are out hunting I know not where, or at night, when storms sweep down from Long's Peak, and the air is full of stinging, tempest-driven snow, and there is barely a probability of any one coming, or of any communication with the world at all, then the stupendous mountain ranges which lie between us and the plains grow in height till they become impassable barriers, and the bridgeless rivers grow in depth, and I wonder if all my life is to be spent here in washing and sweeping and baking. To-day has been one of manual labour. We did not breakfast till 9.30, then the men went out, and I never sat down till two. I cleaned the living-room and the kitchen, swept a path through the rubbish in the passage-room, washed up, made and baked a batch of rolls and four pounds of sweet biscuits, cleaned some tins and pans, washed some clothes, and gave things generally a 'redding up.' There is a little thick buttermilk, fully six weeks old, at the bottom of a churn, which I use for raising the rolls; but Mr. Kavan, who makes 'lovely' bread, puts some flour and water to turn sour near the stove, and this succeeds admirably.

A Lady's Life in the Rocky Mountains

EMILY DICKINSON
1830–86

I am going to learn to make bread to-morrow. So you may imagine me with my sleeves rolled up, mixing flour, milk, saleratus, etc., with a deal of grace. I advise you if you don't know how to make the staff of life to learn with dispatch.

Letters

'AUNT BABETTE'
19th century

In print for more than twenty-five years after its publication in 1889, 'Aunt Babette's' Cook Book rode the wave of the Reform Movement within Judaism. Its recipes are French, English, German, American, Jewish – and decidedly not kosher.

My Dear Ladies: – To begin with, you must have nice rendered butter for baking purposes. I always buy enough butter in June to last all winter, for then it is cheap, say ten cents per pound, which is less than one-third what it is in winter, and it is not the 'fresh May butter' you get then, either. I use the clarified butter for making omelets, frying griddle cakes, buckwheat flapjacks, and for French toast, doughnuts, fritters, greasing cake-pans and numerous other purposes. For the benefit of new housekeepers who are not supplied with last spring's butter, I must give a receipt for clarifying or rendering butter for your French and German 'kuchen': Put the butter in a porcelain-lined or brass kettle, set it on the fire and let boil very slowly, until it becomes quite clear; when you can see the reflection of your spoon in the butter, like a mirror, and you can not hear the butter boil, it is done. Don't let it boil too long, or it will get too brown, and be very careful not to let it run over, and do not stir it with a spoon, nor skim it, else all of the salt will settle at the bottom of the kettle. But every time it rises, which will be about three times, lift it carefully from the stove and when it sinks put it on again to boil. It will not rise as high the second time, and still less the third. Take from the fire, set away for about fifteen minutes or more (being careful where you put it, especially if there are children about), then strain through a clean kitchen towel into a clean stone jar. When cold tie a paper over it and prick holes with a pin through the paper. If you do this and keep the butter in a dry, cool place, it will keep fresh for a year.

'Aunt Babette's' Cook Book

MARY HINMAN ABEL
1850–1938

Living in Germany during the early years of her marriage equipped Mary Hinman Abel for an advisory role during the First World War, when she served (in the US) on the Women's Division of the National Defense Council and made clear the feasibility of offering the public the types of community kitchens and co-operatives she had studied in Europe. Abel wrote this poem around the time of the Chicago World's Fair in 1893 and distributed it there.

Oats, peas, beans, and barley grow,
Wheat and corn and rice for you,
Meat that's cheap, and eggs when low;
Milk with cream, without it too;
Wholesome cabbage, and greens, a few
To cook in the pot with the simmering stew;
And Erin's tuber, in seasons good,
When the price is low for this starchy food.

These are the things that first we buy
When the purse is low but courage high.
We do our work with muscles firm,
And bide the day till the tide shall turn,
But chops and roasts are not for us,
Nor eggs in winter; nor fruit the first

> Of the seasons' gift; and small our share
> Of that which rewards the gardener's care.
>
> 'Good Food for Little Money'

ALICE STONOR
written 1432–3

The Paston letters are better known, but the Stonor letters and papers provide a comparable wealth of detail about the lives of a late mediaeval gentry family.

Die jovis proximo post festum sancti David in vij wytynges frescese, ix. d. Itm., in iij rogettes and in j gournarde, xviij.d. Itm., die cene domini in xij podryd wytyng viij d. Itm., in vj makrel recent. viij d. Itm., in vj rogettes recent., xiiij. d. Itm., in iij botell of wynyger, xv. d. Itm., in vj. bz: avenarum ij. s. Itm., soope iiij. d.

    Summa totalis – xix. s. j. d. facta apud Stonor die lune proximo ante festum Sancti Alphegi et soluta eodem die.

The Stonor Letters and Papers

JAYN STONOR
c. 1470

TO THOMAS S.

[*In dorso*] Ples yt yow to be remembyrde apon genciayn, ruberbe, bays, cappys, pouttys, cheverellaseys, a nounce of flayt selke, lasses, tryacyl.

    To my brodyr Stonor in hast, at þe Swerde in Fletestrete.

The Stonor Letters and Papers

MARGARET PASTON
d. 1484

Margaret Paston often wrote to her travelling son or husband to ask the going price of various cooking ingredients – spices or sugar. Here she implores her husband to send home a pot of treacle in order to cure a parishioner's illness, her daughter's and her own. In the Middle Ages treacle was a medicinal compound said to cure anything from a fever to epilepsy to prolapsed uteruses and plague, rather than the sweet thick syrup we know today.

I have sent my uncle Berney the pot of treacle that you did buy for him. Also I pray you heartily that you will send me a pot with treacle in haste for I have been right evil at ease, and your daughter both, since you rode hence, and one of the tallest young men in this parish lieth sick and has a great myrr [a heavy cold].

Letter 157

BARBARA PYM
1913–80

Barbara Pym never missed the chance to describe what her charac-ters were concocting, or what they wished they were eating. Her catty humour, curiosity and obsession with clerical life are some of the chief joys of her work. She was shortlisted for the Booker Prize in 1978.

23 April 1977. Philip Larkin to lunch. We ate kipper pâté, then veal done with peppers and tomatoes, pommes Anna and celery and cheese (he didn't eat any Brie and we thought perhaps he only likes plain food). He's shy but very responsive and jokey. Hilary took our photo together and he left about 3.30 in his large Rover car (pale tobacco brown).

A Very Private Eye

SYLVIA TOWNSEND WARNER
1893–1978

Novelist Sylvia Townsend Warner loved to cook and peppered her diary with piquant references to memorable meals and details of her baking and jam-making.

24 October 1929. It was a ravishing sou' westerly morning. In the afternoon it poured with rain and I shopped at Barkers, buying a pineapple and half a stilton, and thinking how scandalously easy it was to be kind, when one had money to spend. In the morning I had decided henceforth I only cared for easy loves. It is so degrading to have to persuade people into liking one, or one's works. Let be. Then I made damson pickle three 2lb pots.

15 February 1930. [London] A cold, pretty day, very young – bright sunshine one minute and next everything black and growling. Dorothie Machen to spend the night. We dined off mulligatawney, chicken with almonds and an orange soufflé that was out of breath, but made a good custard. After dinner D.M. and I fell to duets, and the house rocked with our attack of the scherzo and finale of number 5.

Diaries

CHRISTINA HOLE
20th century

Sarah Fell of Swarthmoor paid sixpence for three pounds of butter in 1678; five years before, when prices were slightly higher, she had paid 8¼d. for three-and-a-half pounds. Three neats' tongues cost her ninepence in 1673, four capons and a chicken 2s. 2d.

The English Housewife in the Seventeenth Century

ENCARNACIÓN PINEDO
1848–1902

*It was Ruth Reichl who drew attention to Encarnación Pinedo's El
cocinero español (The Spanish Cook). California's first Spanish-
language cookbook was dedicated to Pinedo's nieces, 'So that you
may always remember the value of a woman's work'.*

MANCHAMANTELES
STEW THAT STAINS THE TABLECLOTH

Take some ripe tomatoes and remove the seeds. Grind them with
soaked toasted dry chiles, cinnamon, and pepper. After they are ground,
fry in lard, mix with warm water, and add chickens or pork, cooked
sausages, olives, vinegar, salt, a lump of sugar, yams, or peanuts.

Encarnación's Kitchen
trans. by Dan Strehl

PATIENCE GRAY
1917–2005

*Honey from a Weed charts Gray's journeys round the Mediterranean
with her sculptor husband. It stresses the importance of seasonal and
local produce, and the recipes are interspersed with legends, local lore,
even politics.*

Beatrice d'Este, writing from a hunting lodge in the Ticino, to her sister
Isabella in Mantua, in 1491: 'And I must tell you that I have had a
whole field of garlic planted for your benefit, so that when you come we
may be able to have plenty of your favourite dishes.'

Honey from a Weed

MONIQUE TRUONG

Monique Truong's debut novel sensuously recreates 1930s Paris and is narrated by the Vietnamese cook who worked for Gertrude Stein and Alice B. Toklas. Truong found her inspiration in these lines from the Alice B. Toklas Cook Book: *'[He] came to us through an advertisement that I had in desperation put in a newspaper. It began captivatingly for those days: "Two American ladies wish . . ."'*

I remember that on the day that I was hired GertrudeStein was present for my first discussion with Miss Toklas about the menus for the coming week. That conversation took place then, as it does now, in the kitchen. GertrudeStein, I now know, never goes into the kitchen. She must have sensed the potential in me from the very beginning. I wanted that afternoon to ask Miss Toklas whether the household budget would allow for the purchase of two pineapples for a dinner to which my Mesdames had invited two guests. I wanted to tell her that I would cut the first pineapple into paper-thin rounds and sauté them with shallots and slices of beef; that the sugar in the pineapple would caramelize during cooking, imparting a faint smokiness that is addictive; that the dish is a refined variation on my mother's favorite. I wanted to tell her that I would cut the second pineapple into bite-sized pieces, soak them in kirsch, make them into a drunken bed for spoonfuls of tangerine sorbet; that I would pipe unsweetened cream around the edges, a ring of ivory-colored rosettes. And because I am vain and want nothing more than to hear the eruption of praises that I can provoke, I wanted to tell her that I would scatter on top the petals of candied violets, their sugar crystals sparkling.

The Book of Salt

FANNIE FLAGG

But, with all of her spooky ways, there wasn't a better cook in the state of Alabama. Even at eleven, they say she could make the most delicious biscuits and gravy, cobbler, fried chicken, turnip greens, and black-eyed peas. And her dumplings were so light they would float in the air and you'd have to catch 'em to eat 'em. All the recipes that were used at the café were hers. She taught Idgie and Ruth everything they knew about cooking.

Fried Green Tomatoes at the Whistle Stop Café

UNRESTRAINED APPETITES

FANNY FERN
1811–72

Born Sara Payson Willis Parton, the saucy Fanny Fern earned the nickname 'Sal Volatile' at school. She became one of America's first women journalists and in 1855 was paid the astonishing salary of $100 for a weekly column with half a million readers.

I believe in eating. The person who affects to despise it either comforts himself with private bits, or is unfitted by disease to eat at all. It does not disenchant me, as it does some, to see 'a woman eat.' I know that the dear creatures cannot keep up their plumpness on saw-dust, or the last 'Lady's Book.' I look at them as the future mothers of healthy little children; and I say mentally, Eat, my dears, and be satisfied; but be sure that you take a good walk after you have digested your food. Still there may be limits to one's tolerance even in this regard. The other morning, at a hotel breakfast, I had been contemplating with great interest a fair creature, who took her seat opposite to me, in all the freshness of a maiden's morning toilette. Smooth hair, tranquil brow, blue eyes, and a little neat white collar finishing off a very pretty morning-robe; and here you will permit me to remark that, if women did but know it, but they don't, and never will, a ball-room toilette is nothing to a neat breakfast dress. Well, my fairy read the bill of fare, while I admired the long eye-lashes that swept her cheek. Straight-way she raised her pretty head, and lisped this order to the colored waiter at her elbow:

'John! Coffee, Fried Pigs' Feet, Fried Oysters, Omelette, Pork Steak.'

Caper-Sauce: A Volume of Chit-chat about Men, Women and Things

GRACE NICHOLS

Born in Guyana, Grace Nichols is an award-winning poet and author of children's books.

Sugarcake, sugarcake
Bubbling in a pot,
Bubble, bubble sugarcake
Bubble thick and hot.

Sugarcake, sugarcake
Spice and coconut,
Sweet and sticky
Brown and gooey,

I could eat the lot.

'Sugarcake Bubble'

VICTORIA GRANOF

Making our way into the center of town, we encountered a very slight, very feeble old widow, cloaked in black, inching her way up the steep hill with the aid of a rickety cane. We approached the little crone and offered up one of our *cannoli*. 'What do you mean, *signorina*!' she barked, slashing the air in front of her with the cane. 'Can't you see I have no teeth?' As I turned to make a sheepish but quick getaway, the end of her cane caught my hand like the rap of a nun's ruler. She gestured at the *cannoli*. '*Però, m'arrangio, signorina*' (I'll manage), she said as her gnarled hands reached for the *cannoli*.

Sweet Sicily: The Story of an Island and Her Pastries

EDWIDGE DANTICAT

Once again, she held the box of cookies in front of me. I took another cookie but she kept the box there, in the same place. I took yet another cookie, and another until the whole box disappeared.

Krik? Krak!

JEANETTE WINTERSON

The novelist owns Verde, an Italian delicatessen on the ground floor of her four-storey Georgian home in London.

The King of Capri had been out to a party. It was just the kind of party that Kings like best. All his friends were there, and somebody had cooked his favourite food. There was royal jelly, crown of lamb, queen of puddings, buns with pearly icing and chocolate soldiers. The King ate as much as he could but not as much as he would have liked. He had a bun in one hand, jelly in the other hand, but try as he might, he couldn't get all the jelly and all the bun into his mouth at once.

'Why have I got two hands but only one mouth?' wondered the King. His advisor stood before him and said, 'Sire, think of all the poor people in your kingdom. They can hardly feed one mouth each. However could they feed two?'

But the King never did think about the poor people. He thought only about himself.

That night a great tempest blew in across the sea . . . Never in all the history of Capri had there been such a wind. Everyone was woken up, except for the King, who was so fat and so weighed down with buns and jelly that even a tempest couldn't so much as blow his hair across the pillow. Perhaps that was because his hair was stuck to the pillow with a jam sandwich he kept underneath it at night, in case he got hungry.

The King of Capri

RUMER GODDEN
1907–98

On and off, all that hot French August, we made ourselves ill from eating the greengages. Joss and I felt guilty; we were still at the age when we thought being greedy was a childish fault, and this gave our guilt a tinge of hopelessness because, up to then, we had believed that as we grew older our faults would disappear, and none of them did. Hester of course was quite unabashed; Will – though he was called Willmouse then – Willmouse and Vicky were too small to reach any but the lowest branches, but they found fruit fallen in the grass; we were all strictly forbidden to climb the trees.

The garden at Les Oeillets was divided into three: first the terrace and gravelled garden round the house; then, separated by a low box hedge, the wilderness with its statues and old paths; and, between the wilderness and the river, the orchard with its high walls. In the end wall a blue door led to the river bank.

The orchard seemed to us immense, and perhaps it was, for there were seven alleys of greengage trees alone; between them, even in that blazing summer, dew lay all day in the long grass. The trees were old, twisted, covered in lichen and moss, but I shall never forget the fruit. In the hotel dining-room, Mauricette built it into marvellous pyramids on dessert plates laid with vine leaves. 'Reines Claudes,' she would say to teach us its name as she put our particular plate down, but we were too full to eat. In the orchard we had not even to pick the fruit – it fell off the trees into our hands.

The greengages had a pale-blue bloom, especially in the shade, but in the sun the flesh showed amber through the clear-green skin; if it were cracked the juice was doubly warm and sweet. Coming from the streets and small front gardens of Southstone, we had not been let loose in an orchard before; it was no wonder we ate too much.

'Summer sickness,' said Mademoiselle Zizi.

'Indigestion,' said Madame Corbet.

I do not know which it was, but ever afterwards, in our family, we called that the greengage summer.

The Greengage Summer

COLETTE
1873–1954

Whether counting the nuts she would collect and eat before sunset or recalling the appetites of her animal friends, Colette had a uniquely sensuous voice.

Jeanne Muhlfeld

Monts-Boucons, mid-July 1902

Do you recognize me, Jeanne? I'm wearing an apron with pockets, a broad-brimmed pink calico hat, little hobnailed boots, no rice powder, buckskin gloves holding large pruning scissors – and the heart of a girl. You cannot imagine the pure – and purgative – joy of eating black cherries which the sun has ripened on the tree. It rains, it shines, I get up at six and am in bed by nine. I am turning the color of a pig-skin valise. My account book is like a well-kept flower bed. It's my annual virtue debauch, almost clandestine, which debases me to the moral level of a day laborer . . . And now I must spray two apple trees which are prone to aphids . . . I can't tell you about the silver dawns and the apricot sunsets today because my mouth is full and I have made a bet with myself to eat four hundred nuts between lunch and dinner. Oh! that's not a record, of course, but when one must gather as well as shell the nuts . . .

Letters
trans. by Robert Phelps

PETA MATHIAS

Seven gastronomic travel books have seen Mathias in France, North Africa, Vietnam, Ireland and her native New Zealand, whose Guild of Food Writers voted hers the best food programme on television.

Profiteroles come from the French word *profit*, to gain. What you gain is the erotic pleasure of sliding hot chocolate and cold ice-cream down your throat at the same time and voluptuous thighs if you keep eating them.

Insatiable

HELEN BAROLINI

An ancient saying has it that 'those who wish to lead virtuous lives should abstain from truffles.' I believe it. With what they cost, weighing in like emeralds, one could be led to beg, borrow, or steal to obtain a respectable amount. King Umberto of Italy was said to be fond of a salad made of thinly sliced white truffle with a few greens and nasturtium blossoms, an aesthetic ultimate.

Living outside New York I would be tempted every so often to go into the city to a shop of Italian imports and plunk down what seemed a huge wad of bills for a 'truffle just arrived from Italy.' It would look like a truffle, it would cost like a truffle, but when the moment of truth came with the grating, it would be utterly disappointing – a mere wisp of scent and taste.

Once Susi located a noted truffle hunter who was said to have con-cocted some secret balsamic elixir which perfectly preserved them out of season. Wanting to indulge me, she sent me a tiny brown lump float-ing in the liquid of a small vial marked *tartufo bianco*. It was not a truffle but a *truffa* – a swindle. The lump was soft and spongy from its balsamic bath, and tasteless, worthless.

It seemed clear that the truffle must be had where it is found and had fresh – dug from the earth that very day.

So it was October when Niki and I drove in sight of that enchanting vision, the twin fairy tale towers of Urbino's Ducal Palace. White truffles were already in the town's speciality shops. And I learned that in local jargon, a *tartufo* is someone who turns up when there is something choice to eat or a bottle of wine has been opened. I thought, if I can't find one, perhaps I can be one.

'In Pursuit of the Great White Truffle'

ELIZABETH ROBINS PENNELL
1855–1936

A close friend of James Abbot McNeill Whistler, Pennell was a well-known journalist and biographer. At a time when women were meant to strap themselves into their corsets and act the maiden, she advocated unashamed greed and left to the Library of Congress a collection of European cookbooks as large as her appetites.

Gluttony is ranked with the deadly sins; it should be honoured among the cardinal virtues. It was in the Dark Ages of asceticism that contempt for it was fostered. Selfish anchorites, vowed to dried dates and lentils, or browsing Nebuchadnezzar-like upon grass, thought by their lamentable example to rob the world of its chief blessing. Cheerfully, and without a scruple, they would have sacrificed beauty and pleasure to their own superstition. If the vineyard yielded wine and the orchard fruit, if cattle were sent to pasture, and the forest abounded in game, they believed it was that men might forswear the delights thus offered. And so food came into ill repute and foolish fasting was glorified, until a healthy appetite passed for a snare of the devil, and its gratification meant eternal damnation. Poor deluded humans, ever so keen to make the least of the short span of life allotted to them!

With time, all superstitions fail; and asceticism went the way of many another ingenious folly. But as a tradition, as a convention, somehow it lingered longer among women. And the old Christian duty became a new feminine grace. And where the fanatic had fasted that his soul might prove comelier in the sight of God silly matrons and maidens starved, or pretended to starve, themselves that their bodies might seem fairer in the eyes of man. And dire, indeed, has been their punishment. The legend was that swooning Angelina or tear-stained Amelia, who, in company, toyed tenderly with a chicken wing or unsubstantial wafer, later retired to the pantry to stuff herself with jam and pickles. And thus gradually, so it is asserted, the delicacy of woman's palate was destroyed: food to her perverted stomach was but a mere necessity to stay the pangs of hunger, and the pleasure of eating she looked upon as a deep mystery, into which only man could be initiated.

In this there is much exaggeration, but still much truth. To-day women, as a rule, think all too little of the joys of eating. They hold lightly the treasures that should prove invaluable. They refuse to recognize that there is no less art in eating well than in painting well or writing well, and if their choice lay between swallowing a bun with a cup of tea in an aerated bread shop, and missing the latest picture show or doing without a new book, they would not hesitate; to the stodgy bun they would condemn themselves, though that way madness lies. Is it not true that the woman who would economize first draws her purse-strings tight in the market and at the restaurant? With her milliner's bill she may find no fault, but in butcher's book, or grocer's, every halfpenny is to be disputed.

The loss is hers, but the generous-hearted can but regret it. Therefore let her be brought face to face with certain fundamental facts, and the scales will fall quickly from her eyes, and she will see the truth in all its splendour.

First, then, let her know that the love of good eating gives an object to life. She need not stray after false gods; she will not burden herself with silly fads, once she realizes that upon food she may concentrate thought and energy, and her higher nature – which to her means so much – be developed thereby. Why clamour for the suffrage, why labour for the redemption of brutal man, why wear, with noisy advertisement, ribbons white or blue, when three times a day there is a work of art, easily within her reach, to be created? All his life a Velazquez devoted to his pictures, a Shakespeare to his plays, a Wagner to his operas: why should not the woman of genius spend hers in designing exquisite dinners, inventing original breakfasts, and be respected for the nobility of her self-appointed task? For in the planning of the perfect meal there is art; and, after all, is not art the one real, the one important thing in life?

And the object she thus accepts will be her pleasure as well. For the gourmet, or glutton, duty and amusement go hand in hand. Her dainty devices and harmonies appeal to her imagination and fancy; they play gently with her emotions; they develop to the utmost her pretty sensuousness. Mind and body alike are satisfied. And so long as this pleasure endures it will never seem time to die. The ancient philosopher thought that time had come when life afforded more evil than good. The good of a pleasantly planned dinner outbalances the evil of daily trials and tribulations.

Here is another more intimate, personal reason which the woman of sense may not set aside with flippancy or indifference. By artistic gluttony, beauty is increased, if not actually created. Listen to the words of Brillat-Savarin, that suave and sympathetic gourmet: 'It has been proved by a series of rigorously exact observations that by a succulent, delicate, and choice regimen, the external appearances of age are kept away for a long time. It gives more brilliancy to the eye, more freshness to the skin, more support to the muscles; and as it is certain in physiology that wrinkles, those formidable enemies of beauty, are caused by the depression of muscle, it is equally true that, other things being equal, those who understand eating are comparatively many years younger than those ignorant of that science.' Surely he should have called it art, not science. But let that pass. Rejoice in the knowledge that gluttony is the best cosmetic.

And more than this: a woman not only grows beautiful when she eats well, but she is bewitchingly lovely in the very act of eating. Listen again, for certain texts cannot be heard too often: 'There is no more pretty sight than a pretty gourmet under arms. Her napkin is nicely adjusted; one of her hands rests on the table, the other carries to her mouth little morsels artistically carved, or the wing of a partridge, which must be picked. Her eyes sparkle, her lips are glossy, her talk cheerful, all her movements graceful; nor is there lacking some spice of the coquetry which accompanies all that women do. With so many advantages she is irresistible, and Cato, the censor himself, could not help yielding to the influence.' And who shall say that woman, declaiming on the public platform, or 'spanking' progressive principles into the child-man, makes a prettier picture?

Another plea, and one not to be scorned, is the new bond of union love of eating weaves between man and wife. 'A wedded pair with this taste in common have once a day at least a pleasant opportunity of meeting.' Sport has been pronounced a closer tie than religion, but what of food? What, indeed? Let men and women look to it that at table delicious sympathy makes them one, and marriage will cease to be a failure. If they agree upon their sauces and salads, what matter if they disagree upon mere questions of conduct and finance? Accept the gospel of good living and the sexual problem will be solved. She who first dares to write the great Food Novel will be a true champion of her sex. And yet women meet and dine together, and none has the courage to whisper the true secret of emancipation. Mostly fools! Alas, that it should have to be written!

And think – that is, if you know how to think – of the new joy added to friendship, the new charm to casual acquaintanceship, when food is given its due, and is recognized as something to be talked of. The old platitudes will fade and die. The maiden will cease to ask 'What do you think of the Academy?' The earnest one will no longer look to Ibsen for heavy small-talk. Pretence will be wiped away, conversational shams abolished, and the social millennium will have come. Eat with understanding, and interest in the dishes set before you must prove genuine and engrossing, as enthusiasm over the last new thing in art or ethics has never been – never can be. The sensation of the day will prove the latest arrangement in oysters, the newest device in vegetables. The ambitious will trust to her kitchen to win her reputation; the poet will offer lyrics and pastorals with every course; the painter will present in every dish a lovely scheme of colour.

Gross are they who see in eating and drinking naught but grossness. The woman who cannot live without a mission should now find the path clear before her. Let her learn first for herself the rapture that lies dormant in food; let her next spread abroad the joyful tidings. Gluttony is a vice only when it leads to inartistic excess.

A Guide for the Greedy by a Greedy Woman

EDNA FERBER
1885–1968

The novel behind the musical Showboat *is Edna Ferber's claim to fame, but she won the Pulitzer Prize in* 1924 *for her novel* So Big. *The first of her two autobiographies,* Peculiar Treasure *evinces pride in her Jewish heritage and her dismay at the discrimination against her people.*

William Allen White knows and loves good food. Anyone who has ever stopped for a meal at the Whites' house in Emporia, Kansas, knows that Bill and Sallie White are epicures. Will shares my distrust of those people who say, dreamily, 'I forgot all about lunch.' Or 'I really never pay any attention to food. I hardly ever know what I'm eating.' I've never seen a really dimensional or important human being who was indifferent to good food and its preparation.

We interviewed the good-natured Negro cook. She was not only willing to cook the breakfast, she was rolling-eyed about it. We volunteered to do the marketing. With a glitter in our eyes and huge Baltimore market baskets on our arms Bill White and I headed toward the big open Lexington Market.

There we went mad. We bought everything in sight – fish, flesh, fowl, fruit, vegetables. As we drove home our eyes could just be seen above the stacked baskets, bundles and boxes.

We had invited as many as the big mahogany dining table could manage, with squeezing, and, as it turned out, a dozen or so humbly stood up or squatted on the floor, plate in hand. I still remember Henry

Beach Needham hanging around sniffing and dreamily closing his eyes while the meal was cooking.

There was no session at the convention hall that morning. There had been an adjournment until half past eight in the evening, according to the strange workings of that political group. We all gathered at about one o'clock. No one in history, including Henry the Eighth at the height of his gustatory powers, ever sat down to such a breakfast. There were no courses and no particular routine. It was all there in Gargantuan profusion. A kind of awe crept into the faces of the visiting correspondents. There were oranges, peaches, grapefruit. There were bacon and eggs for the unimaginative; soft-shell crabs, succulent and sweet; fried chicken, lamb chops, stewed fresh huckleberries (no one knows why. We merely had seen them in the market, bursting black giant huckleberries, and Bill had breathed something about their being elegant with hot popovers). There were waffles with syrup or preserves, little hot biscuits and big hot popovers. Steaming coffee in urns and pitchers of cream. The fat cook kept bringing in fresh supplies. A kind of glaze came into the eyes of the breakfasters. Presently even the cook saw that the famished scribes were replete. At a piled-up platter they only shook their heads, groaning, speechless.

For the rest of the day we sat about blinking and staring at each other like overstuffed pythons who have just swallowed too many rabbits.

A Peculiar Treasure

COLETTE
1873–1954

All was faery and yet simple among the fauna of my early home. You could never believe that a cat could eat strawberries? And yet, because I have seen him so many times, I know that Babou, that black Satan, interminable and as sinuous as an eel, would carefully select in Madame Pomié's kitchen garden the ripest of the Royal Sovereigns or the Early Scarlets. He it was, too, who would be discovered poetically absorbed in smelling newly opened violets.

Have you ever heard tell of Pelisson's spider that so passionately loved music? I for one am ready to believe it and also to add, as my slender contribution to the sum of human knowledge, the story of the spider that my mother kept – as my father expressed it – on her ceiling, in that year that ushered in my sixteenth spring. A handsome garden spider she was, her belly like a clove of garlic emblazoned with an ornate cross. In the daytime she slept, or hunted in the web that she had spun across the bedroom ceiling. But during the night, towards three o'clock in the morning, at the moment when her chronic insomnia caused my mother to relight the lamp and open her bedside book, the great spider would also wake, and after a careful survey would lower herself from the ceiling by a thread, directly above the little oil lamp upon which a bowl of chocolate simmered through the night. Slowly she would descend, swinging limply to and fro like a big bead, and grasping the edge of the cup with all her eight legs, she would bend over head foremost and drink to satiety. Then she would draw herself ceilingwards again, heavy with creamy chocolate, her ascent punctuated by the pauses and meditations imposed by an overloaded stomach, and would resume her post in the centre of her silken rigging.

My Mother's House
trans. by Una Vincenzo Troubridge and Enid McLeod

M.F.K. FISHER
1908–92

Serve It Forth, M.F.K. Fisher's first book, was so 'unwomanly'
that many critics thought it was written by a man. Fisher often
protested that she wasn't a writer, but her books show her to be a
consummate prose stylist.

N IS FOR NAUTICAL

. . . and inevitably for nostalgia, in my own alphabet. Dinners aboard
ship have a special poignancy for me, partly because I have not sailed
anywhere since I went with the *Normandie* on her last fateful crossing,
but mostly because I have always been in love at sea, so that each bit I
took was savored with an intensity peculiar to the moment. I think I am
not alone in this particular juxtaposition of two words for *N.*

The first time I ever rode a ship it was deep down in the shuddering
guts of it, so that dining room silver and china jangled tinnily on the
calmest day – another coupling of two letters: *S* for Student Third
rather than Steerage. It was smart to hop the Atlantic thus cheaply and
uncomfortably in 1929, and a great many bored travelers who could
afford A-deck accommodations titillated themselves by rubbing elbows
with errant priests and broken-down fan dancers and even students in
the renovated holds of a dozen enormous liners (mine was the
Berengaria).

I myself was happily dazed with love, but I do remember one priest,
one dancer, three medical students, and most of all one incongruously
proper middle-class plump Englishwoman who had nothing to do with
anyone at all and seemed non-existent except three times a day in the
dining room. Then it was that she became immortal, at least for me.
With one blind regal stare she picked up the large menu, handed it to the
apparently hypnotized waiter, who hovered over her and almost ignored
the seven other passengers at our table, and said 'Yes.'

It seems to me, when I try to be reasonable about it, that she must
surely have said, 'Yes, pastries,' or 'Yes, soups.' But all I can remember is
'Yes.' All I can remember is sitting for long periods watching her, when

I should rightly have been playing shuffleboard or any other of the games connected with my first honeymoon, while she ate slowly, silently, right through the menu.

Surely it must have been all the soups one meal, and all the roasts another: no human being could eat every dish mentioned on a ship's carte du jour, not even in Student Third where kippered snacks and spiced onions took the place of First Class caviar and bouchées à la Pompadour. But as far as I can say, that woman did. What is more, the waiter seemed to enjoy it almost as much as she; he would hover breathlessly behind her with a dish of apple trifle and a plate of plum heavies while she chewed on through her chocolate sponge with one hand and cut at the crust of an apricot tart with the other.

One day of comparative roughness, when the silver and china clashed noisily to the ocean's roll instead of jingling to the engine's shudderings, I sat almost alone in the room with this relentless eater, feeling that for once in my life I was in the presence of what Rabelais would have called a Gastrolater; insensitive to the elements, unthinking of ordinary human misery, uncaring of the final end to such appetite, she was wrapped in a worship of her belly. 'Yes,' she said simply and sat back for her priest to attend her.

An Alphabet for Gourmets

BARBARA PYM
1913–80

'I suppose old atheists seem less wicked and dangerous than young ones,' said Jane. 'One feels that there is something of the ancient Greeks in them.'

Father Lomax, who evidently thought no such thing, let the subject drop and then somehow he and Nicholas were talking about parish matters, parochial church council meetings, Sunday school teachers and visiting preachers. Jane lay back in her chair lost in thought, wondering about Mr. Mortlake and his friends. Flora got up and quietly refilled the coffee cups, offering a plate of biscuits to Father Lomax. But he refused them with an absent-minded wave of the hand. Meat offered to idols, thought Flora scornfully, taking a biscuit herself and eating it. Then, as nobody seemed to be taking any notice of her, she ate another and another until the clock struck ten . . .

Jane and Prudence

ELIZABETH TAYLOR
1912–75

Margaret was hungry, not tired. She went to the kitchen. As soon as one meal was over, she began to think about the next. Food had started to entrance her.

The kitchen had its scrubbed, afternoon, waiting look. On the rocking-chair lay Nanny's film paper. Margaret took it to read while she stood in the larder eating. On the stone slab was half a gooseberry pie, caved in, and a jam-tart covered with a trellis of pastry; but she had to eat secretly what would not be missed. In the meat-safe was a slab of grey beef, overcooked, a knuckle of veal gleaming with bluish bones. Sage swung from the ceiling, brushing against a net of onions with a lisping sound; there was a brown crock full of cream cheese. She cut a thick slice of wholemeal bread, covered it with butter, then with the cheese, began to eat greedily, dealing craftily with the crumbs, turning the pages of the cinema paper. When she had finished, she was still hungry. She cut another slice and spread it as before. The thought of all this good, wholesome food going into her was pleasing. A fly from outside tried at the perforated zinc over the window. As strategy failed, it tried force. When it flew suddenly away, the silence was complete, perfect. Margaret ate more slowly, with no further sensuous delight. She felt puffed and fagged with eating. 'Grossly, full of bread,' she murmured, thinking she saw what it meant, felt what it meant, for the first time. And then 'crammed with distressful bread,' she remembered.

Shakespeare must have been greedy too. She was sickened now by the food around her on the shelves, pulled off some bits of sage and sniffed at them – aromatic, that was better. She heard her mother calling down through the house; the voice winding thinly down the stairs, along the passages, peevishly.

Palladian

LADY ANNE CLIFFORD
1590–1676

Anne Clifford was born at Skipton Castle during the reign of Elizabeth I. From the age of 60 until her death at 86, she spent her time rebuilding churches and castles in Cumbria. Her descendant Vita Sackville-West was the editor of her remarkably rich and informative diaries. The first of the entries below was written when Anne was 13.

July 1603

Upon the 25th of July the King and Queen were crowned at *Westminster*, my Father and Mother both attended in their robes, my Aunt of *Bath* and my Uncle *Russell*, which solemn sight my Mother would not let me see because the plague was hot in *London*, therefore I continued at *Norbury*, where my cousin did so feed me with breakfasts and pear pies and such things, as shortly after I fell into sickness.

June 1617

The 6th after supper we went in the coach to *Goodwife Syslies* and ate so much cheese there that it made me sick.

Diaries

FANNY TROLLOPE
1779–1863

*Fanny Trollope was the mother of the novelist Anthony Trollope.
Her candid observations about American life and society, published
as* Domestic Manners of the Americans, *launched her career as a
writer in England.*

Where the mansion is of sufficient dignity to have two drawing-
rooms, the piano, the little ladies, and the slender gentlemen are left
to themselves, and on such occasions the sound of laughter is often
heard to issue from among them. But the fate of the more dignified
personages, who are left in the other room, is extremely dismal. The
gentlemen spit, talk of elections and the price of produce, and spit
again. The ladies look at each other's dresses till they know every pin
by heart; talk of Parson Somebody's last sermon on the day of judgment, on Dr. T'otherbody's new pills for dyspepsia, till the 'tea' is
announced, when they all console themselves together for whatever
they may have suffered in keeping awake, by taking more tea, coffee,
hot cake and custard, hoe cake, johny cake, waffle cake, and dodger
cake, pickled peaches, and preserved cucumbers, ham, turkey, hung
beef, apple sauce, and pickled oysters than ever were prepared in any
other country of the known world. After this massive meal is over,
they return to the drawing-room, and it always appeared to me that
they remained together as long as they could bear it, and then they
rise *en masse*, cloak, bonnet, shawl, and exit.

Domestic Manners of the Americans

IRMA ROMBAUER
1877–1962

*Dr Atkins wasn't the first to vilify carbs. They were obviously
thought equally poisonous when Irma Rombauer was writing her
famous cookbook. In 1931, she risked her own savings to publish pri-*

vately 3,000 copies of The Joy of Cooking. *Her witty asides, friendly tone and old-fashioned good sense brought warmth and comfort into Depression kitchens. By 1943* The Joy of Cooking *was America's most popular cookbook and in 1995 the New York Public Library named it one of the 150 most influential books of the century; it was the only cookbook to make the list. Over time, more than fifteen million copies have been sold. Unfortunately, contemporary editions have all but lost the saucy voice – and some of the alarming recipes – that made the earlier editions so entertaining. Julia Child once remarked that if she could keep only one cookbook in English, it would have to be* The Joy of Cooking.

In recent years the mania for girth control has played havoc with the fair name of the potato – bringing 'insinuendoes' against it that are almost as damaging as the charges brought against the erstwhile virtue of bread.

The Joy of Cooking

SUSAN FERRIER
1782–1854

Ferrier, a friend of Sir Walter Scott, remained single, but her witty novel, Marriage, *is the tale of a selfish aristocratic Englishwoman who finds herself in the bosom of a Highland family when she elopes with one of its members.*

'I declare our dear niece has not tasted a morsel,' observed Miss Nicky.

'Bless me, here's charming barley-meal scones,' cried one, thrusting a plateful of them before her. – 'Here's tempting pease-bannocks,' interposed another, 'and oat cakes! I'm sure your ladyship never saw such cakes.'

'I can't eat any of those things,' said their delicate niece, with an air of disgust. 'I should like some muffin and chocolate.'

'You forget you are not in London, my love,' said her husband, reproachfully.

'No, indeed I do not forget it. Well, then, give me some toast,' with an air of languid condescension.

'Unfortunately, we happen to be quite out of loaf bread at present,' said Miss Nicky; 'but we've sent to Drymsine for some. They bake excellent bread at Drymsine.'

'Is there nothing within the bounds of possibility you could fancy, Julia?' asked Douglas. 'Do think, love.'

'I think I should like some grouse, or a beef steak, if it was very nicely done,' returned her ladyship in a languishing tone.

'Beef steak!' repeated Miss Grizzy.

'Beef steak!' responded Miss Jacky.

'Beef steak!' reverberated Miss Nicky.

After much deliberation and consultation amongst the three spinsters, it was at length unanimously carried that the lady's whim should be indulged.

'Only think, sisters,' observed Miss Grizzy in an undertone, 'what reflections we should have to make upon ourselves, if any of our descendants were to resemble a moor-fowl!'

'Or have a face like a raw beef steak!' said Miss Nicky.

These arguments were unanswerable; and a smoking steak and plump moor-fowl were quickly produced; of which Lady Juliana partook, in company with her four-footed favourites.

Marriage

MARY RUSSELL MITFORD
1787–1855

Novelist and dramatist Mary Russell Mitford was the daughter of an extravagant and ultimately impecunious doctor in Alresford, Hampshire, and an early admirer of Jane Austen's novels. Here she describes her nurse's wedding to a local farmer.

Such a dinner . . . Fish from the great pond, Roast beef, Yorkshire pudding. Boiled fowls, and a Gammon of bacon, a Green Goose, and a Sucking pig, plumb puddings, apple pies and custards, followed by home brewed beer and home made wines, by syllabub, by wedding cake. Everybody ate enough for four, and there were four times more than would possibly be eaten.

Our Village

SARAH ORNE JEWETT
1849–1909

Another doctor's daughter, New England writer Sarah Orne Jewett was inspired by the work of Harriet Beecher Stowe.

The feast was a noble feast, as has already been said. There was an elegant ingenuity displayed in the form of pies which delighted my heart. Once acknowledge that an American pie is far to be preferred to its humble ancestor, the English tart, and it is joyful to be reassured at a Bowden reunion that invention has not yet failed. Beside a delightful variety of material, the decorations went beyond all my former experience; dates and names were wrought in lines of pastry and frosting on the tops. There was even more elaborate reading matter on an excellent early-apple pie which we began to share and eat, precept upon precept. Mrs. Todd helped me generously to the whole word *Bowden*, and consumed *Reunion* herself, save an undecipherable fragment; but the most renowned essay in cookery on the tables was a model of the old Bowden house made of durable gingerbread, with all the windows and doors in the right places, and sprigs of genuine lilac set at the front. It must have been baked in sections, in one of the last of the great brick ovens, and fastened together on the morning of the day. There was a general sigh when this fell into ruin at the feast's end and it was shared by a great part of the assembly, not without seriousness, and as if it were a pledge and token of loyalty. I met the maker of the gingerbread house, which had called up lively remembrances of a childish story. She had the gleaming eye of an enthusiast and a look of high ideals.

The Country of the Pointed Firs

ASTRID LINDGREN

1907–2002

At that moment Ella, the maid, came in with the coffee pot, and Mrs. Settergren said, 'Please come and have some coffee.'

'*First!*' cried Pippi and was up by the table in two skips. She heaped as many cakes as she could onto a plate, threw five lumps of sugar into a coffee cup, emptied half the cream pitcher into her cup, and was back in her chair with her loot even before the ladies had reached the table.

Pippi stretched her legs out in front of her and placed the plate of cakes between her toes. Then she merrily dunked cakes in her coffee cup and stuffed so many in her mouth at once that she couldn't have uttered a word no matter how hard she tried. In the twinkling of an eye she had finished all the cakes on the plate. She got up, struck the plate as if were a tambourine, and went up to the table to see if there were any cakes left. The ladies looked disapprovingly at her, but that didn't bother her. Chatting gaily, she walked around the table, snatching a cake here and a cake there.

'It certainly was nice of you to invite me,' she said. 'I've never been to a coffee party before.'

Pippi Longstocking

E. NESBIT
1858–1924

A member of the Fabian Society, Edith Nesbit published under the gender-neutral names of E. Nesbit and Fabian Bland. She wanted recognition as a poet, but turned to children's literature to support her large family.

Jimmy was eagerly unpacking the basket. It was a generous tea. A long loaf, butter in a cabbage leaf, a bottle of milk, a bottle of water, cake, and large, smooth, yellow gooseberries in a box that had once held an extra-sized bottle of somebody's matchless something for the hair and mustache. Mabel cautiously advanced her incredible arms from the rhododendron and leaned on one of her spindly elbows, Gerald cut bread and butter, while Kathleen obligingly ran round, at Mabel's request, to see that the green coverings had not dropped from any of the remoter parts of Mabel's person. Then there was a happy, hungry silence, broken only by those brief, impassioned suggestions natural to such an occasion:

'More cake, please.'

'Milk ahoy, there.'

'Chuck us the goosegogs.'

Everyone grew calmer – more contented with their lot. A pleasant feeling, half tiredness and half restfulness, crept to the extremities of the party. Even the unfortunate Mabel was conscious of it in her remote feet, that lay crossed under the third rhododendron to the north-northwest of the tea party. Gerald did but voice the feelings of the others when he said, not without regret:

'Well, I'm a new man, but I couldn't eat so much as another goosegog if you paid me.'

'I *could*,' said Mabel; 'yes, I know they're all gone, and I've had my share. But I *could*. It's me being so long, I suppose.'

The Enchanted Castle

DIANE MOTT DAVIDSON

*Davidson's series of culinary mysteries are chock full of tempting
recipes and feature a detective who works as a live-in cook and also
runs a catering business.*

Opening a wrapped imported chocolate is like a moment from
Christmas Eve. Your mouth waters. Each tiny crinkle of paper, each
flash of colored foil is agony. You think if you don't get this chocolate
into your mouth in the next five seconds, you're going to die.

The first Mozartkugel dropped into my hand like a smooth, dark ball
from heaven. I bit into it very slowly. As the chocolate melted I closed
my eyes and waited for nirvana.

And oh, it came. When you roll chocolate around on your tongue,
the dark creamy sweetness invades all your senses. Delight worms its
way down your spine. Your ears tingle. You have to say *Mmmm* because
you just can't help it. Some people say the taste of chocolate is second
only to sex. I say putting it second is in dispute.

Dying for Chocolate

MARLENA SPIELER

I was walking down the ever-so-evocative streets of Paris, down rue St.
Honoré, past the Opera and Madeleine, heading toward Ladurée, that
exquisite jewel box of a pastry shop. I had an appointment with a macaroon and was busy mulling over exactly which flavor I was going to
choose. Chocolate and pistachio were two current favorites; I was half
thinking of lemon or raspberry. My mind was absorbed with this important decision.

First of all, I should take a moment to explain that macaroon doesn't
refer to the heavy-ish coconutty things we Americans usually think of
as macaroons. A French macaroon, or *macaron*, is a light-as-air almost

meringue-y almond cookie, or rather two of these light and flavorful cookies sandwiching a filling: creamy chocolate ganache for the chocolate macaroons, buttery caramel for the hazelnut ones, pistachio cream for the pistachio macaroons and tangy raspberry preserves for the raspberry meringues. A delicacy like this is worth being obsessed over.

As I turned the corner I spied a large group of people gathered around the window in front of Ladurée. There were perhaps six or eight Japanese girls – maybe 18 or 19 years old – standing in front of the pastry shop window. They were crying.

An equal number of French adults stood by: women and men, busy raising their shoulders and looking perplexed, shrugging and pouting, giving that particular Gallic downturn of the mouth reflecting an effort to comfort, but helpless nonetheless. No one seemed to have any idea why the girls were crying. Clearly, the French did not understand Japanese, and neither did the Japanese understand French.

I decided to wade in with good ole' all-purpose English.

'Why,' I asked one of the girls, 'are you crying?' A sea of gentle sobs was the only reply. The girls had macaroon crumbs on their faces and didn't look sad at all, they were simply overcome with emotion.

'Ha-ppy,' said the first girl. 'Ha-ppy,' said the second, and the rest joined in, heads bobbing up and down, 'Ha-ppy!' they all chimed in. They were crying because they were happy.

Well, you know, I understand. There we were, on a beautiful street in Paris, the musical sound of the French language in our ears, surrounded by chic women walking little dogs, shop windows filled with fabulous goods arranged in a stunningly artistic manner . . . not to mention those macaroons. Well, who *wouldn't* cry?

'The Roving Feast'

M.M. KAYE
1908–2004

Most of our meals during Bargie and Tony's visits were picnics. Sandwiches, hard-boiled eggs, curry-puffs and cake were packed into rucksacks by Mother and eaten by us on the slopes of the golden, grassy hillsides that looked out across the enormous valleys below us towards the great Himalayan ranges that are the outer bastions of Tibet. Even the nights were exciting when Bargie was a visitor, for we would hold midnight feasts; popular entertainments that were tremendous fun to plan and prepare, though it must be admitted that nine times out of ten by the time midnight struck and our elders and betters were (we hoped) safely asleep, we ourselves were far too drowsy to get much enjoyment out of them. As for the provender that we so carefully collected and hid away in toy-cupboards or under the beds, the best that could be said about it was that it could have been worse. Though not much. This was because the first rule governing such nocturnal bun-fights was that the feast *must* consist of food that had been collected without the knowledge of any grown-up – which restricted it to cold potatoes or soggy lumps of pudding whipped off our plates into a waiting handkerchief during lunch, bits of cake or biscuits filched during tea, and bottles of lemon squash surreptitiously sneaked from the larder when no one was looking. And since the pudding- and/or potato-filled handkerchiefs were then stuffed up our bloomers in order to remove them unseen from the dining-room (children's knickers in those days were invariably bloomers with elastic at the waist and knee) the collected delicacies were not all that appetizing. But then anything eaten by stealth and at an unauthorized hour possessed the charm of forbidden fruit.

These midnight feasts came to be known as 'Chunkychaddles', because Bargie, being of a methodical turn of mind, had on one occasion written down a detailed plan: who was to collect what, the exact time that each one of us left his or her room, etc., etc., in the manner of a military exercise. And having concluded the list, she had thrown her pencil down and said: 'And after that, Chunkychaddle bust!' The newly minted word appealed strongly to her fellow conspirators and from then on, to any member of our own particular circle of friends, a midnight feast was always known by that name.

The Sun in the Morning

HSIANG JU LIN
TSUIFENG LIN
20th century

Tsuifeng Lin was the wife of the artist and writer Yutang Lin; Hsiang Ju Lin was their daughter. Chinese Gastronomy *portrays Chinese cooking as dedicated to the pursuit of flavour and the understanding of certain culinary principles.*

A feast is like a symphony. The rhythm of the great feast comes from the pauses. A pause is very important, and must in itself be tasteful. A feast is like a walk along straight streets, until one comes to a quiet square, where it is possible to rest a moment.

Chinese Gastronomy

FESTIVE FARE

MORAG MURRAY ABDULLAH
20th century

When Morag Murray met an Afghan prince during the First World War, she left her home in Scotland and settled with her new husband in a remote mountain region of her adopted country.

This was the feast night. Every available cook in the district had been lent, and as every chieftain brought his own servants the problem of overwork did not exist.

A cloth was spread on the carpet, and we sat down cross-legged in the rose-decked room. It was amazing how so many people could be accommodated even in relays, though the rooms were large and connected with one another like a series of dining-rooms. Dishes piled up with delicious rice hid tender chickens. Little fat discs of roasted meat eaten with home-made bread; whole sheep disappearing almost magically; roast mutton steeped in butter delicately flavoured; saffron-coloured rice, with each grain soft and yet separated from the rest, strewn with pistachio nuts and small round sultanas; a delicious white pudding like whipped cream covered with what looked like smooth silver paper, which dissolved instantaneously as one ate it; tasty 'candies' and large juicy melons, dried mulberries and walnuts – these are a few scattered recollections of that wonderful meal. The servants waited upon us with tireless energy. As soon as one's plate was empty (and often before) another helping appeared as by magic.

My Khyber Marriage

ELISABETH LUARD

FIRNI AFGHAN BETROTHAL CUSTARD

Quick and easy, a milk custard made without eggs and a minimum of fuss, also served at weddings and for Eid-e-Ramazan, the feast that marks the end of Ramadan. Children love it.

Serves 6–8

4 cups/1 litre whole milk

Generous 1 cup/275g sugar

8 level tablespoons cornstarch

½ teaspoon freshly ground cardamom seeds

1 heaped tablespoon finely chopped pistachios

1 heaped tablespoon finely chopped almonds

1. Heat the milk gently in a heavy pan with the sugar.
2. Meanwhile, mix the cornstarch with a little water, enough to make a thin paste.
3. When the milk is hot, but before it boils, whisk in the cornstarch. Add the cardamom and whisk over the heat till the mixture thickens. Pour into a shallow dish, leave to cool, and sprinkle with the chopped nuts.

Delicious served with little wood strawberries, cherries, and peaches.

Sacred Food: Cooking for Spiritual Nourishment

ANNE FRANK
1929–45

Monday, 8 May 1944

Dear Kitty,

Miep told us this morning about a party she went to, to celebrate an engagement. Both the future bride and bridegroom came from rich families and everything was very grand. Miep made our mouths water telling us about the food they had: vegetable soup with minced meat balls in it, cheese, rolls, hors d'oeuvre with eggs and roast beef, fancy cakes, wine and cigarettes, as much as you wanted of everything (black market). Miep had ten drinks – can that be the woman who calls herself a teetotaler? If Miep had all those, I wonder however many her spouse managed to knock back? Naturally, everyone at the party was a bit tipsy. There were two policemen from the fighting squad, who took photos of the engaged couple. It seems as if we are never far from Miep's thoughts, because she took down the addresses of these men at once, in case anything should happen at some time or other, and good Dutchmen might come in useful.

She made our mouths water. We, who get nothing but two spoonfuls of porridge for our breakfast and whose tummies were so empty that they were positively rattling, we, who get nothing but half-cooked spinach (to preserve the vitamins) and rotten potatoes day after day, we, who get nothing but lettuce, cooked or raw, spinach and yet again spinach in our hollow stomachs. Perhaps we may yet grow to be as strong as Popeye, although I don't see much sign of it at present!

If Miep had taken us to the party we shouldn't have left any rolls for the other guests. I can tell you, we positively drew the words from Miep's lips, we gathered round her, as if we'd never heard about delicious food or smart people in our lives before!

Yours, Anne
The Diary of a Young Girl
trans. by B.M. Mooyaart-Doubleday

IRIS ORIGO
1902–88

*Living at the Villa Medici in Fiesole at the beginning of the twentieth
century, Iris Origo was part of a circle that included the Berensons,
Harold Acton and Edith Wharton. During the Second World War,
she and her husband, the Marchese Antonio Origo, sheltered parti-
sans and refugee children on their rural property, La Foce. Here, in
her classic study of a mediaeval merchant's life, she describes the
betrothal and marriage of the merchant's daughter, Ginevra.*

Francesco must have made up his mind, for in the autumn of 1406,
when Ginevra was fifteen years old, a letter from a friend in Bologna,
Niccolò Compagni, congratulated him on the engagement. In reply,
Francesco remarked that many men had already asked him for Ginevra's
hand – 'not for her own sake, but to get my money' . . .

In Genevra's case there is no record of a betrothal ceremony; it was
probably held on the same day as the wedding feast. . .

The wedding banquet . . . was a very fine one. A special cook, '*Mato
di Stinchese cuoco*', was engaged for the occasion, and was paid 4 florins
10 *soldi* for this single meal – a princely sum, when we consider that a
maid's wages for a whole year were only ten florins. Six extra servants,
besides those of Francesco's regular household, waited at table, and
were supplied with new tunics of scarlet cloth, and new hose. 310 lb. of
fish were brought 'from the lake' at a cost of 14 florins, and 31 lb. of lard
were used. As to the rest of the food, the sumptuary laws forbade more
than three courses, even at a wedding banquet – one of *ravioli*, *tortellini*,
or *bramagiere* (blancmange), one of 'roast with pie', and one dessert –
and specified that there should be no more than 50 dishes for each
course (allowing 20 guests for the bride and 30 for the bridegroom). But
each of the 50 dishes might consist of '7 pounds of veal, or one capon
with a pie, or one goose with a pie, or a couple of fowls with a pigeon,
or a pair of pigeons with a fowl, or a duckling with two pigeons', and,
moreover, the 'pie' in question was itself a most ingenious way of evad-
ing the law-givers' intent, for it was a pasty containing the greatest

possible variety of ingredients: pork, chickens, ham, eggs, dates, almonds, flour, spices, saffron, sugar, and salt. Certainly none of the guests can have left the table hungry! But Ginevra herself, like every refined bride, had only a snack beforehand and did not touch the meal – so that when she dipped her white fingers in the silver washing-bowl, the water should still be clear, and the guests praise her fine manners.

The Merchant of Prato

BUWEI YANG CHAO
20th century

Buwei Yang Chao is credited with being the first to offer an authentic (not Westernised) Chinese cookbook to Americans, and with having coined the term 'stir-frying'. How to Cook and Eat in Chinese was introduced by novelist Pearl Buck whose parents were missionaries in China.

Special foods are associated with special festivals. They are not kinds of dishes, but mostly 'dot-hearts,' or between-meal refreshments. That is one reason why children are always wishing festivals to come around. In the so-called South (Central East), steamed cakes of glutinous rice flour with meat or sweet stuffing is a New Year's 'dot-heart.' On the Fifth of the Fifth Moon on the lunar calendar, the festival food is boiled tetrahedrons of glutinous rice wrapped in leaves of a special kind of rush. The Fifteenth of the Seventh Moon is All Soul's Day, when fried eggplant-tarts are eaten. Around the Mid-Autumn Festival, which is about the time of the harvest moon, mooncake is eaten and sold in Chinatown stores in America. Those with puree-of-jujube stuffing in well-shortened crust are best, though hard to get except in the North.

There are many other ritual meanings of foods besides those eaten at festivals. We don't eat birthday cakes, but eat noodles to wish longevity to the person whose birthday it is. Breads and uncooked noodles are also made into the form of peaches, which are also a symbol of longevity.

If a family moves house, especially into a newly built house, you present them with a very fluffy raised cake called *fa-kao*, 'the flourishing cake.'

How to Cook and Eat in Chinese

ETHEL RAGLAN
1857–1940

On another day a huge fête was given in Canford Park to about three thousand five hundred of the tenants' children; and, besides this, over one thousand four hundred of the cottagers were entertained to dinner, served in a large marquee which had been erected in the grounds. The menu included roast ribs and sirloins of juicy beef, boiled rounds of beef, legs and saddles of mutton, and legs and loins of crisp, crackling-covered pork. There were likewise delicious pies made of ham and tongue, and veal and pork.

In front of the terrace an old-fashioned incident was taking place, which was the roasting whole of an ox. The animal had been placed in its temporary fireplace as early as six o'clock in the morning. Sir Ivor Guest carved the first slice, and the carcase was then dismembered by Mr. Luff, the steward, who served it out to those around. (The latter, be it said, were not among those villagers already busily feasting inside the marquee.)

By the time the evening arrived, not a vestige of the ox remained; even its bones had been removed.

Memories of Three Reigns

ELIZA POTTER
19th century

Potter was a U.S. society hairdresser of African-American descent.

I was invited to a very beautiful place called Weehawken; it was the prettiest place I ever saw in the woods for any amusement of the kind. When we arrived at Weehawken, we found a handsome house fitted up for the season; in front was a platform about one hundred feet square, with a railing round it and seats; outside this railing was a place erected for a full band of music. All commenced dancing the instant they arrived; some even before they got their things off. While I, with some others who did not dance, went to see the preparations for cooking the clams.

I was very much pleased, as it was something I had never seen before. First, they put on the ground thirty or forty logs of wood, with plenty of kindling; when these logs were burning, they put on a cart load of large stones; when these became red hot, they covered them with sea-weed. They then took fish of all kinds that could be baked sweet, and Irish potatoes, corn in the ear; rolled them all up in separate pieces of paper, laid them on the sea-weed; then they made another row of sea-weed, on which about three barrels of clams were put; then another covering of sea-weed; and so on, till there was a pile four or five feet high, and all was in a short time beautifully baked. In the meantime there was quite a circle of boards erected round this bed of clams, where the people stood around and received from those inside this circle bowls, butter, pepper and salt, and anything else they might require; then last came along a number of forks to eat with. Then commenced such an opening of clams, handing round of sweet potatoes and corn – just which you pleased to have – and all seemed to eat as if they were the most elegant things imaginable.

I sat aside and looked on, an amused spectator, as, though pressed by many to eat, and told how good they were, I could not eat them. There was an immense kettle of chowder, which they all seemed to enjoy very much. They all ate with such a relish as if they never had eaten anything so good before. There was a good deal of fun and merriment going on.

After they had finished their clams, they took another dance; then all retired to dress for a ball which was to be inside the house. They kept it up till eleven o'clock at night.

A Hairdresser's Experience in High Life

EDNA LEWIS

SUNDAY REVIVAL DINNER
Baked Virginia Ham
Southern Fried Chicken
Braised Leg of Mutton
Sweet Potato Casserole
Corn Pudding
Green Beans with Pork
Platter of Sliced Tomatoes with Special Dressing
Spiced Seckel Pears
Cucumber Pickles
Yeast Rolls
Biscuits
Sweet Potato Pie
Summer Apple Pie
Tyler Pie
Caramel Layer Cake
Lemonade
Iced Tea

Although I didn't think about it at the time, I wonder how my mother made it each year to Revival Sunday, with so much to do and without ever varying from the calm and quiet manner that was her nature . . .

My mother never started her cooking until late on the eve of Revival

Sunday. By this time she would have everything gathered in and laid out that she would need, and, I guess, a carefully planned schedule laid out in her mind as well. When we were bathed and turned into bed, no pies or cakes had yet been made. But when we came hurrying down on Sunday morning, the long, rectangular dining-room table would be covered with cakes ready to be iced and pie dishes lined with pastry dough to be filled and baked. While we counted them and excitedly discussed our special favorites and how many slices of each we could eat, my mother was out in back feeding her fowl. When she came in she would make us breakfast, standing at the stove with her everyday calm. Then she would help us dress, tie on our ribbons, and send us to sit on the porch until noontime with firm warning to sit quietly so that our new clothes would not get mussed. It would seem a very long morning.

Mother would return to the kitchen to continue her cooking. Because she liked to arrive at the church with the food piping hot, my father would attend the morning service alone and then come back for us as soon as it was over. We would be so excited as we climbed into the surrey. I remember how very special I felt in my new dress which helped me overcome the discomfort of having to wear shoes for the first time since March when school had let out. After we were all squeezed in, my father would load on the carefully packed baskets of food. The savory aroma of fried chicken, so warm and close, always pricked our appetites and long before we reached the church, which was only two miles distant, we would be squirming impatiently, though silently.

The churchyard would be filled with people as we drove up; I felt as though everyone was looking at us. My father would drive straight up to one of the long tables that were stretched out in a line under the huge, shady oak trees alongside the church. My mother would spread out a white linen tablecloth before setting out the baked ham, the half-dozen or more chickens she had fried, a large baking pan of her light, delicate corn pudding, a casserole of sweet potatoes, fresh green beans flavored with crisp bits of pork, and biscuits that had been baked at the last minute and were still warm. The main dishes were surrounded with smaller dishes of pickled watermelon rind, beets and cucumbers and spiced peaches. The dozen or so apple and sweet potato pies she had made were stacked in tiers of three, and the caramel and jelly layer cakes placed next to them. Plates, forks, and white damask napkins and gallon jars of lemonade and iced tea were the last things to be unpacked.

All along the sixty-foot length of tables, neighbors were busy in the same way setting our their own specialties. There were roasts and casseroles, cole slaw and potato salads, lemon meringue, custard, and Tyler pies, chocolate and coconut layer, lemon cream, and pound cakes.

When all the food had been placed on the tables, an unspoken signal would ripple down the line and we would all stand quietly while the minister spoke a grace of thanksgiving. We always liked him, for he knew to keep it short.

The Taste of Country Cooking

ISABELLA BIRD
1831–1904

We spent the afternoon cooking the Thanksgiving dinner. I made a wonderful pudding, for which I had saved eggs and cream for days, and dried and stoned cherries supplied the place of currants. I made a bowl of custard for sauce, which the men said was 'splendid;' also a rolled pudding, with molasses; and we had venison steaks and potatoes, but for tea we were obliged to use the tea-leaves of the morning again. I should think that few people in America have enjoyed their Thanksgiving dinner more.

A Lady's Life in the Rocky Mountains

LIZETTE WOODWORTH REESE
1865–1935

This holiday and all others included a constant and savory procession of cakes, from crisp, round, clove-spiced ginger ones, and thick, sugar-topped loaves, fat and black with raisins, to the flat sheets baked in shallow pans, and concocted from a recipe which my grandmother had brought with her from the German country town where she had been born. This incomparable creation of dead and gone Saxon cooks consisted of two layers, the bottom one of sweetened dough, the other a mixture of cornmeal, butter, sugar, cinnamon and handfuls of currants. You took a mouthful, and wished for nothing better in this world. In comparison to this a sack of gold was but puny dross. You forgave your enemies; you meditated giving of your goods to the poor. It was indigestible to the last degree; it had the faculty – at the first touch of lips – of crumbling into small bits and dropping down to the floor.

A Victorian Village

CHRISTINA HOLE

At Christmas the ancestor of our modern Christmas pudding was composed of neats'-tongues, chickens, eggs, candied peel, raisins, sugar, and spices, and with this rather liquid mixture went mince pies, which also contained meat. Fruit tarts of various kinds were very popular, and became increasingly so as the price of sugar slowly fell from *1s. 6d.* a pound at the beginning of the century to *5d.* or *6d.* a pound at its end. Leaches made of seethed cream, almonds, rosewater and ising-glass were favourite sweet dishes, and so were Imbals, which were a kind of shortcake made from fine flour mixed with pulped fruit or almonds, rolled out very thinly, baked, and sometimes iced with sugar and rose-water. On ceremonial occasions there might be marchpane, gilded and flavoured with pistachio nuts, or sugar-plate moulded into elaborate shapes. This was a confection of double-refined sugar, starch, gum-dragagant dissolved in rosewater, and white of egg, all made into a stiff paste and put into carved wooden moulds to set. Such delicacies were often coloured and flavoured with flowers.

The English Housewife in the Seventeenth Century

ELIZABETH DAVID
1913–92

The time she spent working and researching local eating habits in France, Italy, Greece and Egypt during World War II profoundly influenced Elizabeth David's views on cooking. When she published A Book of Mediterranean Food *in 1949, David changed British cuisine for ever.*

If I had my way – and I shan't – my Christmas Day eating and drinking would consist of an omelette and cold ham and a nice bottle of wine at lunch time, and a smoked salmon sandwich with a glass of champagne on a tray in bed in the evening. This lovely selfish anti-gorging, un-Christmas dream of hospitality, either given or taken, must be shared by thousands of women who know it's all Lombard Street to a China orange that they'll spend both Christmas Eve and Christmas morning peeling, chopping, mixing, boiling, roasting, steaming. That they will eat and drink too much, that someone will say the turkey isn't quite as good as last year, or discover that the rum for the pudding has been forgotten, that by the time lunch has been washed up and put away it'll be tea-time, not to say drink or dinner time, and tomorrow it's the week-end and it's going to start all over again.

Is There a Nutmeg in the House?

DELLA LUTES
1872–1942

Dessert, of course, on Christmas Day, consisted of plum pudding, and plum pudding only. On Thanksgiving there were pies – pumpkins and mince. On New Year's there would be pies, mince and apple and pumpkin, but on Christmas the pudding stood alone, a monarch amongst desserts.

It had been made weeks before, in fact at the same time that the mincemeat for Thanksgiving pies was in preparation. Contrary to her usual custom, my mother had a rule for making her plum pudding. In general her cookery was of so simple an order, consisting of dishes frequently repeated, as to need no rules, but this pudding was made but once a year, and so when the time came for its concoction she took down from its place beside the clock an old cookbook and opened it to a page slightly discolored from a tracing finger rich with fruity contact.

I think, perhaps, she also liked to read the words, for she spoke them aloud, and I can remember seeing my father draw his chair within hearing distance, adjust his spectacles, craftily lift a newspaper before his face, and give ear to the rich phrasing which fell alluringly upon the air:—

'Take of cold beef suet one pound, string it, and crumble into a wooden bowl and chop very fine. Mix with one cup of brown sugar. Into an earthen bowl put half a pound of currants, an equal amount of raisins, seeded; one-fourth pound each of candied citron, lemon, and orange peel, sliced to transparent thinness with a very sharp knife on a board; one ounce each of cinnamon, ginger, nutmeg, cloves; one teaspoonful salt (or more); cover these with one pound of flour and stir with fingers until fruit is coated.

'Now add two cups of fine bread crumbs, four eggs well beaten, one cup of milk, one-half cup of brandy. Mix and stir to a stiff dough. Now set this aside to *assimilate flavors* for two hours or more.

'Have ready a large flannel pudding bag, square in shape. Wet this, wring as dry as possible; lay the cloth on the table, butter the centre, and sprinkle with flour. Place this over a bowl and pour in the pudding. Tie firmly with string, leaving a little room for the swell but not much. Put a plate in bottom of a large kettle of boiling water, set the pudding on it, and let boil for seven hours. Serve on a round platter with a small amount of brandy poured over, to which a light is applied after the room is darkened. A sprig of holly adds to its tastiness. This pudding (*if not eaten*) will last for weeks and is as good cold as it was hot.'

Could anything afford pleasanter reading than that? Is it any wonder that my father's newspaper dropped and sagged, or that his spectacles were pushed impatiently to the top of his head, the better to hear?

Upon one occasion I remember his remarking to my mother as her voice dropped, regretfully, the last phrase, 'We might try that "applying a light" sometime, maybe, 'Miry, huh?'

'Yes, and likely burn the whole pudding up,' was her unsympathetic retort.

When the pudding, after the proper 'assimilation of flavors,' was finally consigned to the pot, the kitchen became of all rooms that could be imagined the most desirable. Every corner, every inch and ell, was permeated with the rich bouquet of 'assimilated' raisins, currants, lemon, ginger, citron, and spice borne upon a cloud of steam, while the pudding on its plate, with its woolly ears protruding above the boisterous, ebullient seas of darkening water, danced and bubbled, puffed and swelled, in its own juices. Perhaps it would last for weeks 'if not eaten,' but its chances for longevity beyond the date set for its proper consumption were slim indeed.

The Country Kitchen

CHERRY RIPE

When Nanny came back to the farm from town carrying a basket of tins, Cherry's father insisted that 'No daughter of mine is going to eat anything I haven't grown myself' and swept them all into the rubbish bin. In this extract Cherry describes the Australian tradition of picnicking on Christmas Day.

It's not like finding hubcaps under the ruins of ancient Rome, but nevertheless it might come as a surprise to many that Australia once had its own indigenous Christmas celebration – the public picnic.

For most of the last century, people would adjourn to the shadiest spot they could find, preferably near water, where games like three-legged races would be played, and cold food consumed, outdoors . . .

There are delightful depictions of 19th-century Christmas picnics in Maisy Stapleton and Patricia McDonald's *Christmas in the Colonies*. 'Starting for the Christmas Picnic' from the *Illustrated Australian News*, 23 December 1860, shows a canopied wagon being loaded with huge covered baskets of provisions, bottles and stoppered jugs, and parties of people waiting to set off – men in suits and waistcoats with shadecloths hanging from the backs of their hats, and women in their Sunday best, complete with hats and parasols. Another engraving from 1865 shows families spread out on rugs in what appears to be a rainforest, under huge tree ferns, again in their Sunday best. There are children playing shuttlecock, men and women reading, cricket bats stacked up against a tree trunk, buggies in the background. The centrepiece is a large tablecloth spread out on the ground with baskets and platters – on one, a pineapple, bottles and a flagon . . .

These days, wherever you are in the world, Christmas has become homogenised. Whether on terra firma, or 30,000 feet above it, you're as likely to be offered roast turkey on Qantas as on Air India.

Nevertheless, picnics were always a part of the Aussie way of eating.

Goodbye Culinary Cringe

GEORGE ELIOT
1819–80

Fine old Christmas, with the snowy hair and ruddy face, had done his duty that year in the noblest fashion, and had set off his rich gifts of warmth and colour with all the heightening contrast of frost and snow . . .

And yet this Christmas day, in spite of Tom's fresh delight in home, was not, he thought, somehow or other, quite so happy as it had always been before. The red berries were just as abundant on the holly, and he and Maggie had dressed all the windows and mantlepieces and picture-frames on Christmas eve with as much taste as ever, wedding the thick-set scarlet clusters with branches of the black-berried ivy. There had been singing under the windows after midnight . . . and then there were the smell of hot toast and ale from the kitchen, at the breakfast hour; the favourite anthem, the green boughs, and the short sermon gave the appropriate festal character to the church-going; and aunt and uncle Moss, with all their seven children, were looking like so many reflectors of the bright parlour-fire, when the church-goers came back, stamping the snow from their feet. The plum-pudding was of the same handsome roundness as ever, and came in with the symbolic blue flames around it, as if it had been heroically snatched from the nether fires, into which it had been thrown by dyspeptic Puritans; the dessert was as splendid as ever, with its golden oranges, brown nuts, and the crystalline light and dark of apple-jelly and damson cheese; in all these things Christmas was as it had always been since Tom could remember; it was only distinguished, if by anything, by superior sliding and snow-balls.

The Mill on the Floss

ANNA MᶜNEILL WHISTLER
1804–81

Mr Ingersoll and Wm. Winans dined with father and I, we had a
Baltimore ham to relish turkey and _pea nuts_ for dessert, but mince pies
or plum pudding I have not ventured to propose since the Cholera
season . . .

I had about sixteen to make tea for . . . Cook had made some of her
most transparent jelly in lieu of fruit which one does not offer in these
Cholera times, & if English palates did not fancy Pea-nuts the
American lads were not slow to help themselves, & Stuarts sugar plums
& candy went around.

Whistler's Mother's Cook Book

JAN STRUTHER
1901–53

New Year's Eve was the only day of the year on which Mrs. Adie really
unbent. Christmas she held to be of little account, though she cooked
the turkey and the mince-pies faithfully enough and took a benign
interest in the children's presents. Boxing Day made her, if anything,
more tight-lipped than usual, for on that day the Minivers were in the
habit of eating a 'June dinner' as a respite from Christmas food: a practice which Mrs. Adie looked upon as unnatural and faintly sacrilegious.
There was a no-good-can-come-of-this expression on her face as she
served up the clear soup, the fish mayonnaise, and the summer pudding
(made of bottled currants and raspberries); but up till now nobody had
so much as choked on a fish-bone.

On New Year's Eve, however, Mrs. Adie always invited the whole
family into the kitchen for a Hogmanay tea. There were scones and oatcakes and shortbread and rowan jelly; and a Melrose sponge-cake sent
down by her brother, and a Selkirk bannock sent down by her sister; and
in addition to all these she managed to provide a constant supply of

fresh drop-scones all through the meal. She let the children take turns in pouring spoonfuls of batter on to the hot girdle, and in watching each little sizzling yellow pool go beautifully brown round the edges. She even let Gladys make a few, on condition that she gave up her regrettable Sassenach habit of calling them 'flapjacks.'

Mrs Miniver

SALLY CLARKE

Elizabeth David's memorial feast was provided by Sally Clarke.

In Venice, in celebration of Epiphany, almost every baker on every street is found to be frying these delicious little spiced buns [*frittelle*] throughout the cold weeks. In order to stay warm as one walks along the canals, it is imperative to make a pit stop once in a while to purchase a hot cup of frothy cappuccino and a frittella to go with it. Often the pastry cream which fills these buns is flavoured with vanilla, but I prefer the ones which have the added shot of Marsala, which results in an extra inner glow as one continues the promenade.

Sally Clarke's Book

LADY ANNE CLIFFORD
1590–1676

January 1617
Upon the 6th being Twelfth Day I went about 4 o'clock to the Court with my Lord. I went up with my Lady *Arundel* and ate a scrambling supper with her and my Lady *Pembroke* at my Lord *Duke's* lodgings. We stood to see the Masque in the box with my Lady *Ruthven*.

Diaries

CLAUDIA RODEN

Like Colette Rossant, Claudia Roden grew up in Egypt. Her books on Mediterranean and Jewish food have introduced western food lovers to the magic of orange flower water, bulghur and tamarind.

Oriental New Year meals end with fresh dates, figs, and above all pomegranates – all of which are mentioned in the Bible – as the new fruits of the season. In Egypt, we thought pomegranates would cause our family to bear many children. We ate the seeds sprinkled with orange-blossom water and sugar. Pastries were made with sesame or aniseed, which also symbolized fecundity, or were stuffed with nuts or dates and soaked in syrup. Jams were made with quince, figs, dates, and apples. White things – such as milk puddings, coconut jam, and the sharope blanco (an almost all-sugar jam) – evoke purity, whereas golden-pumpkin jam, like all saffron-coloured foods, evokes joy and happiness.

Nothing sharp or bitter is served – there is no vinegar or lemon or tamarind – and nothing black – no eggplants or chocolate. Green, not black olives are eaten, and mint or green tea is drunk instead of black coffee.

The Book of Jewish Food

'AUNT BABETTE'
19th century

HOW TO SET THE TABLE FOR THE SERVICE OF THE 'SEDAR' ON THE
EVE OF PESACH OR PASSOVER

Set the table as usual, have everything fresh and clean; a wineglass for
each person, and an extra one placed near the platter of the gentleman
who is to give the sedar. Then get a large napkin; fold it into four parts,
set it on a plate, and in each fold put a perfect matzo; that is, one that
is not broken or unshapely; in short, one without a blemish. Then place
the following articles on a platter: One hard-boiled egg, a bone that has
been roasted in ashes, the top of a nice stick of horseradish (it must be
fresh and green), a bunch of nice curly parsley and some bitter herb (the
Germans call it lattig), and, also, a small vessel filled with salt water.
Next to this platter place a small bowl filled with חרוסת, prepared as follows: Pare and chop up a few apples; add sugar, cinnamon, pounded
almonds, some white wine and grated lemon peel, and mix thoroughly.
Place these dishes in front of the one that gives the sedar, and to his left
place two pillows, nicely covered, and a small table or chair, on which
you have placed a wash-bowl with a pitcher of water and clean towel. In
some families hard-boiled eggs are distributed after the sedar (Easter
eggs).

MATZO-KUGEL

Soak about six matzos; heat some fat in a spider, press all the water
out of the matzos with your hands and dry them in a spider of heated
fat. Now add about half a pound of matzo-meal; stir the matzo and
matzo-meal well with a large spoon; add by degrees the yelks of ten
eggs and three or four ounces of pounded almonds, and the grated
peel of a lemon. Add also two large sour apples, grated, a pinch of
salt, and, last, the stiff-beaten whites of the eggs. Line a kugeltopf
well with fat, and pour about half a pound of hot fat over the kugel.
Bake immediately.

MATZOS PUDDING, OR SCHALET

Soak about three matzos, press out every drop of water, and stir the matzos in a bowl with a tablespoonful of goose fat and a saltspoonful of salt. Stir at least ten minutes, or until it looks like a mass of cream; then add gradually the yelks of eight or ten eggs, the grated peel of a lemon and juice; half a pound of sifted sugar, and, last, the beaten whites of the eggs. Have the pudding form well greased, and bake immediately. Time required, about half an hour.

'Aunt Babette's' Cook Book

ON THE HOOF

CELIA FIENNES
1662–1741

From 1685 to 1703 Celia Fiennes travelled extensively around England, alone apart from her two servants. Her record of the journeys was first published in 1888 as Through England on a Side Saddle. Hundreds of years later both Florence White and Dorothy Hartley catalogued regional food specialities in a similar, if more comprehensive manner.

[FROM NEWTON TONEY TO PURBECK]

At a place 4 mile off called Sea Cume [Seacombe] the rockes are so craggy and the creekes of land so many that the sea is very turbulent, there I pick'd shells and it being a springtide I saw the sea beat upon the rockes at least 20 yards with such a foame or froth, and at another place the rockes had so large a cavity and hollow that when the sea flowed in it runne almost round, and sounded like some hall or high arch. In this Island are severall pretty good houses though not very large, att Kingston Sir William Muex [Meux] has a pretty house, and att Income [Encombe] Mr. Coliffords Doonshay [Downshay] Mr. Dollings, and 7 mile off Quare att Tinnum [Tyneham] Lady Larences there is a pretty large house but very old timber built, there I eate the best lobsters and crabs being boyled in the sea water and scarce cold, very large and sweet.

*

In most part of Sommer-setshire it is very fruitfull for orchards, plenty of apples and peares, but they are not curious in the planting the best sort of fruite, which is a great pitty; being so soone produced, and such quantetyes, they are likewise as careless when they make cider, they press all sorts of apples together, else they might have as good sider as in any other parts, even as good as the Herriffordshire; they make great quantetyes of cider their presses are verye large, so as I have seen a Cheese, as they call them, which yeilded 2 hoddsheads; they pound their apples then lay fresh straw on the press, and on that a good lay of pulp of the apples then turne in the ends of the straw over it all round, and lay fresh straw, then more apples up to the top.

*

In this town [Scarborough] we had good accomodations and on very reasonable terms; they drye a large fish like Codlings and salt them and, when you dress them, water them, then they string them on wire and so rost them before the fire and make good sauce for them, they eate very well and as tender as a fresh Codling and very sweete iff they were well cured when they were first taken, else they will taste strong.

*

They have much rhye in Lancashire Yorkshire and Stafford and Shropshire and so Herriford and Worcestershire which I found very troublesome in my journeys, for they would not own they had any such thing in their bread but it so disagrees with me as allwayes to make me sick, which I found by its effects when ever I met with any tho' I did not discern it by the taste; in Suffolke and Norfolke I also met with it – but in these parts its altogether the oatbread . . .

At the Kings Arms one Mrs. Rowlandson she does pott up the charr fish the best of any in the country, I was curious to have some and so bespoke some of her . . .

Mr. Majors was the best entertaining house where I was [Windermere]; the Isle did not looke to be so bigg at the shore but takeing boate I went on it and found it as large and very good barley and oates and grass; the water is very cleer and full of good fish, but the Charr fish being out of season could not easily be taken so I saw none alive, but of other fish I had a very good supper; the season of the Charrfish is between Michaelmas and Christmas, at that tyme I have had of them which they pott with sweete spices, they are as big as a small trout rather slenderer and the skinn full of spotts some redish, and part of the whole skinn and the finn and taile is red like the finns of a perch, and the inside flesh looks as red as any salmon; if they are in season their taste is very rich and fatt tho' not so strong or clogging as the lamprys are, but its as fatt and rich a food . . .

Here it was I saw the oat Clap bread made: they mix their flour with water so soft as to rowle it in their hands into a ball, and then they have a board made round and something hollow in the middle riseing by degrees all round to the edge a little higher, but so little as one would take it to be only a board warp'd, this is to cast out the cake thinn and so they clap it round and drive it to the edge in a due proportion till drove as thinn as a paper, and still they clap it and drive it round, and then they have a plaite of iron same size with their clap board and so shove off the cake on it and so set it on coales and bake it; when enough on one side they slide it off and put the other side; if their iron plaite is smooth and they take care their coales or embers are not too hot but just to make it looke yellow, it will bake and be as crisp and pleasant to eate as any thing you can imagine; but as we say of all sorts of bread there is a vast deale of difference in what is housewifely made and what is ill made, so this is if its well mixed and rowled up and but a little flour on the outside which will drye on and make it mealy is a very good sort of food; this is the sort of bread they use in all these countrys, and in Scotland they breake into their milk or broth or else sup that up and bite of their bread between while, they spread butter on it and eate it with their meate; they have no other sort of bread unless at market towns and that is scarce to be had unless the market dayes, soe they make their cake and eate it presently for its not so good if 2 or 3 dayes old; it made me reflect on the description made in scripture of their kneeding cakes and bakeing them on the hearth when ever they had Company come to their houses, and I cannot but thinke it was after this maner they made their bread in the old tymes especially those Eastern Countryes where their bread might be soone dry'd and spoil'd.

*

[THROUGH DEVONSHIRE TO LAND'S END]

I went over the heath and commons by the tinn mines, 3 miles and halfe to St. Austins [St. Austell] which is a little Market town where I lay, but their houses are like barnes up to the top of the house; here was a pretty good dineing-roome and chamber within it, and very neate country women; my Landlady brought me one of the West Country tarts, this was the first I met with, though I had asked for them in many places in Sommerset and Devonshire, its an apple pye with a custard all on the top, its the most acceptable entertainment that could be made me; they scald their creame and milk in most parts of those countrys and so its a sort of clouted creame as we call it, with a little sugar, and soe put on the top of the apple pye; I was much pleased with my supper.

Through England on a Side Saddle in the Time of William and Mary,
being the Diary of Celia Fiennes

DOROTHY WORDSWORTH
1771–1855

Dorothy regularly recorded in her journals what she cooked for and ate with her brother William. In the summer of 1803 she made a six-week journey to the Highlands with William and their friend Coleridge.

Saturday, August 27th. – Before I rose, Mrs. Macfarlane came into my room to see if I wanted anything, and told me she should send the servant up with a basin of whey, saying, 'We make very good whey in this country;' indeed, I thought it the best I had ever tasted; but I cannot tell how this should be, for they only make skimmed-milk cheeses. I asked her for a little bread and milk for our breakfast, but she said it would be no trouble to make tea, as she must make it for the family; so we all breakfasted together. The cheese was set out, as before, with plenty of butter and barley-cakes, and fresh oaten cakes, which, no doubt, were made for us: they had been kneaded with cream, and were excellent. All the party pressed us to eat, and were very jocose about the necessity of helping out their coarse bread with butter, and they themselves ate almost as much butter as bread . . .

When breakfast was ended the mistress desired the person whom we took to be her husband to 'return thanks.' He said a short grace, and in a few minutes they all went off to their work.

Thursday, September 1st. – We were glad when we reached Taynuilt, a village of huts, with a chapel and one stone house, which was the inn. It had begun to rain, and I was almost benumbed with the cold, besides having a bad headache; so it rejoiced me to see kind looks on the landlady's face, and that she was willing to put herself in a bustle for our comfort; we had a good fire presently, and breakfast was set out – eggs, preserved gooseberries, excellent cream, cheese, and butter, but no wheat bread, and the oaten cakes were so hard I could not chew them. We wished to go upon Loch Etive; so, having desired the landlady to prepare a fowl for supper, and engaged beds, which she promised us willingly – a proof that we were not in the great road – we determined to find our way to the lake and endeavour to procure a boat. It rained heavily, but we went on, hoping the sky would clear up.

Recollections of a Journey Made in Scotland

SYLVIA TOWNSEND WARNER
1893–1978

17 September. I visited every counter of the domestic Woolworth, even to buying boot-polish, and refreshed myself with a sixpenny fish tea – plaice, of course. Cheap low-class meals are such a pleasure, I wonder I don't take to chewing-gum.

23 September. We went by Guildford and beyond Alton lunched in a nut copse, talking about great aunts. A delicious lunch: cold chicken, beer, pears and madiera [sic]. And midges. And ash-trees. Their green fronds so flatly distinct on a grey sky that they looked like transfer patterns on china.

Diaries

FANNY CRADOCK
1909–94

The woman who named her dog Mademoiselle Lolita Saltina Cradock was prone to embellishing her own name as well. Born Phyllis Nan Sortain Pechey, she styled herself Frances Dale when she wrote romantic novels and sometimes used Primrose-Pechey as her surname. Fanny was expelled from school for dabbling in the occult. As the first British TV chef, in ballgowns and pancake makeup she dominated not only her husband Johnnie, but television ratings for twenty years. Fanny and Johnnie were also the country's first restaurant critics under the guise of 'Bon Viveur' in the Daily Telegraph. French cuisine was for Fanny, as for Julia Child, the best.

If gastronomy in all its forms and origins attracts you it will not be possible to leave Barcelona without spending an hour in the city's largest covered market on the Rambla San Jose. This market offers up a pageant of colour and succulence. We wandered along, cancelling out the careful correctness of our town clothing by buying and munching fat, honey-sweet black figs with coral centres and lamenting all the while. It was *torture* to be surrounded by such an *embarras de choix* and be hundreds of miles removed from a stove or chafing dish. Alas! Those masterpieces we could not create . . . fish soups rich in both octopus and squid . . . inky brews of rice impregnated with the dark juice of cuttle fish . . . bombes of frozen fruit pulps, sweet cream and perfumed liqueurs . . . fondue variations based on the pungent Minorcan cheeses . . .

All this recollection of wandering compells us to recall that in all Barcelona we never discovered a public lavatory.

Holiday in Barcelona and the Balearics

GEORGE ELIOT
1819–80

To lie on the wool-packs, with a cranny left between the curtains of the awning to let in the air, was luxury to Hetty now, and she half-slept away the hours till the driver came to ask her if she wanted to get down and have 'some victual'; he himself was going to eat his dinner at this 'public.' Late at night they reached Leicester, and so this second day of Hetty's journey was past. She had spent no money except what she had paid for her food, but she felt that this slow journeying would be intolerable for her another day . . . she hated going into the public houses, where she must go to get food and ask questions, because there were always men lounging there, who stared at her and joked her rudely. Her body was very weary too with these days of new fatigue and anxiety; they had made her look more pale and worn than all the time of hidden dread she had gone through at home. When at last she reached Stony Stratford, her impatience and weariness had become too strong for her economical caution; she determined to take the coach for the rest of the way, though it should cost her all her remaining money. She would need nothing at Windsor but to find Arthur. When she had paid the fare for the last coach, she had only a shilling; and as she got down at the sign of the Green Man in Windsor at twelve o'clock in the middle of the seventh day, hungry and faint, the coachman came up, and begged her to 'remember him.' She put her hand in her pocket and took out the shilling, but the tears came with the sense of exhaustion and the thought that she was giving away her last means of getting food, which she really required before she could go in search of Arthur. As she held out the shilling, she lifted up her dark tear-filled eyes to the coachman's face and said, 'Can you give me back sixpence?'

'No, no,' he said, gruffly, 'never mind – put the shilling up again.'

The landlord of the Green Man had stood near enough to witness this scene, and he was a man whose abundant feeding served to keep his good nature, as well as his person, in high condition. And that lovely tearful face of Hetty's would have found out the sensitive fibre in most men.

'Come, young woman, come in,' he said, 'and have adrop o' something; you're pretty well knocked up, I can see that.'

He took her into the bar and said to his wife, 'Here, missis, take this young woman into the parlour; she's a little overcome' – for Hetty's tears were falling fast. They were merely hysterical tears: she thought she had no reason for weeping now, and was vexed that she was too weak and tired to help it. She was at Windsor at last, not far from Arthur.

She looked with eager, hungry eyes at the bread and meat and beer that the landlady brought her, and for some minutes she forgot everything else in the delicious sensations of satisfying hunger and recovering from exhaustion.

Adam Bede

IRMA ROMBAUER
1877–1962

In Switzerland we had a vile tempered cook named Marguerite. Her one idea, after being generally disagreeable, was to earn enough to own a small chalet on some high peak where she could cater to mountain climbers. While she was certainly not born with a silver spoon in her mouth – although it was large enough to accommodate several – I am convinced she arrived with a cooking spoon in her hand. If she has attained her ideal, many a climber will feel it worth while to scale a perilous peak to reach her kitchen.

The Joy of Cooking

ISABELLA BIRD
1831–1904

Just at nightfall the descent of a steep hill took me out of the forest and upon a clean log cabin, where, finding that the proper halting-place was two miles farther on, I remained. A truly pleasing, superior-looking woman placed me in a rocking-chair; would not let me help her otherwise than by rocking the cradle, and made me 'feel at home.' The room, though it serves them and their two children for kitchen, parlour, and bedroom, is the pattern of brightness, cleanliness, and comfort. At supper there were canned raspberries, rolls, butter, tea, venison, and fried rabbit, and at seven I went to bed in a carpeted log room, with a thick feather-bed on a mattress, sheets, ruffled pillow slips, and a pile of warm white blankets! I slept for eleven hours. They discourage me much about the route which ex-Governor Hunt has projected for me. They think that it is impassable, owing to snow, and that another storm is brewing.

A Lady's Life in the Rocky Mountains

LAURA SCHENONE

ANCIENT FRUIT PRESERVES

Women were preserving berries long before the rise of glass mason jars. Gitksan women of the Northwest, present-day Canada, went out and gathered berries on expeditions that could last for weeks. They then boiled, smoked, and pressed them into rolls, which could be transported home in wood boxes and stored. Later the rolls were cut into cakes to be eaten plain or dipped in grease – perfect for traveling while hunting.

A Thousand Years Over a Hot Stove

EDITH WHARTON
1862–1937

When the tea came he watched her in silent fascination while her hands flitted above the tray, looking miraculously fine and slender in contrast to the coarse china and lumpy bread. It seemed wonderful to him that any one should perform with such careless ease the difficult task of making tea in public in a lurching train . . . [S]ecure in the shelter of her conspicuousness, he sipped the inky draught with a delicious sense of exhilaration.

Lily, with the flavour of Selden's caravan tea on her lips, had no great fancy to drown it in the railway brew which seemed such nectar to her companion; but, rightly judging that one of the charms of tea is the fact of drinking it together, she proceeded to give the last touch to Mr. Gryce's enjoyment by smiling at him across her lifted cup.

The House of Mirth

MARY RENAULT
1905–83

Opposite her sat a stout man in a navy suit and bowler, smoking a miniature cigar. He had given her the only bad moment of the trip by boarding the carriage at a panting run, just as they left Reading. Her mother had warned her most carefully against men who employed this technique. They did it, after having marked down a woman sitting alone, in order to make sure that it would be too late for her to change her compartment. It was a local train too, with no rescuing corridor. Clammy with panic, and pretending to look fixedly out of the window, she watched him out of the tail of her eye open an attaché case and take out typewritten matter, which he proceeded to mark heavily in pencil. The lid of the case was raised towards her, so that anything might have been inside it still; chloroform, for instance, on a handkerchief, a weapon which played a most important part in her mother's cautionary tales.

Five minutes later, her worst suspicions were confirmed. They were passing the blank wall of an embankment, and, reflected in the window, she could see that he was looking at her fixedly, and groping in the case at the same time. She shot a lightning glance at the communication cord above her head. Once he had seized her, she would not be able to reach it. But what if she pulled it in time, and when the guard came he pretended to be perfectly innocent? She would have to pay five pounds for its improper use: which would leave her with only half the price of a second pull.

'Excuse me,' said the man.

Elsie turned, with the rigid compulsion of a bird fascinated by a serpent. He was bringing his hand out of the case, and in it was something wrapped in a white cloth. She did not even look at the communication cord. It was too late now; it would only accelerate his spring.

'You'll pardon a liberty, I hope, miss. But being there's no tea-car on this train, it crossed my mind if you'd care to help me out with these sandwiches.' He unfolded the wrapping and displayed them, a thick, juicy pile, the top half filled with sardine and the bottom half with egg. Could one drug sardines, and if drugged, did they smell so good? 'My better half puts them up for me,' he added apologetically. 'Can't bear to think of me missing my tea. Fact is, if I get a good filling meal at midday, like what I had at Oxford to-day, they spoil my appetite for my supper, and that upsets her. But she'll have me on the carpet just the same, if she finds any left.'

'Thank you,' said Elsie, 'very much.'

The sandwiches were moist and delicious, most comforting to a stomach frugally sustained since morning with odd cups of tea and buns in railway refreshment rooms. The man lent her the *Daily Mail*, and she responded with *John o' London*, which she had bought because she had felt it would be a cultured object to have with her on arrival. Her spirits mounted. Here she was, mature and sophisticated, emerging triumphant from a situation fraught with danger, conversing with a strange man on a train, and honour intact. She felt ready to cope with anything, even her destination.

The Friendly Young Ladies

CONSTANCE SPRY 1886–1960
ROSEMARY HUME 1907–

A florist by trade, Constance Spry became joint principal, with Rosemary Hume, of London's Cordon Bleu Cookery School. They teamed up to write a witty and engaging cookery book that has become a classic.

I well remember the first time I had a luncheon basket on a train; ordered ahead by wire it was brought to the carriage at some main-line station *en route*. Now, I thought, I really am grown up, no more packets of sandwiches for me. Someone must have tipped off the guard, for I remember he brought in a fresh footwarmer and inquired if I was comfortable. Hair up, long skirts, luncheon basket, the *Strand Magazine*, on my way to my first house party – I was beginning life. In the basket was a wing of chicken, roll, butter, biscuits, cheese and, I think, celery and possibly cake or a jam tart and an apple, and I have an idea that it cost 2s. 6d., though it may have been less. Later, with less precision, I remember meals taken in restaurant cars, food of good quality with reasonable variety, albeit served in the somewhat regimented way adopted in railway dining-cars . . . I should like to give you the details of a delicious meal made by one of the family for a small party going up to the far north.

Each of us was handed when we got into our sleepers a small, neat cardboard box containing two little screw-top cartons and other small packages. In one carton was a perfect freshly made lobster salad in a delicious dressing, the second carton contained fresh fruit salad of peaches, strawberries, and orange. Crisp poppy-seed-sprinkled rolls were quartered and buttered, and a Porosan bag held the crisp heart of a cos lettuce. There were small cream cheese rolls made by taking two short pieces of celery, filling the hollow made when they were put together with cream cheese, and rolling the whole in brown bread and butter. Porosan bags are a boon for carried meals; one heart of lettuce not used on this long journey was fresh and crisp when it was taken out of its bag eighteen hours or so after it had been packed up.

The Constance Spry Cookery Book

SHOBA NARAYAN

The most important thing when traveling by train in India is not the location of your seat (first-class is more comfortable, second-class more congenial), whether you have confirmed tickets, or even your destination. The crucial element is the size of your neighbor's tiffin carrier. If you're lucky, you will be seated near a generous Marwari matron whose method of making your acquaintance is to hand you a hot roti stuffed with potato *saag*.

I was twelve when this happened to me, and I still remember biting into the soft, ghee-stained roti and feeling the explosion of spices in my mouth as I encountered cumin, cilantro, ginger, green chiles, pungent onions, and finally – like a sigh – a comfortingly soft potato. It was dawn. The train whistled mournfully as it click-clacked its way through the misty countryside. A cool breeze wafted through the open window and teased the curls behind my ear. Fragrant turmeric-yellow *saag* dribbled down the corner of my mouth. A perfect symphony for the senses . . .

If my school lunch box with its measly two containers was a Manhattan town house, the Marwari matron's tiffin carrier was the Empire State Building, with more than a dozen impressively stacked stainless steel containers. She opened each one at strategic points during our train journey together. At dawn we had roti and potato *saag*. At ten o'clock, a snack of crisp *kakda* wafers speckled with pepper. For lunch, a bounty of *parathas* (flat breads stuffed with mashed potatoes, spinach, radish, *paneer*, and other such goodies).

My mother had brought our lunch in a tiffin carrier too: petal-soft *idlis* wrapped in banana leaf and slathered with coconut chutney. She always made *idlis* for train travel because, among their other virtues, they keep well. The Marwari boys scooped them up with gusto when my mother offered them, and wolfed them down with gentle satisfied grunts . . .

Almost every station in India sells a regional specialty that causes passengers to dart in and out of trains. My parents have woken me up at

3:00 A.M. just to taste the hot milk at Erode Station in Tamil Nadu. Anyone passing by Nagpur Station is entreated to buy its glorious oranges. Allahabad, home to Hinduism on the banks of the River Ganges, is famous for its guavas. Agra, home of the Taj Mahal, has wonderful *pedas* (milk sweets). Shimla, called Queen of Hill Stations by the British, was known for its apples. North of Delhi we could buy thick yogurt in tiny terra-cotta pots. The earthenware pots sucked the moisture from the yogurt, leaving it creamy enough to be cut with a knife. Kerala, where my father spent his childhood and still leaves his heart, is where I've eaten the best banana *appams*, fried in coconut oil on the platform. A few stations down on our journey to Bombay was the summer resort of Lonavla, where my mother would hop out of the train to buy *chikkis* (peanut brittle) . . .

Sated and tired, we arrived at Bombay station around 4:00 P.M. But there was still one more ritual left before we got into the car to head home. At a corner of the station was a tiny, smoky stall that served the best *vada-pav* in all of Bombay and therefore all of India. *Vada-pav* is Bombay's version of a hamburger, a deep-fried potato pancake spiced with ginger, garlic, green chiles, and cumin and served on a sliced bun with spicy chutneys on the side.

The stall at Dadar Station was always crowded, and we waited in line surrounded by bulging bags and suitcases. A potbellied man stood behind a giant black wok, frying round *vadas*, balls of mashed potato, until they turned golden brown. With quick, deft actions, he removed the *vadas* from the oil using a large sieve and stuffed them between a sliced bun generously coated with butter. A dollop of green chutney, some red sauce, and sometimes a tart tamarind relish, and the *vada-pav* was ready. We slathered the chutneys on the bun and took a bite. It was tongue-scalding hot, gloriously spicy, crisp on the outside, and melting soft on the inside. It tasted piquant and spicy. It tasted like India. Pure heaven!

Monsoon Diary: A Memoir with Recipes

DARRA GOLDSTEIN

Darra Goldstein is the editor of Gastronomica: The Journal of Food and Culture *and the food editor of* Russian Life Magazine.

No picture of the Russian peasant is quite complete unless it also depicts a handful of sunflower seeds. The love of these crisp seeds is near-universal, and even though it is considered gauche to crunch them in public, the floors of public buildings – especially waiting rooms – bear testimony to their popularity. The careful observer can always spot the site of an erstwhile line from the sunflower hulls strewn over the ground. One of my favorite memories of Russia is of a tiny girl boarding a train, her hair done up in bright ribbons, proudly clutching her refreshment for the long train ride ahead, a sunflower head almost as big as herself.

A Taste of Russia

MARGARET VISSER

Visser's comment that 'The British meal is all to do with a hard thing and two soft things' reveals her almost structuralist concern with the pattern and symbolism of food.

An airline dinner is a useful device to keep passengers pinned to their places and occupied for an appreciable length of time. People hurtling through the air in a metal tube, both uneasily aware of what could go wrong and stupefied with boredom, are deemed to require solace. Eating is comfort – provided that nothing untoward or unexpected occurs during dinner. In the early days of air travel, until the early thirties, travellers ate at tables set out in the plane, as in a restaurant. There were wine bottles, flowers, cloths on the tables, and male stewards (then called couriers) in white jackets, serving the meals. The shuddering and dipping of the aircraft caused spills, and the noise was so infernal that conversation had often to be carried on by means of written notes – but still things were done 'properly,' which is to say as far as possible as they were done on earth . . .

The 'companions' close to our sides (we face other people's backs) are likely to be strangers. Meals are provided in strict accustomed sequence: breakfast, lunch, dinner, with 'proper' tea-breaks and drinks, in spite of time changes, and regardless of the fact that eating events may take place with very short periods of sedentary time between them. An airline meal is not large: who would expect a large meal in our cabined and confined state? But it is invariably complete, and as complex as possible. It tries to carry all the connotations of a shared, comforting, 'proper' dinner. It is supposed to supply a nostalgic link with the cultural presuppositions with which flying conflicts, such as warm kitchens, stable conditions, and the products of the earth. Manners, here, impose passivity and constraint; ornamentation is taken care of by the oddity of our being served dinner at all in such circumstances. There is no question of argument, and only very limited choice. Airline passengers are extraordinarily docile and uncomplaining.

The Rituals of Dinner

AMANDA HESSER

Amanda Hesser studied culinary history with Barbara Wheaton at Radcliffe. Her bestselling Cooking for Mr Latte *was based on the* Food Diary *she introduced in the* New York Times Magazine.

[W]hen I fly, I am convinced that I will die. So I put a lot of energy into creating a kind of cocoon around myself. I wear Bose headphones, which block out the roar of the engines (and any signs of malfunction), wrap myself in a blanket, and wear one of those blow-up neck pillows. Food in the cocoon is most important. I want the meal to be delicious and civilized: if it's going to be my last, it's certainly not going to be some rubbery chicken suffocating in tinfoil . . .

For the main course, I often bring a sandwich. They were designed for eating on the road, after all. A good sandwich contains the best foods in the world: excellent cured meats and cheeses, aged vinegars, nut oils, roasted onions, herbs and homemade mayonnaise.

One of my favorite sandwiches for the air is a thin baguette spread with sweet butter and draped with prosciutto. I also love a similar version with olive oil, roasted red pepper and creamy mozzarella cheese.

This time, since I was on my way to Spain, the land of ham, I needed to think outside the box. It was spring, and the season's first asparagus was popping up, so I leapt on it at Fairway. There, I also picked up some fresh goat curd (regular soft goat cheese would have been fine), blood oranges and arugula. I bought big, plump Medjool dates and a ripe pear. For breakfast, I chose an almond croissant from a nearby pastry shop.

A few hours before my flight, I blanched the asparagus and let it cool, then sliced it into inch-long pieces. I whisked blood orange juice and vinegar with a few teaspoons of Dijon mustard, salt and pepper, dripping in grapeseed oil a little at a time. It was sweet and a moody shade of purple, which stained the arugula and bled all over the lumps of goat curd. I could have added tuna instead of goat curd, and some green beans or chickpeas, but I liked the salad's simplicity, its tangle of pure vivid flavors. I packed the salad in a plastic container and brought a napkin and a real fork (which disturbingly, makes it through the X-ray machine every time).

For dessert, almost any tart, cake or petit four may be packed. Don't bother making anything. Buy a treat. It will give you something to look forward to, deep into the flight, after being forced to watch 'Shallow Hal.' I picked up some cornmeal almond biscotti and dark chocolates and went on my way.

For those hours that stretch between meals, I sometimes bring along sliced fennel, radishes, olives or figs. And for breakfast, I like to have a ripe banana, yogurt (my own; the stuff on planes is loaded with stabilizers), plums and a small, decadent pastry. A humble bagel will not do . . .

It never hurts to be a fussy gourmet, even in coach.

Cooking for Mr Latte

M.F.K. FISHER
1908–92

Once, I remember, we sat for hours in a cool bar with a dirt floor, drinking milk from coconuts which the boss pulled up from a deep covered well in the center of the room. He would get down on his knees as he saw us tipping the shells back further, and haul up the nuts in a kind of seine, cold and dripping. He could poke the eyes out with his thumb. We drank in a kind of frenzy. The milk was like balm after the coarse wines and the sea air. We felt a little sick for a few hours, but it was good to sit there so quietly with the earth under our feet.

Another time everybody on ship went to a palmy courtyard for a dinner. It was inside a hotel, a small dirty place without any doors, where the toilet was a hole in one corner of a room with several hammocks in it and several sleeping men in the hammocks.

We walked through a few little streets where every house was open, with a handsome Sears-Roebuck bed under a lithograph of the Sacred Heart, like the whores' rooms in Cristobal, and then hammocks swung for the real family life.

We started to eat, in a patio filled with vines and parrots and our long table, before the light left. A tiny gray-bearded man in white cotton trousers and a pink silk polo-shirt served us, helped by two children only a little taller than he.

We ate and ate. I can't remember much of it except avocados in several different manners. There was meat, though, probably found at great cost and, for me at least, impossible either to chew or swallow. There were dozens of little dishes of sweet cooked fruits and flat tidbits which could have been bats' ears or sliced melon-rind. The man, his large eyes devoutly veiled, slid them in front of us, hour after hour.

Occasionally came a dish of chicken boiled with peppers and chocolate ... something like that, as loud as a trumpet call in all the sweetness.

We sat eating, big pale strangers, and the patio grew dark. By the time we had drunk coffee and finished our beer and paid, the night was black. Under a streetlight three prisoners stumbled past us. Their irons rang the occasional pavements, and sucked at the mudholes. And outside the village, before we came to the dock, fireflies taunted us in the forest, like mischievous candles, the biggest in the world.

The Gastronomical Me

PETA MATHIAS

I had always been fascinated by the life of a sailor on the high seas, so when I was offered a position as chef on a luxury hotel barge in the Loire, I thought, now is my chance to stop being a landlubber. The idea of swanning around calm canals in quiet countryside appealed greatly after the madness of Paris and Rose Blues. I saw myself as Bruce Chatwin's shadow – adventurous, fearless and kind to the natives. It turned out to be everything I had hoped for except that it was very hard work. The chef alone was responsible for a huge buffet lunch, a four-course evening meal and a cooked breakfast for those who requested it from the twenty-two passengers and eight staff . . . Passengers spent three to six days with us, eating, mostly, and going on excursions to vineyards, castles, abbeys and walking or bicycling along the towpaths and country lanes.

There was very much an atmosphere of 'upstairs-downstairs' with the stewardesses being gushingly polite on one side of the kitchen door and utterly vile on the other. The kitchen was open plan, so while I was preparing smoked country ham, ratatouille, taboulé, endive, beetroot and walnut salad, white asparagus with lemon and butter sauce and stuffed artichokes for lunch, I got to be witness to all the gossip, dramas and romances of the staff . . .

The worst torture for all the chefs on the barges was having to go out and explain to the assembled starving mass what they had prepared for them that day. I would go out dry and speak about the secret pleasures of raw oysters with shallot and red-wine vinegar, roquefort quiche, the regional *charcuterie* and cheeses, salmon and dill muffins, crisp little radishes dipped in butter and salt, and cauliflower, cucumber and potato salad, and come back drenched, with tears of perspiration running through my lipstick. Americans, who have been educated to diet as part of their culture, often made my job difficult, but the English were always absolutely thrilled to be eating anything and were unfailingly courteous and appreciative.

Fête Accomplie

IRIS ORIGO
1902–88

Apparently, according to a memorandum 'of all the things that are required at sea', most travellers, in addition to their wares, took their own food and cooking pots with them. The list (which does not specify the number of travellers or the length of the journey) includes 3 large oil-jars, 6 bowls, 6 basins, 2 earthenware saucepans, 2 pewter cups, 12 glasses, and 6 knives, while the food consists of 250 white loaves for making biscuits, 1 sheep, 2 shoulders of salted meat, several pairs of fowls, 50 eggs, 1 lb. of salt, 4 lb. of sugar, 1 little flask of oil, 2 flasks of strong vinegar, 100 sweet oranges, ½ lb. of spices, 1 lb. of cassia in beans, 2 lb. of comfits (*tregea*), 1 lb. of rosewater, and an unspecified amount of onions, garlic, saffron, pepper, clove, and ginger. And finally, to keep up the traveller's courage, there were 2 barrels of red wine and 2 flasks of 'good Corsican' – and the list ended with 2 lb. of wax candles and 'comfits to set the stomach right'.

The Merchant of Prato

DOROTHY HARTLEY
1892–1985

We have special interest in the share womenfolk had in providing food for long voyages, because an aunt was one of the first women travelling to the West Indies in sailing ships. She had the minute memory and zestful interest of her period and remembered voyages of several months' duration: 'We took goats for milk and hens for eggs, and pigs and sheep, the butcher looked after all animals and they were all eaten by the end of the voyage. Regular diet was salt meat, dried peas and beans, and forms of beans and bacon. We also had boiled salt beef with dumplings, carrots, and root vegetables. Cabin passengers used to take watercress growing in jars, and a few dozen new-laid eggs greased with hot lard and packed in sawdust. The ship provided lemons – against scurvy, and for 'punch'. We took eating apples and conserves in jars. I remember cook used to make a most delicious conserve of fresh apricots and red-currant juice, and we took black-currant cordial. Salves and ointments we always took. I always took a ham as a present to the Captain, as we sat at his table; we cooked it specially with cider and cloves. The cloves helped to keep it. We used to take poultry, potted in tubs and potted trout and salmon done in vinegar, and potted meat in jars. We grew to be very clever! It was our pride. We had apple sauce and onion with the pork. The pig was first to go – the goats and hens last. Cream we boiled with sugar till it was quite stiff; it kept excellently.'

Food in England

HANNAH GLASSE
1708–70

FOR CAPTAINS OF SHIPS

To make Catchup to keep twenty Years.

Take a gallon of strong stale beer, one pound of anchovies washed from the pickle, a pound of shalots peeled, half an ounce of mace, half an ounce of cloves, a quarter of an ounce of whole pepper, three or four large races of ginger, two quarts of the large mushroom-flaps rubbed to pieces; cover all this close, and let it simmer till it is half wasted, then strain it through a flannel bag; let it stand till it is quite cold, then bottle it. You may carry it to the Indies. A spoonful of this to a pound of fresh butter melted makes a fine fish-sauce, or in the room of gravy sauce. The stronger and staler the beer is, the better the catchup will be.

The Art of Cookery, Made Plain and Easy

LADY MARY WORTLEY MONTAGU
1689–1762

Her mother having died young, Mary took carving lessons three times a week in order to assume the duty of presiding at the family table. She taught herself Latin, and also learned to speak Italian, French and Turkish. Though the family tried to suppress them, her Turkish Embassy Letters were an overnight sensation.

To Lady Mar,

Pera, Constantinople, 10 March 1718

I have not writ to you, dear sister, these many months; a great piece of self-denial, but I know not where to direct or what part of the world you were in . . .

I went to see the Sultana Hafise, favourite of the last Emperor Mustafa, who, you know (or perhaps you don't know) was deposed by his brother the reigning Sultan, and died a few weeks after, being poisoned, as it was generally believed . . .

She gave me a dinner of fifty dishes of meat, which, after their fashion, was placed on the table but one at a time, and was extremely tedious, but the magnificence of her table answered very well to that of her dress. The knives were of gold, the hafts set with diamonds, but the piece of luxury that grieved my eyes was the table cloth and napkins, which were all tiffany, embroidered with silks and gold in the finest manner in natural flowers. It was with the utmost regret that I made use of these costly napkins, as finely wrought as the finest handkerchiefs that ever came out of this country. You may be sure that they were entirely spoilt before dinner was over. The sherbet, which is the liquor they drink at meals, was served in china bowls, but the covers and salvers massy gold. After dinner water was brought in a gold basin and towels of the same kind of the napkins, which I very unwillingly wiped my hands upon, and coffee was served in china with gold soûcoupes.

The Turkish Embassy Letters

GIOVANNA GIUSTI GALARDI

The report on the religious and secular celebrations held for the wedding of Prince Ferdinando III de' Medici with Violante of Bavaria in the Cathedral of Santa Maria del Fiore and at Pitti Palace in January 1689, also gives an account of the journey undertaken by the Princess in that harsh, frozen winter in order to arrive at Florence. We can just imagine her entourage, proceeding slowly towards Florence and growing thicker along the way as they collect the many gifts of food offered – for the most part, sweets and sugar figures! Thus, we know that on December 13th, 1688, Monsignor Alberti, Bishop and Prince of Trento, gives a gift of 40 basinfuls containing, amongst the capons, partridges, grouse, turkeys and wine, 6 basins of *various preserves*.

The following 16th of December, passing through Verona, the Princess receives as a present of the *Serenissima* Republic of Venice: 2 cases containing 42 boxes of 'CANDIED BEANS AND PISTACHIOS, CITRON BLOSSOMS, coriander, CANDIED CITRON, orange blossoms, melon seeds, candied persimmons, moscadelle pears, candied *moselle*, *ruzzolati*, CANDIED FIGS, 8 TALL SUGAR CENTREPIECES, 250 MOULDED SUGAR *PERSICATE*, 60 BLOCKS OF SUGAR TRUFFLE, 2 barrels of oysters and 6 cases of Spanish wine and Venetian muscatel'.

Three days later, on the 19th, the duke of Mantua gives to Violante: '1 CASE OF BOXES OF PRESERVES, 1 case with 6 boxes of GENOAN CANDIED FRUITS, 6 boxes of GENOAN PASTRIES, 6 boxes of ROYAL PASTRIES, 1 box of SUGAR BLOCKS'.

Some of the richest gifts come from the duke of Modena on the 21st:

'45 basins of various preserves, 2 basins of sugars, . . . 1 basin of Portuguese oranges, 1 basin of CHOCOLATE, 1 basin of white meal in glass vases, 2 basins of oysters (. . .)' apart from the game, fish, wines, and so forth.

Sweets at Court

MONICA ALI

They sat on the grass in St James's Park and Nazneen laid the picnic out on four tea towels. Chicken wings spread in a paste of yoghurt and spices and baked in the oven, onions sliced to the thickness of a fingernail, mixed with chillies, dipped in gram flour and egg and fried in bubbling oil, a dry concoction of chickpeas and tomatoes stewed with cumin and ginger, misshapen chapattis wrapped while still hot in tinfoil and sprinkled now with condensation, golden hard-boiled eggs glazed in a curry seal, Dairylea triangles in their cardboard box, bright orange packets containing shamelessly orange crisps, a cake with a list of ingredients too long to be printed in legible type. She arranged them all on paper plates and stacked up the plastic tubs inside the carrier bags.

'It's ready,' she cried, as though calling them to the table.

Shahana extricated a Dairy Lea and picked the foil apart. She rolled the cheese inside a chapatti. Bibi sat on her feet and chewed at a chicken wing. Chanu took his time loading a plate with each item, including three crisps and a slice of the cake. He balanced it on his knee. 'It's quite a spread,' he said in English. 'You know, when I married your mother, it was a stroke of luck.' He gestured at the tea towels as if his luck were plainly on display. Then he ate with a fervour that ruled out conversation.

Brick Lane

MAYA ANGELOU

The summer picnic gave ladies a chance to show off their baking hands. On the barbecue pit, chickens and spareribs sputtered in their own fat and a sauce whose recipe was guarded in the family like a scandalous affair. However in the ecumenical light of the summer picnic every true baking artist could reveal her prize to the delight and criticism of the town. Orange sponge cakes and dark brown mounds dripping

Hershey's chocolate stood layer to layer with ice white coconuts and light brown caramels. Pound cakes sagged with their buttery weight and small children could no more resist licking the icings than their mothers could avoid slapping the sticky fingers.

I Know Why the Caged Bird Sings

RUTH LOWINSKY
1892–1958

Ruth Lowinsky found living in the country without her French cook 'a nightmare' during the war but compensated by serving every dish with about nineteen sauces. Her granddaughter remembers her as 'a marvellous toad in ruched Schiaparelli and fantastical mille-feuille hats'. Her recipes did not provide measurements.

A picnic lunch and dinner. This is what your guests expect when they refuse your invitation to a picnic!

SARDINES   HARD-BOILED EGGS
HAM OR BEEF SANDWICHES
UNDRESSED CUCUMBER
SEED CAKE   JAM SANDWICHES
SWISS ROLL   CORKED COFFEE

This is what you would have given them:

Picnic Lunch
FISH PIE
OR
BRAZILIAN OMELETTE
*

SPICED BEEF
*

TOMATO SALAD IN JELLY
*

CHOCOLATE CAKE
*
FRUIT

Picnic Dinner
COLD CONSOMMÉ WITH KULIBYAKA
OR
CHEESE FLAN
*

RUSSIAN HERRING SALAD
*

TONGUE AND PÂTÉ
*

NORTHAMPTONSHIRE GOOSEBERRY FOOL
*

BLACK COFFEE

More Lovely Food

ELIZABETH VON ARNIM
1866–1941

Yesterday, by way of a change, we went for a picnic to the shores of the Baltic, icebound at this season, and utterly desolate at our nearest point. I have a weakness for picnics, especially in winter, when the mosquitoes cease from troubling and the ant-hills are at rest; and of all my many favourite picnic spots this one on the Baltic is the loveliest and best . . .

[W]e started off in the gayest of spirits, even Minora being disposed to laugh immoderately on the least provocation. Only our eyes were allowed to peep out from the fur and woollen wrappings necessary to our heads if we would come back with our ears and noses in the same places they were in when we started, and for the first two miles the mirth created by each other's strange appearance was uproarious . . .

It was a hoar-frost day, and the forest was an enchanted forest leading into fairyland, and though Irais and I have been there often before, and always thought it beautiful, yet yesterday we stood under the final arch of frosted trees, struck silent by the sheer loveliness of the place. For a long way out the sea was frozen, and then there was a deep blue line, and a cluster of motionless orange sails; at our feet a narrow strip of pale yellow sand; right and left the line of sparkling forest; and we ourselves standing in a world of white and diamond traceries. The stillness of an eternal Sunday lay on the place like a benediction . . .

I warmed soup in a little apparatus I have for such occasions, which helped to take the chilliness off the sandwiches, – this is the only unpleasant part of a winter picnic, the clammy quality of the provisions just when you most long for something very hot. Minora let her nose very carefully out of its wrappings, took a mouthful, and covered it up quickly again. She was nervous lest it should be frost-nipped, and truth compels me to add that her nose is not a bad nose, and might even be pretty on anybody else; but she does not know how to carry it, and there is an art in the angle at which one's nose is held just as in everything else, and really noses were intended for something besides mere blowing.

It is the most difficult thing in the world to eat sandwiches with immense fur and woollen gloves on, and I think we ate almost as much fur as anything, and choked exceedingly during the process. Minora was angry at this, and at last pulled off her glove, but quickly put it on again.

'How very unpleasant,' she remarked after swallowing a large piece of fur.

'It will wrap round your pipes, and keep them warm,' said Irais.

'Pipes!' echoed Minora, greatly disgusted by such vulgarity.

'I'm afraid I can't help you,' I said, as she continued to choke and splutter; 'we are all in the same case, and I don't know how to alter it.'

'There are such things as forks, I suppose,' snapped Minora.

'That's true,' said I, crushed by the obviousness of the remedy; but of what use are forks if they are fifteen miles off? So Minora had to continue to eat her gloves.

By the time we had finished, the sun was already low behind the trees and the clouds beginning to flush a faint pink. The old coachman was given sandwiches and soup, and while he led the horses up and down with one hand and held his lunch in the other, we packed up – or, to be correct, I packed, and the others looked on and gave me valuable advice.

Elizabeth and Her German Garden

MARY ELIZABETH BRADDON
1835–1915

During the course of her fifty-five-year career, Mary Elizabeth Braddon adopted a variety of literary styles. This extract is from The Doctor's Wife, *an English version of Flaubert's* Madame Bovary.

It was nearly three o'clock now, and high time for the opening of the hampers, Mr Raymond declared, when he rejoined the rest of the party, much to the delight of the orphans, who were always hungry, and who ate so much, and yet remained so pale and skeleton-like of aspect, that they presented a pair of perpetual phenomena to the eye of the physiologist. The baskets had been carried to a little ivy-sheltered arbour, perched high above the waterfall; and here Mr Raymond unpacked them, bringing out his treasures one after another; first a tongue, then a pair of fowls, a packet of anchovy sandwiches, a great poundcake (at sight of which the eyes of the orphans glistened), delicate caprices in the way of pastry, semi-transparent biscuits, and a little block of stilton cheese, to say nothing of sundry bottles of Madeira and sparkling Burgundy.

Perhaps there never was a merrier party. To eat cold chicken and drink sparkling Burgundy in the open air on a bright May afternoon is always an exhilarating kind of thing, though the scene of your picnic may be the bleakest of the Sussex Downs, or the dreariest of the Yorkshire Wolds; but to drink the sparkling wine in that little arbour at Hurstonleigh, with the brawling of the waterfall keeping time to your laughter, the shadows of patriarchal oaks sheltering you from all the outer world, is the very *ultima Thule* of bliss in the way of a picnic.

The Doctor's Wife

ENID BLYTON
1897–1968

Famous children's author Enid Blyton was the daughter of a one-time cutlery salesman.

'I'll get you some supper,' said Anne to everyone. 'We're all famished. We can talk while we eat. George, come and help. Julian, can you get some ginger-beer? And, Dick, do fill up the water-bowl for me.'

The boys winked at one another. They always thought that Anne was very funny when she took command like this, and gave her orders. But everyone went obediently to work.

Nobby went to help Anne. Together they boiled ten eggs hard in the little saucepan. Then Anne made tomato sandwiches with potted meat and got out the cake the farmer's wife had given them. She remembered the raspberry syrup, too – how lovely!

Soon they were all sitting on the rocky ledge, which was still warm, watching the sun go down into the lake. It was a most beautiful evening, with the lake as blue as a cornflower and the sky flecked with rosy clouds. They held their hard-boiled eggs in one hand and a piece of bread and butter in the other, munching happily. There was a dish of salt for everyone to dip their eggs into.

'I don't know why, but the meals we have on picnics always taste so much nicer than the ones we have indoors,' said George. 'For instance, even if we had hard-boiled eggs and bread and butter indoors, they wouldn't taste as nice as these.'

'Can everyone eat two eggs?' asked Anne. 'I did two each. And there's plenty of cake – and more sandwiches and some plums we picked this morning.'

'Best meal I've ever had in my life,' said Nobby, and picked up his second egg. 'Best company I've ever been in too!'

'Thank you,' said Anne, and everyone looked pleased. Nobby might not have their good manners, but he always seemed to say just the right thing.

Five Go Off in a Caravan

THE FOOD OF LOVE

SYLVIA THOMPSON

In The Gastronomical Me, *M.F.K. Fisher describes her goddaughter, Sylvia Thompson, as hating 'sensuous dishes'. Something must have changed over time. The Norah of this tale was M.F.K. Fisher's sister.*

Cooking in love is not like cooking under any other circumstances. Cooking in an apartment you could put in your eye makes cooking in love the more delicate . . . on our third date (Gene had begun to propose on our second date, a picnic, but I asked him to wait), I made him spaghetti in his apartment. It was one room big enough for a bed, a desk, a phonograph, and a gas heater. Up three steps was a closet converted to an alcove with a two-burner hotplate on the left and a refrigerator on the right. Beyond that was the bathroom.

I suppose I've never cooked anything I wanted so much to be sublime nor ended up laughing so much in the making as that spaghetti. I chopped the onions, carrots, celery, parsley, and garlic on a plate on my lap sitting on the bed – the only free surface was a corner of Gene's desk, which is where he usually ate, but I was afraid of scattering onions and carrots through his papers. Then I simmered the ground beef, vegetables, and tomatoes on one burner of the hotplate, brought the pasta water to a boil on the other burner, and sautéed mushrooms for the sauce on top of the heater (it was February, thank heaven). When the pasta was ready, Gene drained the pot in the tub while I grated Parmesan into a bowl in the sink. I'd already tossed lettuce with olive oil and vinegar, and dinner was served. Gene meanwhile had taken his typewriter and papers off his desk and set two places for dinner. Which was marvelous. Except he kept staring at me.

I said to him finally, 'Now you can ask me.'

'Ask you what?'

'To marry you!'

He did and I accepted. We went upstairs to tell Norah. We rapped on the kitchen door and she opened it. 'We're going to be married,' Gene said.

She stared at us. 'Um,' she said, and closed the door. We stood there for a moment, then walked silently down the outside stairs to Gene's apartment. Five minutes later, there was a knock on the door. It was Norah, with a bottle of champagne.

Feasts and Friends

SUE GRAFTON

Grafton's detective heroine Kinsey Millhone is no cook, and famously fond of junk food, but here she realises how seductive a good meal can be.

We drove down to the Ranch House in Ojai, one of those elegant restaurants where the waiter stands at your table and recites the menu like a narrative poem.

'Shall I order for us or would that offend your feminine sensibilities?'

'Go ahead,' I said, feeling oddly relieved, 'I'd like that' . . .

The meal that followed was one of the most sensual I ever experienced: fresh, tender bread with a crust of flaky layers, spread with a buttery pâté, Boston lettuce with a delicate vinaigrette, sand dabs sautéed in butter and served with succulent green grapes. There were fresh raspberries for dessert with a dollop of tart cream, and all the time Charlie's face across the table from me, shadowed by that suggestion of caution, that hint of something stark and fearful held back, pulling me forward even while I felt myself kept in check.

A Is for Alibi

SHOBA NARAYAN

My grandfather fell in love with my grandmother over *idlis*. As a child bride, Nalla-ma was put to work on the granite grinding stone (*aatu-kal* in Tamil). She was twelve and spent her morning turning the stone to make *idli* batter. Enter my grandfather, a strapping lad of twenty-two. Desperate to ease the burden of his beautiful bride yet fearful of being taunted as a henpecked husband if caught beside her, he came up with an ingenious solution. He donned a sari, covered his head like any dutiful daughter-in-law, sat down beside my grandmother, and turned the heavy granite stone himself. They gazed into each other's eyes, didn't say a word, and together made the fluffiest *idli* batter imaginable.

Monsoon Diary: A Memoir with Recipes

LAURA ESQUIVEL

With its remedies and recipes, Esquivel's bestseller is much like a household book from the seventeenth or eighteenth century.

Ingredients
12 roses, preferably red
12 chestnuts
2 teaspoons butter
2 teaspoons cornstarch
2 drops attar of roses
2 tablespoons anise
2 tablespoons honey
2 cloves garlic
6 quail
1 pitaya

Preparation

Remove the petals carefully from the roses, trying not to prick your fingers, for not only are the little wounds painful but the petals could soak up blood that might alter the flavor of the dish and even produce dangerous chemical reactions . . .

With Nacha dead, Tita was the best qualified of all the women in the house to fill the vacant post in the kitchen, and in there flavors, smells, textures, and the effects they could have were beyond Mama Elena's iron command.

Tita was the last link in a chain of cooks who had been passing culinary secrets from generation to generation since ancient times, and she was considered the finest exponent of the marvelous art of cooking. Naming her official ranch cook was a popular decision with everyone. Tita was pleased to receive the post, in spite of the sorrow she felt at losing Nacha.

Her unfortunate death had left Tita in a very deep depression. With Nacha dead she was completely alone. It was as if her real mother had died. To help her get over it, Pedro thought it would be nice to bring her a bouquet of roses to celebrate her first year as ranch cook. But Rosaura – who was expecting her first child – did not agree, and when she saw him walk in carrying a bouquet for Tita, instead of her, she burst into tears and ran from the room.

With just a look Mama Elena sent Tita away to get rid of the roses. Now, too late, Pedro realized his foolhardiness. Again with a look, Mama Elena informed him there was still time to repair the damage. Such a look it was that he excused himself and went off to look for Rosaura. Tita clasped the roses to her chest so tightly that when she got to the kitchen, the roses, which had been mostly pink, had turned quite red from the blood that was flowing from Tita's hands and breasts. She had to think fast what to do with them. They were beautiful. She couldn't just throw them in the trash; in the first place, she'd never been given flowers before, and second, they were from Pedro. All at once she seemed to hear Nacha's voice dictating a recipe, a prehispanic recipe involving rose petals. Tita had nearly forgotten it because it called for pheasants, which they didn't raise on the ranch.

The one bird they did have was quail. She decided to revise the recipe slightly, just so she could use the flowers . . .

Everyone was a little tense as they sat down at the table, but that's as far as it went until the quail was served. It wasn't enough he'd made his wife jealous earlier, for when Pedro tasted his first mouthful, he couldn't help closing his eyes in voluptuous delight and exclaiming:

'It is a dish for the gods!'

Mama Elena knew that the quail was exquisite; nonetheless, Pedro's remark did not sit well with her, and she replied:

'It's too salty.' . . .

Something strange had happened . . . even though [Tita's] body was sitting up quite properly in her chair; there wasn't the slightest sign of life in her eyes. It was as if a strange alchemical process had dissolved her entire being in the rose petal sauce, in the tender flesh of the quails, in the wine, in every one of the meal's aromas. That was the way she entered Pedro's body, hot, voluptuous, perfumed, totally sensuous . . .

Pedro didn't offer any resistance. He let Tita penetrate to the farthest corners of his being, and all the while they couldn't take their eyes off each other. He said:

'Thank you, I have never had anything so exquisite.'

It truly is a delicious dish. The roses give it an extremely delicate flavor.

After the petals are removed from the roses, they are ground with the anise in a mortar. Separately, brown the chestnuts in a pan, remove the peels, and cook them in water. Then, puree them. Mince the garlic and brown slightly in butter; when it is transparent, add it to the chestnut puree, along with the honey, the ground pitaya, and the rose petals, and salt to taste. To thicken the sauce slightly, you may add two teaspoons of cornstarch. Last, strain through a fine sieve and add no more than two drops of attar of roses, since otherwise it might have too strong a flavor and smell. As soon as the seasoning has been added, remove the sauce from the heat. The quail should be immersed in this sauce for ten minutes to infuse them with the flavor and then removed.

The smell of attar of roses is so penetrating that the mortar used to grind the petals will smell like roses for several days.

Like Water for Chocolate

RUTH REICHL

Formerly restaurant critic for the New York Times, *Reichl is currently the editor of* Gourmet *magazine.*

When Michael asked if I would bake a cake for his fortieth birthday party, I could not say no. It was what I would have done for any friend. But as I watched myself cream ten pounds of sugar into seven pounds of butter I began to understand what I was really up to. My unconscious had taken over; I had made a decision. The cake took rivers of chocolate and dozens of eggs, and by the time it was finished I needed four men to help me lift it into the car.

Michael blanched when he saw my creation coming toward him. This was more than a cake; it was a declaration of love in front of three hundred people, and we both knew it.

Comfort Me with Apples

PHILIPPINE WELSER
1527–80

When he fell in love with the commoner Philippine Welser, Archduke Ferdinand II of Augsburg married her secretly rather than risk scandalising the court at Vienna. The marriage was upheld on condition that Philippine's children renounce their right of succession. It is said that Philippine died of liver failure. In any event her cookbook is possibly the first in western Europe to have been compiled by a woman.

SPAETZLE NOODLES WITH-LARD/DRIPPING (SAMALZIC NUDELIN)

Ingredients
(Enough for 4)
350g flour
4-5 eggs
20g butter
Pinch of nutmeg
Salt
50g lard/dripping
Chopped parsley
2 litres of salted water

Method
Sift the flour into a bowl. Add the eggs one at a time and mix to form a heavy dough. Melt the butter and add to the dough, mixing well. Add the nutmeg and salt and mix to form an elastic dough. Leave the dough to rest for half an hour.

Put the salted water to boil in a pan. Dip the pastry board into the water, place some of the dough onto the board and with a sharp knife scrape fine strips of dough into the water which should be at a fast boil. Keep dipping the knife into cold water. The noodles should be moving freely in the water so it is important not to scrape too many into the pot at one go.

When the noodles surface they are done. Remove them with a slotted spoon/ladle, run cold water over them for a second (to stop the cooking process), drain them and fry them in a pan with melted lard/dripping.

Serve with chopped parsley.

BREADCRUMB TART (SEMELDORTEM)

Ingredients
(For 4 portions)
5 eggs
250g breadcrumbs
Rusks
250g ground almonds
Salt and pepper
50g fat (butter)

Method
Whisk up the eggs and mix in the breadcrumbs, season with salt and pepper and knead with the ground almonds to form a pliable dough.

Warm the fat or lard until melted, and use it to coat the inside of a rectangular cake tin. Put the dough in the tin and place in a pre-heated oven (present-day oven setting: electric 200°C) for about 30–50 minutes. With a pastry brush put some of the fat on top of the mixture several times during the baking process. When ready, paint a final layer of the fat and add a pinch of salt and leave in the oven for another two minutes.

Check with a wooden skewer. If the skewer comes out clean the cake is done. While still warm it should be cut into thick slices (as thick as a thumb).

From an original recipe dated 1557 by Duchess Philippine Welser
trans. by Sheelagh Neuling

MARY ELIZABETH BRADDON
1835–1915

They all went down-stairs presently, and were ushered into an oak-panelled room, where there was an oval table laid for luncheon, and where Isabel found herself seated presently on Mr Lansdell's right hand, and opposite to Lady Gwendoline Pomphrey.

This was life. There was a Lance-like group of hothouse grapes and peaches, crowned with a pine-apple, in a high Dresden basket in the centre of the table. Isabel had never seen a pine-apple out of the celebrated Edith-Dombey picture until to-day. There were flowers upon the table, and a faint odour of orange-blossoms and apricots pervaded the atmosphere. There were starry white glasses, so fragile-looking that it seemed as if a breath would have blown them away; cup-shaped glasses, broad shallow glasses like water-lily leaves, glasses of the palest green, and here and there a glimpse of ruby glass flashing in the sunshine. Mrs Gilbert had a very vague idea of the nature of the viands which were served to her at that wonderful feast. Somebody dropped a lump of ice into the shallow glass, and filled it afterwards with a yellow bubbling wine, which had a faint flavour of ripe pears, and which some one said was Moselle. Mr Lansdell put some white creamy compound on her plate, which might or might not have been chicken; and one of the servants brought her an edifice of airy pastry, filled with some mysterious concoction in which there were little black lumps. She took a spoonful of the concoction, seeing that other people had done so; but she was very doubtful of the little black lumps, which she conjectured to be a mistake of the cook's. And then some one brought her an ice, a real ice, – just as if Mordred Priory had been a perpetual pastrycook's shop, – a pink ice in the shape of a pear, which she ate with a pointed gold spoon; and then the pine-apple was cut, and she had a slice of it, and was rather disappointed in it, as hardly realising the promise of its appearance.

But all the dishes in that banquet were of 'such stuff as dreams are made of.' So may have tasted the dew-berries which Titania's attendants gave to Bottom. To Isabel there was a dream-like flavour in every thing. Was not *he* by her side, talking to her every now and then? The subjects of which he spoke were commonplace enough, certainly, and he talked to other people as well as to her. He talked about the plans of the Cabinet and the hunting-season to Lord Ruysdale, and he talked of books and pictures with Mr Raymond and Lady Gwendoline, and of parish matters with George Gilbert. He seemed to know all about every thing in the world, Isabel thought. She could not say much; *how* to admire was all the art she knew. As to the orphans, those young ladies sat side by side, and nudged each other when the sacrificial knife was plunged into any fresh viand, and discoursed together every now and then in rapturous whispers; nothing came amiss to them, from rout-cakes and preserved ginger to lobster-salad or the wall of a fricandeau.

It was four o'clock by the time the pine-apple had been cut, and the banquet concluded.

The Doctor's Wife

JANE AUSTEN
1775–1817

FROM CHAWTON TO CASSANDRA AT STEVENTON

24 January 1813

I could see nothing very promising between Mr P & Miss P.T. She placed herself on one side of him at first, but Miss Benn obliged her to move up higher; & she had an empty plate, & even asked him to give her mutton twice without being attended to for some time. There might be design in this, to be sure, on his side; he might think an empty stomach more favourable to love.

Letters

JENNIE FONTANA

I want to eat watercress now
in a doorstep sandwich
with you outside a ramshackle pub
with only the sound of skylarks

and our teeth crunching through thick crusts
our tongues startled by the pepper
of freshly picked watercress

'Watercress Beds'

ALICE ADAMS PROCTOR
20th century

HONEYMOON SPECIAL

Ingredients

Three thin slices of Wonder Bread cut in heart shape. One heart-shaped piece of green pepper about ¾ inch across. Arrow 1¼-inch long, cut from pimento. Cream cheese. Egg yolk mixed with mayonnaise. Sardine or anchovy paste.

Directions

Spread bread with creamed butter. Between first and second slices spread fish paste. Between second and third slices spread egg-yolk mixture. On center top, place small decorative pepper heart with pimento arrow thrust through it. Edge top with a frill of cream cheese. Sprinkle with paprika.

NOTE: Minced ham or chicken may be used instead of fish paste.

The Wonder Sandwich Book

JUDI BENSON

You can make a meal of me any day, big boy.
I'm ripe and juicy, nectarine sweet
a tangy little kick on the top of the tongue.

I'm smooth as an avocado
slippery as a trout,
soft as mashed potatoes.

Turn me over-easy, baby.
Look into my golden eye
but don't cut me up.

No dicing, no chopping
just squeeze me, knead me
grind your pepper mill all over my flesh.

A complementary blend
a pinch of this, a knob of that.
Now sprinkle me with culinary kisses.

Keep me on a low heat till I blush pink.
Whisper honey, up and down my spine.
Decorate my naked body with parsley.

Now serve me up on the honeysuckle platter
steaming hot, waiting for you to cool me down.
Hungry now? Bon appetit, big boy.

'Cooking with Mae West'

SYLVIA TOWNSEND WARNER
1893–1978

Here she describes an anniversary meal enjoyed with her lover,
Valentine Ackland.

12 January 1933

Our second anniversary. A most brilliant day, with frost and sun bargaining. In the morning (the proper morning, for already in early light my darling had got up, seen the moon setting behind Granny, and sat reading Pocahontas by candlelight, while I drowsed and burrowed beside her) she gave me my aquamarine pendant. An aquamarine, very deep through, cut to a point behind, and ice-burning blue, dangling from a diamond the colour of a drop of champagne; and a sleek compact silver cigarette-case, with the falcon; and Mrs Gaskell's Letters to Ch. Eliot Norton, who must have been the father of my Mr Norton in New York; and I gave her a new-faced watch, with a scientific expression, and an inscription in a wedding-ring on the back.

We drove to Dorchester to fetch the oysters. After lunch we walked to see the lambs in Child's meadow, and then took William as far as the thorn. Elder, and spindle-berry tree already showing their leaves. Our ceremonial dinner was oysters, champagne, truffles cooked gently in cream, and coffee.

Diaries

M.F.K. FISHER
1908–92

W IS FOR WANTON

It is an agelong rumor, apparently fairly well founded, that the great procuresses and madams have always been the great teachers in 'la cuisine d'amour.' Such proficient pupils as Du Barry and the Countess of Louveciennes bear out this theory, and recipes ascribed to both of them are reprinted annually in various undercover publications dedicated to the somewhat dubious encouragement of libertinage.

Most of the culinary secrets told in them, at a high price and 'in plain wrappers for mailing,' lean heavily on the timeworn knowledge that dishes made with a great deal of mustard and paprika and other heating spices, and ones based on the generous use of shrimps and other fish high in phosphorus, are usually exciting to both human sexes but particularly to the male. Sometimes a more complicated significance, straight from Freud, is given to recipes thought of long before his day. The dish of eel innocently prepared for a gathering of good pastors by a former brothel cook, which Brillat-Savarin describes so lightly in his *Physiology of Taste*, is a perfect example of this: there is a phallic rightness about the whole thing, visual as well as spiritual, which has more to do with the structure of the fish than the possible presence of a mysterious and exotic spice.

In general, however, the great courtesans have paid less attention to the Freudian appearance of their kitchens' masterpieces, from what I can gather, than to the temperaments of the men they have willed to please. They have studied the appetites of their prey.

This is, in a way, a paraphrase of the old saying, 'First catch your hare, then cook him': wolf or even goose can be substituted for the little wild rabbit.

Once caught, a human male is studied by the huntress as thoroughly as if he were a diamond. She looks at his ear lobes and his fingernails after he has eaten of rare beef, and if the former are plump and ruddy, and the latter rosy pink, she knows his glands to be both satisfied and active. She analyzes his motor reflexes after he has downed a fair portion of jugged venison, and if instead of showing a pleasurable skittishness he yawns and puffs and blinks, she nevermore serves that gamy dish. She notes coldly, calculatingly, his reactions to wine and ale and heady spirits, as well as to fruits, eggs, cucumbers, and such; she learns his dietetic tolerance, in short, and his rate of metabolism, and his tendencies toward gastric as well as emotional indigestion. And all this happens whether she be a designing farm girl in Arkansas or a slim worldly beauty on the Cap d'Antibes.

An Alphabet for Gourmets

FANNY FERN
1811–72

'The hand that can make a pie is a continual feast to the husband that marries its owner.'

Well, it is a humiliating reflection, that the straightest road to a man's heart is through his palate. He is never so amiable as when he has discussed a roast turkey. Then's your time, 'Esther,' for 'half his kingdom,' in the shape of a new bonnet, cap, shawl, or dress. He's too complacent to dispute the matter. Strike while the iron is hot; petition for a trip to Niagra, Saratoga, the Mammoth Cave, the White Mountains, or to London, Rome, or Paris. Should he demur about it, the next day cook him another turkey, and pack your trunk while he is eating it.

There's nothing on earth so savage – except a bear robbed of her cubs – as a hungry husband. It is as much as your life is worth to sneeze till dinner is on the table, and his knife and fork are in vigorous play. Tommy will get his ears boxed, the ottoman will be kicked into the corner, your work-box be turned bottom upwards, and the poker and tongs will beat a tattoo on that grate that will be a caution to dilatory cooks.

After the first six mouthfuls you may venture to say your soul is your own; his eyes will lose their ferocity, his brow its furrows, and he will very likely recollect to help you to a cold potato! Never mind – *eat it.* You might have to swallow a worse pill – for instance, should he offer to kiss you, for of course you couldn't love such a carnivorous animal!

Well, learn a lesson from it – keep him well fed and languid – live yourself on a low diet, and cultivate your thinking powers; and you'll be as spry as a cricket, and hop over all the objections and remonstrances that his dead-and-alive energies can muster. Yes, feed him well, and he will stay contentedly in his cage, like a gorged anaconda. If he was *my* husband, wouldn't I make him heaps of *pison* things! Bless me! I've made a mistake in the spelling; it should have been *pies-and-things!*

Ruth Hall and Other Writings

NORA EPHRON

POTATOES AND LOVE: SOME REFLECTIONS

The beginning

I have made a lot of mistakes falling in love, and regretted most of them, but never the potatoes that went with them.

Not just any potato will do when it comes to love. There are people who go on about the virtues of plain potatoes – plain boiled new potatoes with a little parsley or dill, or plain baked potatoes with crackling skins – but my own feeling is that a taste for plain potatoes coincides with cultural antecedents I do not possess, and that in any case, the time for plain potatoes – if there is ever a time for plain potatoes – is never at the beginning of something. It is also, I should add, never at the end of something. Perhaps you can get away with plain potatoes in the middle, although I have never been able to.

All right, then: I am talking about crisp potatoes . . . There are two kinds of crisp potatoes that I prefer above all others. The first are called Swiss potatoes, and they're essentially a large potato pancake of perfect hash browns; the flipping of the pancake is so wildly dramatic that the potatoes themselves are almost beside the point. The second are called potatoes Anna; they are thin circles of potato cooked in a shallow pan in the oven and then turned onto a plate in a darling mound of crunchy brownness. Potatoes Anna is a classic French recipe, but there is something so homely and old-fashioned about them that they can usually be passed off as either an ancient family recipe or something you just made up . . .

The middle (II)

Sometimes, when a loved one announces that he has decided to go on a low-carbohydrate, low-fat, low-salt diet (thus ruling out the possibility of potatoes, should you have been so inclined), he is signalling that the middle is ending and the end is beginning.

The end

In the end, I always want potatoes. Mashed potatoes. Nothing like mashed potatoes when you're feeling blue. Nothing like getting into bed with a bowl of hot mashed potatoes already loaded with butter, and methodically adding a thin cold slice of butter to every forkful. The problem with mashed potatoes, though, is that they require almost as much hard work as crisp potatoes, and when you're feeling blue the last thing you feel like is hard work. Of course, you can always get someone to make the mashed potatoes for you, but let's face it: the reason you're blue is that there *isn't* anyone to make them for you. As a result, most people do not have nearly enough mashed potatoes in their lives, and when they do, it's almost always at the wrong time.

Heartburn

DIANE MOTT DAVIDSON

I bustled around the kitchen making breakfast. The forty-degree weather demanded a quick bread. I had developed a recipe for Arch's preschool that had become a favorite with clients. Perhaps the idea of eating something called Montessori muffins made people think they were learning something. Food can substitute for so many things.

I got out whole wheat flour and molasses and began to chop prunes. I supposed Schulz had the right to hang up without saying good-bye. After my business nearly collapsed last fall, we had started to date. But not for long.

I broke an egg and swirled it into oil and milk.

Schulz had been attentive, God knew. On my birthday, on Arch's birthday, on Julia Child's birthday, he had sent cards with pictures of mice eating cookies, rabbits downing carrot cakes, French poodles dancing through french fries. Valentine's Day brought the arrival of the most sumptuous box of candy I had ever received. For this gift I had written him a thank-you note. When he called I told him Arch was taking a carefully wrapped piece in his lunch each day.

'What about you?' he had asked. 'Did you like it?'

'Of course,' I'd said carefully. 'It's wonderful.' And then I'd begged off with a catering assignment.

Finally he had asked the dreaded question: Do you see our relationship going anywhere? How could I say I didn't know? How could I say stop being so nice? How could I admit to running against stereotype, the first woman afraid to commit?

There are many bad ways that relationships end, I reflected as I mixed together the wet and dry ingredients. Death. Divorce. I knew all about the latter. But I had deliberately let the relationship with Schulz wane until there was little left. We had been like the hot chocolate they sell at the ski resorts. For your buck fifty, a machine first spews dark, thick syrup into a cup. This liquid gradually turns to a mixture of chocolate and hot water. Soon there is just a stream of hot water, and in a moment, drops. You wish the chocolate part would go on gushing forever, but it doesn't.

Dying for Chocolate

BARBARA PYM
1913–80

'But surely liking the same things for dinner is one of the deepest and most lasting things you could possibly have in common with anyone,' argued Dr Parnell. 'After all, the emotions of the heart are very transitory, or so I believe; I should think it makes one much happier to be well-fed than well-loved.'

Some Tame Gazelle

SOLITARY PLEASURES

AMANDA HESSER

People believe that dining alone will mark them as a loser or a desperate soul, one who can't find a friend in all the world to eat with them. But the reality is that other diners hardly notice you. And if they do, they probably think you are from another country.

In the same way that you should get massages and take naps or meditate, you should, everyone should, make a point to eat out by yourself from time to time. You should be kind enough to yourself to lavish your appetite with good food without the interruptions of company.

When you are by yourself, you have the chance to read the entire menu, take in the décor, observe the theater of the place and, most important, pay attention to the food. You can concentrate on the interplay of flavors rather than having to make a mental note to do so in between delivering anecdotes about your vacation. (If the company is good, I often come home forgetting what wine we drank or what the spice was in the cake.) You may sit by yourself, but you are never lonely.

Which is why some of the best meals of my life have been solitary. In Europe, dining alone is much more common than it is here. When I turned twenty-three, I took myself to lunch at La Côte St. Jacques, then a three-star restaurant in Joigny, France. During the six-course menu dégustation, none of the army of waiters in tuxedos seemed to pity me. None of the other diners in the room expressed disapproval. The only person disturbed by the event was my mother, when she got the bill.

Cooking for Mr Latte

SYLVIA THOMPSON

It was midnight by the time our boat train arrived in Paris. We found the Hôtel de l'Avenir – my French professor had recommended it – and fell into bed. But I couldn't sleep. At dawn, I began to dress, my heart pounding. I shook my friend and asked if she didn't want to get up and come with me to see Paris. Pharumph. By six I could stand it no longer and called the concièrge – my professor had said that as soon as I woke up, *petit déjeuner* would be brought to my room. When the tray arrived, my knees grew weak as I took it from the plump pink *bonne* who smiled and gave a flick of a curtsey at the door.

On my tray, service for one: a ceramic pitcher of hot milk, a thick brown pitcher of dark-roasted coffee (I had come to love its bitter flavor on the ship), a flute of bread faintly warm from the oven, a saucer with pats of sweet butter, another saucer with bright red cherry preserves, and another saucer with cubes of brown sugar. Nothing, not the sumptuous breakfasts on the *Liberté*, not the French books I had read nor the French movies I had seen, nothing prepared me for that tray. In its Gallic simplicity (what the French regard as essentials for starting the day), tearing hunks from the slim shiny loaf, spreading every crevice with butter and spooning over tart cherries, pouring milk with one hand and coffee with the other into the enormous white bowl of a cup (a lesson learned on the ship), plopping in cubes of brown sugar, stirring until I could feel the sugar dissolve, then sipping and chewing as I looked down from my perch and saw the early morning bustle of the Left Bank – Paris, imagine! – it was one of the dearest meals of my life.

The three sisters were sleeping soundly, so I closed the door and climbed down the creaking old stairs to the street.

Feasts and Friends

KATHERINE MANSFIELD
1888–1923

Saturday: This joy of being alone. What is it? I feel so gay and at peace –
the whole house takes the air. Lunch is ready. I have a baked egg, apricots and cream, cheese straws and black coffee. How delicious! A baby
meal! Athenaeum is asleep and then awake on the studio sofa. He has
a silver spoon of cream – then hides under the sofa frill and puts out a
paw for my finger. I gather the dried leaves from the plant in the big
white bowl, and because I must play with something, I take an orange
up to my room and throw it and catch it as I walk up and down.

Journal

NIGELLA LAWSON

Eating alone, for me, is most often a prompt to shop. This is where self-
absorption and consumerism meet – a rapt, satisfyingly convoluted
pleasure. The food I want most to buy is the food I most often try not to
eat – a swollen-bellied tranche of cheese, a loaf of bread. These constitute the perfect meal. A slither of gorgonzola or coulommiers sacrificed
on the intrusive and unyielding surface of a biscuit at the end of dinner
is food out of kilter. Just bread and cheese is fine to give others if you've
shown the consideration of providing variety. But I want for myself the
obsessive focus of the one huge, heady *baveuse* soft cheese, or else a
wedge of the palate-burning hard stuff, a vintage Cheddar or strong
blue – too much, too strong. If I'm eating a salty blue cheese, its texture
somewhere between creamy and crumbly, I want baguette or a bitter,
fudge-coloured *pain au levain*; with Cheddar, real Cheddar, I want
doughier white bread – whichever, it must be a whole loaf. I might eat
tomatoes with the bread and cheese, but the tomatoes mustn't be in a
salad, but left whole on the plate, to be sliced or chopped, *à la minute*.

How to Eat

BARBARA PYM
1913–80

I made myself what seemed an extravagant lunch of scrambled eggs, preceded by the remains of some soup, and followed by cheese, biscuits and an apple. I was glad that I wasn't a man, or the kind of man who looked upon a meal alone as a good opportunity to cook a small plover, though I should have been glad enough to have someone else cook it for me.

Excellent Women

FAY MASCHLER
ELIZABETH JANE HOWARD

ABANDONED MAN

A man accustomed to being cooked for is a helpless thing. Abandoned by his cook, either temporarily or permanently, his first instinct is to find someone else to make his meals. This conditioned response may be because women, from his mother onwards, have not only spoiled him, but woven an air of mystery around cooking. They have whispered of barding and basting and double boilers. Like cats, they have spat at frying pans to test the heat or, in apparent ungovernable rage, flung strands of spaghetti at the wall to see if they would stick. The whole performance, from the shopping that seems to require arcane and distressingly female talk – phrases like a pound of skirt or a bag of Desirées – to choosing the one dish of the thirty available, that in some talismanic way his cook will have decreed the only one suitable, could have made a man craven in the kitchen.

On the other hand, he may just have been arrogant and idle or simply not interested. But friends will soon tire of providing for him and he must turn to the fridge and stove and think conscientiously about cooking for himself and for others, because nothing is more lowering than too many solitary meals, and a man left to cook for his children will find they grow fractious on uninterrupted junk food.

Men who cook, particularly those new to the activity, want to make dishes that either have the quality of immediacy, or ones where alchemy in the oven will transform them. Men, on the whole, are not good at diddling about waiting for one thing to happen before proceeding with the next. For this reason, a stew which can be left alone to cook for hours and requires no cosseting is a favourite. Most men, even abandoned ones, believe it improves with keeping and that it can be jazzed up with curry powder and raisins towards the end of its life. This is not so, although the sauce of a stew does mellow when it is cooked on one day, heated up and eaten the next.

Cooking for Occasions

MARJORIE HILLIS
1889–1971

Provider of advice for the young singleton, the budget conscious, the traveller and the widow, Marjorie Hillis was also a Vogue *editor.*

We can't say too much about dinner in the grand manner for a woman by herself. Not a pompous meal at a lonely dining-room table, like a *grande dame* of the nineties, but dinner at a little table beside the fire, or dinner on the chaise longue, or dinner in bed, or dinner on a balcony – or any place else that is comfortable and attractive. Dress up a bit for it. Here is the perfect place for a trailing négligée and frou-frou. The woman who always looks at night as though she were expecting a suitor is likely to have several. (One of the pleasantest things about modern life is the increased span of beaux.)

Among the problems for the diner-alone is the dread of left-overs. They are all very well once, but we feel no enthusiasm ourselves for seventh-day chicken. Yet a little ingenuity can overcome this, with no fear of monotony. Lots of good things to eat come in small packages.

We are not going into the matter of menus, which you can find in any magazine or newspaper. But just to prove our point, here are a few dishes that won't hang on and on. First, of course, the old familiar lamb-chop, or any other kind of chop. There are also chicken livers or calf's liver, which you can buy in small quantities and serve with its partner, bacon. There are sweetbreads, and squabs for days when you feel like being elegant. There is corned-beef, which you can buy in one thick slice at the delicatessen store and make into delectable hash. There are very small pork tenderloins, which are specially good boiled first, then baked with canned peaches.

Then the good books (on things to eat) tell us that we don't eat half enough fish – which is a perfect solution for the small purchaser. Crab-meat, lobster meat, scallops, fillet of sole, and a variety of other fish can be bought in as small quantities as you please. So can mushrooms – delectable when creamed and baked. And what about eggs baked in ramekins with cheese, or eggs Benedict, or eggs à la king, or scrambled eggs with tomatoes or perhaps asparagus?

Any of these as a basis, with soup, a vegetable, and some green salad with French dressing and a little cheese, makes a dinner at which you wouldn't mind having your worst friend drop in. Or you might substitute fruit for the salad – melon or chilled berries or a compote. (A very special one combines big black cherries, which you can get in cans, with canned pears. And did you ever try fresh peaches with raspberry sauce over them?)

Though you may have no maid and are definitely anti-domestic, things are not hopeless. There is the great army of canned things – and we don't mean just tomato soup and green peas. We mean shad roe, and green turtle soup, for instance, and a great many other things, too. The possibilities in canned soup alone will make you famous as a cook. And lots of the cans now come in one-woman size.

There are, also, the Exchanges for Woman's Work, dotted all over the country, at which all sorts of home-cooking delicacies are sold, and more other places to help you meet your problem that we can name. There are even firms that will deliver your dinner all hot and steaming, at the moment you want it, though we don't know how.

Live Alone and Like It

M.F.K. FISHER
1908–92

H IS FOR HAPPY

Lone meals, which can be happy too, are perhaps the hardest to put on paper, with a drop of cyanide on their noses and a pin through their guts. They are the fleetingest of the gastronomical butterflies. I have known some. We all have. They are compounded in almost equal parts of peace, nostalgia, and good digestion, with sometimes an amenable touch of alcohol thrown in.

An Alphabet for Gourmets

KATE CHOPIN
1850–1904

Edna was not so consciously gratified at her husband's leaving home as she had been over the departure of her father. As the day approached when he was to leave her for a comparatively long stay, she grew melting and affectionate, remembering his many acts of consideration and his repeated expressions of an ardent attachment. She was solicitous about his health and his welfare. She bustled around, looking after his clothing, thinking about heavy underwear, quite as Madame Ratignolle would have done under similar circumstances. She cried when he went away, calling him her dear, good friend, and she was quite certain she would grow lonely before very long and go to join him in New York.

But after all, a radiant peace settled upon her when she at last found herself alone . . .

Even the kitchen assumed a sudden interesting character which she had never before perceived. She went in to give directions to the cook, to say that the butcher would have to bring much less meat, that they would require only half their usual quantity of bread, of milk and groceries. She told the cook that she herself would be greatly occupied during Mr. Pontellier's absence, and she begged her to take all thought and responsibility of the larder upon her own shoulders.

That night Edna dined alone. The candelabra, with a few candles in the center of the table, gave all the light she needed. Outside the circle of light in which she sat, the large dining-room looked solemn and shadowy. The cook, placed upon her mettle, served a delicious repast – a luscious tenderloin broiled *à point*. The wine tasted good; the *marron glacé* seemed to be just what she wanted. It was so pleasant, too, to dine in a comfortable *peignoir*.

She thought a little sentimentally about Léonce and the children, and wondered what they were doing. As she gave a dainty scrap or two to the doggie, she talked intimately to him about Etienne and Raoul. He was beside himself with astonishment and delight over these companionable advances, and showed his appreciation by his little quick, snappy barks and a lively agitation.

Then Edna sat in the library after dinner and read Emerson until she grew sleepy. She realized that she had neglected her reading, and determined to start anew upon a course of improving studies, now that her time was completely her own to do with as she liked.

After a refreshing bath, Edna went to bed. And as she snuggled comfortably beneath the eiderdown a sense of restfulness invaded her, such as she had not known before.

The Awakening

MARY WILKINS FREEMAN
1852–1930

It was late afternoon and the light was waning . . . Louisa tied a green apron round her waist, and got out a flat straw hat with a green ribbon. Then she went into the garden with a little blue crockery bowl, to pick some currants for her tea. After the currants were picked she sat on the back door-step and stemmed them, collecting the stems carefully in her apron, and afterwards throwing them into the hen-coop. She looked sharply at the grass beside the step to see if any had fallen there.

Louisa was slow and still in her movements; it took her a long time to prepare her tea; but when ready it was set forth with as much grace as if she had been a veritable guest to her own self. The little square table stood exactly in the centre of the kitchen, and was covered with a starched linen cloth whose border pattern of flowers glistened. Louisa had a damask napkin on her tea-tray, where were arranged a cut-glass tumbler full of teaspoons, a silver cream-pitcher, a china sugar-bowl, and one pink china cup and saucer. Louisa used china every day – something which none of her neighbors did. They whispered about it among themselves. Their daily tables were laid with common crockery, their sets of best china stayed in the parlor closet, and Louisa Ellis was no richer nor better bred than they. Still she would use the china. She had for her supper a glass dish full of sugared currants, a plate of little cakes, and one of light white biscuits. Also a leaf or two of lettuce, which she raised to perfection in her little garden. She ate quite heartily, though in a delicate, pecking way; it seemed almost surprising that any considerable bulk of the food should vanish.

After tea she filled a plate with nicely baked thin corn-cakes, and carried them out into the back-yard.

'Cæsar!' she called. 'Cæsar! Cæsar!'

There was a little rush, and the clank of a chain, and a large yellow-and-white dog appeared at the door of his tiny hut, which was half hidden among the tall grasses and flowers. Louisa patted him and gave him the corn-cakes. Then she returned to the house and washed the tea-things, polishing the china carefully. The twilight had deepened now; the chorus of the frogs floated in at the open window wonderfully loud and shrill, and once in a while a long sharp drone from a tree-toad pierced it. Louisa took off her green gingham apron, disclosing a shorter one of pink and white print. She lighted her lamp, and sat down again with her sewing.

'A New England Nun'

COOKING UP MAGIC

ELSA SCHIAPARELLI
1890–1973

Born in Rome, Schiaparelli studied philosophy before working as a scriptwriter in the US. In the 1920s she opened a fashion boutique in Paris, where she became famous for her use of shocking pink and ice blue and for her surreal hat designs, including one in the shape of a giant lamb chop.

A good cook is like a sorceress who dispenses happiness.

Shocking Life

JOANNE HARRIS

There is a kind of sorcery in all cooking; in the choosing of ingredients, the process of mixing, grating, melting, infusing, and flavouring, the recipes taken from ancient books, the traditional utensils – the pestle and mortar with which my mother made her incense turned to a more homely purpose, her spices and aromatics giving up their subtleties to a baser, more sensual magic. And it is partly the transience of it that delights me; so much loving preparation, so much art and experience, put into a pleasure that can last only a moment, and which only a few will ever fully appreciate. My mother always viewed my interest with indulgent contempt. To her, food was no pleasure but a tiresome necessity to be worried over, a tax on the price of our freedom. I stole menus from restaurants and looked longingly into patisserie windows. I must have been ten years old – maybe older –

before I first tasted real chocolate. But still the fascination endured. I carried recipes in my head like maps. All kinds of recipes: torn from abandoned magazines in busy railway stations, wheedled from people on the road, strange marriages of my own confection. Mother with her cards, her divinations, directed our mad course across Europe. Cookery cards anchored us, placed landmarks on the bleak borders. Paris smells of baking bread and croissants; Marseille of bouillabaisse and grilled garlic. Berlin was *Eisbrei* with sauerkraut and *Kartoffelsalat*, Rome was the ice cream I ate without paying in a tiny restaurant beside the river . . .

There is a kind of alchemy in the transformation of base chocolate into this wise fool's-gold, a layman's magic that even my mother might have relished. As I work, I clear my mind, breathing deeply. The windows are open, and the through-draft would be cold if it were not for the heat of the stoves, the copper pans, the rising vapour from the melting *couverture*. The mingled scents of chocolate, vanilla, heated copper, and cinnamon are intoxicating, powerfully suggestive; the raw and earthy tang of the Americas, the hot and resinous perfume of the rain forest. This is how I travel now, as the Aztecs did in their sacred rituals: Mexico, Venezuela, Columbia. The court of Montezuma. Cortez and Columbus. The Food of the Gods, bubbling and frothing in ceremonial goblets. The bitter elixir of life.

Chocolat

DIANE PURKISS

Many folk stories warn of the dangers of accepting a gift of food, especially a luxury food such as fruit or cake, from a woman outside the immediate family. In 'Snow Drop', the earliest version of the tale which became better-known as 'Snow White', the wicked queen, who plainly has magical powers, prepares one last trap for her victim: a poisoned apple. 'The outside looked very rosy and tempting, but whoever tasted it was sure to die'. 'Hansel and Gretel' is the best known of a group of stories in which two children are victims of their own and their parents' terrible hunger. These two children, abandoned by their (step)mother, find an alternative and apparently miraculous source of food, a house made of luxury items: 'the cottage was made of bread and cakes, and the windowpanes were of clear sugar'. The magic house is inhabited by a witch; it embodies and represents her magical power that she can create such an impossible dwelling and symbol of plenitude. The witch at first seems kind and considerate, but later reveals herself to be the opposite of the nurturer she seems; she is a devourer, not a substitute mother but an antimother:

> The old woman, nodding her head, said 'Ah, you dear children, what has brought you here? Come in and stop with me, and no harm shall befall you; and so saying she took them both by the hand and led them into her cottage. A good meal of milk and pancakes, with sugar, apples and nuts, was spread on the table, and in the back room were two little beds, covered with white where Hansel and Gretel laid themselves down, and thought themselves in heaven . . .

The witch decides to eat Hansel and to keep Gretel to work, and as a result it is Gretel's feminine linkage with the kitchen and cooking that allows her to take the witch from consumer to meal, baking her in the oven she prepares for Hansel.

The Witch in History

CHRISTINA ROSSETTI
1830–94

Morning and evening
Maids heard the goblins cry:
'Come buy our orchard fruits,
Come buy, come buy:
Apples and quinces,
Lemons and oranges,
Plump unpecked cherries,
Melons and raspberries,
Bloom-down-cheeked peaches,
Swart-headed mulberries,
Wild free-born cranberries,
Crab-apples, dewberries,
Pine-apples, blackberries,
Apricots, strawberries; –
All ripe together
In summer weather, –
Morns that pass by,
Fair eves that fly;
Come buy, come buy:
Our grapes fresh from the vine,
Pomegranates full and fine,
Dates and sharp bullaces,
Rare pears and greengages,
Damsons and bilberries,
Taste them and try:
Currants and gooseberries,
Bright-fire-like barberries,
Figs to fill your mouth,
Citrons from the South,
Sweet to tongue and sound to eye;
Come buy, come buy.'

'Goblin Market'

ELIZA ACTON
1799–1859

Though she sought fame as a poet, Acton found it through the cookery books her publisher pressed her to publish instead. Her great innovation was to list ingredients separately rather than in the body of the recipe. Mrs Beeton is known to have pilfered her work.

FAIRY FANCIES
Fantaisies de Fées

A small, but very inexpensive set of tin cutters must be had for this pretty form of pastry, which is, however, quite worthy of so slight a cost. The short crust answers for it better than puff paste. Roll it thin and very even, and with the larger tin, shaped thus, cut out a dozen or more of small sheets; then, with a couple of round cutters, of which one should be about an inch in diameter, and the other only half the size, form four times the number of rings, and lay them on the sheets in the manner shown in the engraving. The easier mode of placing them regularly is to raise each ring without removing the small cutter from it, to moisten it with a camel's hair brush dipped in white of egg, and to lay it on the paste as it is gently loosened from the tin. When all the pastry is prepared, set it into a very gentle oven, that it may become crisp and yet remain quite pale. Before it is sent to table, fill the four divisions of each *fantaisie* with preserve of a different colour. For example: one ring with apple or strawberry jelly, another with apricot jam, a third with peach or green-gage, and a fourth with raspberry jelly. The cases may be iced and ornamented in various ways before they are baked. They are prettiest when formed of white almond-paste, with pink or pale green rings: they may then be filled, at the instant of serving, with well-drained whipped cream.

Modern Cookery for Private Families

EMILY DICKINSON
1830–86

I cooked the peaches as you told me, and they swelled to beautiful fleshy halves and tasted quite magic. The beans we fricasseed and they made a savory cream in cooking that 'Aunt Emily' liked to sip.

Letters

ELIZABETH ELLICOTT LEA
1793–1858

Domestic Cookery, Useful Receipts and Hints to Young Housekeepers *was simple in focus – not religious or scientific, as was then the fashion – and it became one of the best-loved cookbooks of the time. Lea, in later life an invalid, would sit by a large window next to the stairs above her kitchen and call out her recipes to a loyal assistant, who tried them out until they were perfect. Lea's parents were flour manufacturers and her husband, from a prominent Quaker family, owned flour mills.*

SNOW CREAM

Take the richest cream you can procure, season it with a few drops of essence of lemon, or syrup of lemon peel, and powdered white sugar, and if you choose a spoonful of preserve syrup, and just as you send it to table, stir in light newly fallen snow till it is nearly as stiff as ice cream.

OPAL WHITELEY
1897–1991

Liar? Lunatic? Saint? The case of Opal Whiteley remains fascinating. Opal claimed to have written a diary at the age of five. When it was published in 1920 by Atlantic Monthly, it was hailed variously as a hoax, the work of a poetical genius and the story of a magical and heartbreaking childhood. Opal, 'the flower child of Oregon literature', was born in the United States, but spent much of her adult life in an English mental hospital. She is buried in London's Highgate Cemetery.

Sometimes I share my bread and jam with yellow jackets.*
They have a home on a bush
distant from the garden twenty trees and one.
Today I climbed the fence close to their home
with a piece and a half of bread and jam.
The half piece for them
and the piece for myself.
They all wanted to be served at once.

I broke it all into little pieces
and they had a royal feast there on the fence.
Yellow jackets are such interesting fairies
being the world's first paper-makers.

*wasps (Am.)

Opal

HANNAH GLASSE
1708–70

TO MAKE THE MOON AND STARS IN JELLY
Take the dish you intend for the table, have ready some white jelly, the

same as for flummery; likewise a mould the shape of half a moon and two or three the shape of stars, fix them on your dish before you put in your white jelly, which is to represent the sky; have ready some clear jelly such as is for glasses, when your white jelly is cold on the dish, take out the moulds of the moon and stars carefully, and fill up the places with the clear jelly, but not hot, least it dissolves the white: it is a pretty dish by candle-light.

TO MAKE FAIRY BUTTER

Take the yolks of two hard eggs, and beat them in a marble mortar, with a large spoonful of orange-flower water, and two tea-spoonfuls of fine sugar beat to powder; beat this all together till it is a fine paste, then mix it up with about as much fresh butter out of the churn, and force it through a fine strainer full of little holes into a plate. This is a pretty thing to set off a table at supper.

The Art of Cookery, Made Plain and Easy

E. NESBIT
1858–1924

When you are young so many things are difficult to believe, and yet the dullest people will tell you that they are true – such things, for instance, as that the earth goes round the sun, and that it is not flat but round. But the things that seem really likely, like fairy tales and magic, are, so say the grown-ups, not true at all. Yet they are so easy to believe, especially when you see them happening. And, as I am always telling you, the most wonderful things happen to all sorts of people, only you never hear about them because the people think that no one will believe their stories, and so they don't tell them to anyone except me. And they tell me, because they know that I can believe anything.

When Jimmy had awakened the Sleeping Princess, and she had invited the three children to go with her to her palace and get something to eat, they all knew quite surely that they had come into a place of magic happenings. And they walked in a slow procession along the grass towards the castle. The Princess went first, and Kathleen carried her shining train; then came Jimmy, and Gerald came last. They were all quite sure that they had walked right into the middle of a fairy tale, and they were the more ready to believe it because they were so tired and hungry. They were, in fact, so hungry and tired that they hardly noticed where they were going, or observed the beauties of the formal gardens through which the pink silk Princess was leading them. They were in a sort of dream, from which they only partially awakened to find themselves in a big hall, with suits of armor and old flags round the walls, the skins of beasts on the floor, and heavy oak tables and benches ranged along it.

The Princess entered, slow and stately, but once inside she twitched her sheeny train out of Jimmy's hand and turned to the three.

'You just wait here a minute,' she said, 'and mind you don't talk while I'm away. This castle is crammed with magic, and I don't know what will happen if you talk.' And with that, picking up the thick goldy pink folds under her arms, she ran out, as Jimmy said afterwards, 'most unprincesslike,' showing as she ran black stockings and black strap shoes.

Jimmy wanted very much to say that he didn't believe anything would happen, only he was afraid something would happen if he did, so he merely made a face and put out his tongue. The others pretended not to see this, which was much more crushing than anything they could have said. So they sat in silence, and Gerald ground the heel of his boot upon the marble floor. Then the Princess came back, very slowly, and kicking her long skirts in front of her at every step. She could not hold them up now because of the tray she carried.

It was not a silver tray, as you might have expected, but an oblong tin one. She set it down noisily on the end of the long table and breathed a sigh of relief.

'Oh! It *was* heavy,' she said. I don't know what fairy feast the children's fancy had been busy with. Anyhow, this was nothing like it. The heavy tray held a loaf of bread, a lump of cheese, and a brown jug of water. The rest of its heaviness was just plates and mugs and knives.

'Come along,' said the Princess, hospitably. 'I couldn't find anything but bread and cheese – but it doesn't matter, because everything's magic here, and unless you have some dreadful secret fault the bread and cheese will turn into anything you like. What *would* you like?' she asked Kathleen.

'Roast chicken,' said Kathleen, without hesitation.

The pinky Princess cut a slice of bread and laid it on a dish. 'There you are,' she said, 'roast chicken. Shall I carve it, or will you?'

'You, please,' said Kathleen, and received a piece of dry bread on a plate.

'Green peas?' asked the Princess, cutting a piece of cheese and laid it beside the bread.

Kathleen began to eat the bread, cutting it up with knife and fork, as you would eat chicken. It was no use owning that she didn't see any chicken and peas, or anything but cheese and dry bread, because that would be owning that she had some dreadful secret fault.

'If I have, it *is* a secret, even from me,' she told herself.

The others asked for roast beef and cabbage – and got it, she supposed, though to her it only looked like dry bread and Dutch cheese.

'I *do* wonder what my dreadful secret fault is,' she thought, as the Princess remarked that, as for her, she could fancy a slice of roast peacock. 'This one,' she added, lifting a second mouthful of dry bread on her fork, 'is quite delicious.'

'It's a game, isn't it?' asked Jimmy, suddenly.

'What's a game?' asked the Princess, frowning.

'Pretending it's beef – the bread and cheese, I mean.'

'A game? But it *is* beef. Look at it,' said the Princess, opening her eyes very wide.

'Yes, of course,' said Jimmy feebly. 'I was only joking.'

Bread and cheese is not perhaps so good as roast beef or chicken or peacock (I'm not sure about the peacock. I never tasted peacock, did you?); but bread and cheese is, at any rate, very much better than nothing when you have gone on having nothing since breakfast (gooseberries and ginger beer hardly count), and it is long past your proper dinnertime. Every one ate and drank and felt much better.

'Now,' said the Princess, brushing the bread crumbs off her green silk lap, 'if you're sure you won't have any more meat you can come and see my treasures. Sure you won't take the least bit more chicken?'

The Enchanted Castle

J.K. ROWLING

Around half past twelve there was a great clattering outside in the corridor and a smiling, dimpled woman slid back their door and said, 'Anything off the trolley, dears?'

Harry, who hadn't had any breakfast, leapt to his feet, but Ron's ears went pink again and he muttered that he'd brought sandwiches. Harry went out into the corridor.

He had never had any money for sweets with the Dursleys, and now that he had pockets rattling with gold and silver he was ready to buy as many Mars Bars as he could carry – but the woman didn't have Mars Bars. What she did have were Bertie Bott's Every Flavour Beans, Drooble's Best Blowing Gum, Chocolate Frogs, Pumpkin Pasties, Cauldron Cakes, Liquorice Wands, and a number of other strange things Harry had never seen in his life. Not wanting to miss anything, he got some of everything and paid the woman eleven silver Sickles and seven bronze Knuts.

Harry Potter and the Philosopher's Stone

FRANCES HODGSON BURNETT
1849–1924

Born in Manchester in 1849, Frances and her family moved to Knoxville, Tennessee after the death of her father. Frances became a U.S. citizen in 1905.

'Oh, Sara!' she cried. 'What a silly thing I am not to have thought of it!'

'Of what?'

'Something splendid!' said Ermengarde, in an excited hurry. 'This very afternoon my nicest aunt sent me a box. It is full of good things. I never touched it, I had so much pudding at dinner, and I was so bothered about papa's books.' Her words began to tumble over each other. 'It's got cake in it, and little meat-pies, and jam tarts and buns, and oranges and red-currant wine, and figs and chocolate. I'll creep back to my room and get it this minute, and we'll eat it now.'

Sara almost reeled. When one is faint with hunger the mention of food has sometimes a curious effect. She clutched Ermengarde's arm.

'Do you think – you *could?*' she ejaculated.

'I know I could,' answered Ermengarde, and she ran to the door – opened it softly – put her head out into the darkness, and listened. Then she went back to Sara. 'The lights are out. Everybody's in bed. I can creep – and creep – and no one will hear.'

It was so delightful that they caught each other's hands and a sudden light sprang into Sara's eyes.

'Ermie!' she said. 'Let us *pretend!* Let us pretend it's a party! And oh, won't you invite the prisoner in the next cell?'

'Yes! Yes! Let us knock on the wall now. The jailer won't hear.'

Sara went to the wall. Through it she could hear poor Becky crying more softly. She knocked four times.

'That means, "Come to me through the secret passage under the wall,"' she explained. '"I have something to communicate."'

Five quick knocks answered her.

'She is coming,' she said.

Almost immediately the door of the attic opened and Becky

appeared. Her eyes were red and her cap was sliding off, and when she caught sight of Ermengarde she began to rub her face nervously with her apron.

'Don't mind me a bit, Becky!' cried Ermengarde.

'Miss Ermengarde has asked you to come in,' said Sara, 'because she is going to bring a box of good things up here to us.'

Becky's cap almost fell off entirely, she broke in with such excitement.

'To eat, miss?' she said. 'Things that's good to eat?'

'Yes,' answered Sara, 'and we are going to pretend a party.'

'And you shall have as much as you *want* to eat,' put in Ermengarde. 'I'll go this minute!' . . .

As the things were taken out of the hamper – the frosted cakes – the fruits – the bonbons and the wine – the feast became a splendid thing.

'It's like a real party!' cried Ermengarde.

'It's like a queen's table,' sighed Becky.

Then Ermengarde had a sudden brilliant thought.

'I'll tell you what, Sara,' she said. 'Pretend you are a princess now and this is a royal feast.'

'But it's your feast,' said Sara; 'you must be the princess, and we will be your maids of honor.'

'Oh, I can't,' said Ermengarde. 'I'm too fat, and I don't know how. *You* be her.'

'Well, if you want me to,' said Sara.

But suddenly she thought of something else and ran to the rusty grate.

'There is a lot of paper and rubbish stuffed in here!' she exclaimed. 'If we light it, there will be a bright blaze for a few minutes, and we shall feel as if it was a real fire.' She struck a match and lighted it up with a great specious glow which illuminated the room.

'By the time it stops blazing,' Sara said, 'we shall forget about its not being real.'

She stood in the dancing glow and smiled.

'Doesn't it *look* real?' she said. 'Now we will begin the party.'

She led the way to the table. She waved her hand graciously to Ermengarde and Becky. She was in the midst of her dream.

'Advance, fair damsels,' she said in her happy dream-voice, 'and be seated at the banquet table. My noble father, the king, who is absent on a long journey, has commanded me to feast you.' She turned her head slightly toward the corner of the room. 'What, ho, there, minstrels! Strike up with your viols and bassoons. Princesses,' she explained rapidly to Ermengarde and Becky, 'always had minstrels to play at their feasts. Pretend there is a minstrel gallery up there in the corner. Now we will begin.'

A Little Princess

CHITRA BANERJEE DIVAKARUNI

I am a Mistress of Spices.

I can work the others too. Mineral, metal, earth and sand and stone. The gems with their cold clear light. The liquids that burn their hues into your eyes till you see nothing else. I learned them all on the island.

But the spices are my love.

I know their origins, and what their colors signify, and their smells. I can call each by the true-name it was given at the first, when earth split like skin and offered it up to the sky. Their heat runs in my blood. From *amchur* to *zafran*, they bow to my command. At a whisper they yield up to me their hidden properties, their magic powers.

The Mistress of Spices

FAUX FOOD

MAY BYRON
d. 1936

PARSNIPS FRIED TO LOOK LIKE TROUT (Yorkshire, 1769)
Take a middling sort of parsnips, not over thick, and boil them as soft as
you would do for eating; peel, and cut them in two the long way. You must
only fry the small ends, not the thick ones. Beat two or three eggs, put to
them a tablespoonful of flour, dip in your parsnips, and fry them a light
brown in butter. Have for your sauce a little vinegar and butter.

Pot-Luck

LADY HARRIET ST CLAIR
1837–67

ROAST-LEG OF BEAVER
Beavers are found by several rivers in Prussia, the Oder, the Elbe, and
several of its tributary streams. It is a favourite diet in some places with
Roman Catholics on fast-days, being allowed to pass as fish, as is also
otter, which latter is held in so much esteem, that it is considered a
valuable present to offer to a Bishop.

Dainty Dishes

REBECCA PRICE
1660–1740

TO PICKLE COLLYFLOWERS, TO EAT LIKE MUSHROONS

Take the whitest colyflowers you can gett, and cutt them into little bunches like Elder Budds, you will find they grow in little bunches but do not cutt them too bigg, take away all the green leaves that grow between them, then lay them in a gallypott [gallipot] and strew a little peper and sliced ginger and a little gemacoe [Jamaica?] peper and a blade of mace, then boyle some vineger and pour it on them hott, you must not put in any salt at all: cover them close and they will eat like mushroons.

The Compleat Cook: or
The Secrets of a Seventeenth-Century Housewife

HANNAH GLASSE
1708–70

MUTTON-CHOPS IN DISGUISE

Take as many mutton-chops as you want, rub them with pepper, salt, nutmeg, and a little parsley; roll each chop in half a sheet of white paper, well buttered on the inside, and rolled on each end close. Have some hog's-lard, or beef-dripping, boiling in a stew-pan; put in the steaks, fry them of a fine brown, lay them in your dish, and garnish with fried parsley; throw some all over, have a little good gravy in a cup; but take great care you do not break the paper, nor have any fat in the dish; but let them be well drained.

ELDER-SHOOTS, IN IMITATION OF BAMBOO

Take the largest and youngest shoots of elder, which put out in the middle of May, the middle-stalks are most tender and biggest; the small ones are not worth doing. Peel off the outward peel or skin, and lay them in a strong brine of salt and water for one night, then dry them in a cloth, piece by piece. In the mean time, make your pickle of half white wine and half beer vinegar: to each quart of pickle you must put an ounce of white or red pepper, an ounce of ginger sliced, a little mace, and a few corns of Jamaica pepper; when the spice has boiled in the pickle, pour it hot upon the shoots, stop them close immediately, and set the jar two hours before the fire, turning it often. It is as good a way of greening pickles as often boiling; or you may boil the pickle two or three times, and pour it on boiling hot, just as you please: if you make the pickle of the sugar-vinegar, you must let one half be spring-water.

The Art of Cookery, Made Plain and Easy

ELIZABETH RAFFALD
1733–81

TO DRESS COD SOUNDS LIKE LITTLE TURKEYS

Boil your sounds as for eating but not too much. Take them up and let them stand till they are quite cold. Then make a forcemeat of chopped oysters, crumbs of bread, a lump of butter, nutmeg, pepper, salt and the yolks of two eggs. Fill your sounds with it and skewer them up in the shape of a turkey, then lard them down each side as you would do a turkey's breast. Dust them well with flour and put them in a tin oven to roast before the fire, and baste them well with butter. When they are enough pour on them oyster sauce. Three are sufficient for a side dish. Garnish with barberries.

It is a pretty side dish for a large table, for a dinner in Lent.

The Experienced English Housekeeper

HSIANG JU LIN
TSUIFENG LIN
20th century

TEXTURAL VARIATIONS OF BEAN CURD: VEGETARIAN HAM

Many people treat bean curd with contempt because it is so cheap, and after all it *is* made of beans, and it *is* a curd. Could anything be more unappetizing? They cannot believe that insipid curd can be interesting.

The curd in its natural form is very much like custard. But it can be made crisp; juicy and spongy; like noodles, firm and tasty, or, dried in sheets and cooked with sauce, into Vegetarian Ham. Buddhists are vegetarians, consequently a small pocket of gastronomy has developed, fascinating in its attempt to create the ordinary flavours and appearance of fish and meat by use of vegetarian ingredients. For the fancy which caused Central Europeans to make marzipan pigs and babies of embryonic size and pinkness had its Chinese counterpart . . . The Buddhists, whether monks or ordinary people, mingled freely with the non-vegetarians, and because the manners of Chinese society are all-embracing and diffuse, felt obliged to provide food which looked and almost tasted like meat. This was a sign of hospitality. Their cuisine was based on nuts, spices, vegetables, sauces, sesame, peanut and vegetable oils, and bean curd. The last was the factotum, now appearing as duck, then as chicken, then as fish. Its very lack of personality made it an excellent actor . . .

'duck'	=	*fried dried bean curd*
'crab'	=	*sautéed fresh walnuts with sauce*
'chicken'	=	*sautéed cabbage*
'fish'	=	*bean curd and potatoes*
'fried eel'	=	*turnips, mushrooms and bamboo*
'prawns'	=	*potatoes*

Chinese Gastronomy

MINNIE, LADY HINDLIP
20th century

CARROT JAM INTO APRICOT JAM

Boil three pounds of fresh young carrots till quite tender, strain off the water, which is useless, and rub the carrots through a sieve. Boil three pounds of apple till quite soft and add the juice extracted from them to the carrots in proportion of one pint to each pound of carrots. Then add four and a half pounds of sugar and the juice of nine lemons, with the peel finely grated without any of the white part. Boil the whole over a gentle fire twenty minutes, skim it carefully, and add three ounces of bitter almonds cut small.

Minnie, Lady Hindlip's Cookery Book

MARTHA WASHINGTON
1731–1802

ANOTHER WAY TO MAKE BEEF LIKE RED DEARE

Take a piece of ye clod of beefe next ye legg & cut ye sinews from it; then put it in a clean cloth & beat it extremely; yn lard it very well, & season it with nutmegg, pepper, & salt; then lay it on a clean dish & poure upon it halfe a pinte of white wine & as much wine vinegar. let it ly in steepe all night, & ye next day poure away ye vinegar & wine. put ye meat in a round coffin of paste crust & lay 2 or 3 bay leaves under & as many above it. put in store of butter, & let it stand 6 hour in ye oven. make a hole in ye lid & fill it up with buter when it comes out of ye oven.

TO CULLER YOUR ARTIFICIALL FRUIT AFTER THE LIFE

To culler yr artifitiall fruit: If it must be a light red, take vermillion & grinde it with gum water. If it must be a dark red, culler it with lake, ground in gum water in a brass morter or on a marble stone. & If it must be green, take sap green & steep it in gum water or else ye Juice of spinnage or green wheat. If it must be yellow, take white rose leaves & beat them in a morter wth a little roach allome, & then strayne ye Juice out, which will be a perfect yellow; or else steep saffron in [rose] water. these are all the cullers yt you need to [culler artific]iall fruit withall.

TO MAKE BIRDS & BEASTS

Take a pound of vallentine almonds & blanch ym & beat them in a morter till they come to perfect paste, then put to them a pound of searsed sugar. soe beat it alltogether A little while, & then you may make yr conceits by hand, & print some in moulds. soe gild them, & stove them before the fire.

Martha Washington's Booke of Cookery and Book of Sweetmeats

MARY TAYLOR SIMETI

Here marzipan is known as *pasta reale* or as *frutta di Martorana*, from the convent of the Martorana in Palermo, where the nuns excelled in the preparation of almond paste. It is said that once their mother superior, Sister Gertrude, wishing to celebrate the pastoral visit of the bishop, instructed the nuns to mold the paste into apples, peaches, pears, and oranges, which were then hung on the trees growing in the cloister garden. Strolling in the cloister before dinner with the mother superior, the bishop marveled to see so many different trees bearing fruit all in the same season. Still greater was his surprise when, at the dinner table, he bit into a bright red apple and discovered that it was made of almond paste.

Today it is still possible to play a practical joke with *pasta reale*, even if it would be difficult to invent one as enchanting as Sister Gertrude's: you can buy cakes of soap, sandwiches with the filling dribbling out, even complete meals served on paper plates. I once gave my children fried eggs and peas for supper, and it wasn't until they put their forks to it that they realized it was made of marzipan.

On Persephone's Island

REAY TANNAHILL

Between 1851 and 1854 the two commissioners – Dr Arthur Hill Hassall, a chemist, and Dr Henry Lethaby, a dietician – published a long series of articles reporting on the extraneous matter to be found in samples of staple foods bought at random in London shops. Hassall analysed forty-nine loaves from various sources, not one of which proved to be free from alum, the mineral-salt whitening agent, and reported that coffee was almost invariably diluted with chicory, acorns or mangel-wurzel (a kind of beet). Other researchers also discovered that publicans put the froth on their beer by doctoring it with green vitriol or sulphate or iron, and that cocoa powder often contained a large admixture of brick dust. In 1860, as a direct result of the *Lancet*'s investigations, the first British Food and Drugs Act was passed. It was drastically revised and strengthened in 1872.

Despite subsequent regulations on food purity in almost every country, however, independent venturers have continued to sidestep the law. Among the more disarming twentieth-century cases was that of an Italian gentleman who was charged in 1969 with selling a product described as grated Parmesan cheese – which turned out, on analysis, to consist of grated umbrella handles (Malacca, presumably). Another was the firm selling salami that not only looked like plastic and tasted like plastic, but *was* plastic.

Food in History

POISONS & PANACEAS

PETA MATHIAS

Some people think that sugar is white death, the consumption of which will result in mental and physical morbidity or worse. Some parents think sugar makes their children hyperactive and aggressive. It is the parents who are driving the children nuts, not the sugar. Sweets make you happy, stop you from fainting in church and we are born with only one innate taste preference, a desire for sweetness.

Insatiable

HANNAH WOOLLEY
1622?–75

Woolley's second book, The Cook's Guide, *offers valuable insights into food habits in the early modern period. Woolley was unusual in establishing herself as a female author of cookbooks at a time when women often did the cooking, and men the writing.*

Sugar is neither so hot and dry as Honey; the brownest or coarsest is most cleansing, and is good for absterstions in diseases of the Breast or Lungs; but as it is opening and cleansing, so the immoderate use thereof is dangerous; for it will rot the Teeth, and taint the Breath, ingender Jaundies and Consumptions; and Physicians verily believe, that the major part of those who die of the Consumption in the City (the constantly great numbers whereof may be seen in the Weekly Bills of Mortality) are such who eat Confections, and such-like sweet things immoderately.

And since I have spoken of Sugar, pray take special notice of this remark, That the most part of our finest Sugar, and which is most coveted, is refined and whitened by the means of the Lee of Lime; how prejudicial that may be to the body, I will leave it to the Rational to consider.

The Gentlewoman's Companion or,
A Complete Guide to the Female Sex

BARBARA CARTLAND

1901–2000

The Queen of Romance manifested a keen interest in health during her lifetime and was elected President of the National Association for Health. Three of her 723 books are about food.

Acacia honey comes from Hungary and always makes me think of the beautiful, unhappy Empress Elizabeth of Austria galloping across the plains beside the Prime Minister Count Julius Andrássy, whom she loved.

Acacia honey is gathered from the blossom of trees grown on the romantic Danube. It contains a broad spectrum of trace elements and is much appreciated by athletes as an extra source of energy. I feel I must quote here from my book *The Magic of Honey*:

What I am certain of is that honey possesses some magic quality which can help us to feel young, so that old age is never troublesome. It doesn't matter being old in years, and I do believe that honey, if taken every day, can help us to feel, look and be young whatever our birth certificate says.

The Health Food Cookery Book

MAY BYRON
d. 1936

TEA FOR A HEADACHE (Surrey)
This is a special remedial tea, an expensive one, and not for ordinary use: but it will cure, or ameliorate, in most cases, the nervous headaches which otherwise yield to nothing.

Take half a pound of a *good* Congou blend, about 2s. 2d. or 2s. 6d. per pound, such as Ridgway's, two ounces of a good China Tea, not less than 3s. per pound, and one ounce of a good green tea, about 4s. 6d. per pound. Blend these thoroughly well and keep in a closed tin in a dry place. Do not entrust the making of this (or any other tea) to servants. The 'scalding' of the teapot and making of tea with *freshly boiling* water are essential: and this is just what servants usually ignore. Water that has been boiling some time will not 'draw' tea properly: much less so, water that 'has boiled,' which is too frequently made use of.

Pot-Luck

JULIANNE BELOTE

VIRTUES OF COFFEE
Coffee accelerates digestion corrects crudities, removes colic and flatulencies. It mitigates headaches, cherishes the animal spirits, takes away listlessness and languor, and is serviceable in all obstructions arising from languid circulation. It is a wonderful restorative to emaciated constitutions, and highly refreshing to the studious and sedentary.

The habitual use of coffee would greatly promote sobriety being in itself a cordial stimulant; it is a most powerful antidote to the temptation of spirituous liquors.

It will be found a welcome beverage to the robust labourer, who would despise a lighter drink.

The Compleat American Housewife: 1787

REAY TANNAHILL

Caffeine, the natural stimulant in coffee, is fatal at a dose of about one-third of an ounce. Nutmeg can be hallucinogenic. Two pounds of onions a day are enough to cause anaemia. Both rhubarb and spinach contain oxalic acid, which builds kidney stones. Carotene, which puts the colour in egg yolks and carrots, can result in jaundice. Cabbage in excess can help to cause goitre. Too much white bread in childhood (a new one, this) may cause shortsightedness in later life. Bran, promoted in the high-fibre diet that is advocated as helping to protect against coronary and colon diseases, can in excess prevent absorption of iron and calcium. Red kidney beans, inadequately boiled, can be toxic. Watermelon seeds are claimed to damage the liver and kidneys. People have been poisoned by the solanin in green potatoes, the prussic acid in bitter almonds, the cyanide in lima beans.

Food in History

ABBY FISHER
c. 1832–?

A former mulatta slave from Alabama (her father was French), Mrs Fisher worked as a cook and caterer in San Francisco in the 1870s. Her cookbook was thought to be the first by an African American woman until the discovery in 2001 of Malinda Russell's A Domestic Cookbook *(1866).*

TONIC BITTERS

A Southern Remedy for Invalids

Take one ounce of cardamom seed, one ounce of Peruvian bark bruised, two ounces of Gentian root bruised, half ounce of dry orange peel, one ounce of aloes, and put the whole into half a gallon of best whiskey or brandy; let it come to a boil, then strain or filter it through a fine cloth or filtering paper.

Dose half wineglassfull three times a day before meals. Will strengthen and produce an appetite.

What Mrs Fisher Knows About Old Southern Cooking

HANNAH WOOLLEY
1622?-75

We have a spice growing here at home called Saffron, which need not give place to any of the former; it is hot in the second, and dry in the first degree: It is a great Cordial, and a help against obstructions; it is good against the Jaundies, and unstuffs the pipes of the Lungs: It is good to bring down the Menstruum, and facilitates the Birth, if taken moderately. And since I have spoken of a thing of our own growth, let me add another, which is Honey, hot and dry in the second degree, and is better boiled than raw; it is very restorative, and therefore good against Consumptions, and Phlegmatick Constitutions, but dangerous to be used much by hot Complexions, for thereby it is soon converted into Choler. The best is very sweet, pleasant of smell, of a cleer and yellowish colour, pretty stiff and firm, and yieldeth but little scum on the top when boiled. Garden-honey is the best and is clarified by adding a little water to it, about the fourth part, and so scum it whilst any froth ariseth, or till the water be evaporated, which is known by the bubbles rising from the bottom; if you will have it more pure, put into every pound of Honey the white of an Egg, and afterwards scum it again in the boiling; then use it against all pectoral infirmities, as the Cough, shortness of breath, the Pleurisie &c.

The Gentlewoman's Companion or,
A Complete Guide to the Female Sex

MARGARET VISSER

Tasting for poison is still etiquette in some modern societies. In Papua New Guinea, it is good manners for a host to sip water before offering it to a guest; in several African societies, food is ritually tasted by the host before guests receive it. The person who splits and shares the cola nut in Nigeria must kiss it first, reputedly to reassure everyone present that poison is out of the question. There is normally no real anxiety among the guests; the act is initiatory and honorific, a polite flourish like publicly washing one's hands even if they are clean. Our custom of having the host taste the wine before approving it for his guests seems merely practical and entirely in the interests of the palate, but it is often at the same time a purely ceremonial expression of concern for the well-being of the guests.

The Rituals of Dinner

MADDISON AND MORISON FAMILIES
1663–88

My Lady Widderington ressett for a Looseness
Take hogs dung newly dunged and boyle it in a pint of milke prity well the Straine and drink it off – to make the hog dung you may turne him round severall times and falloe him till he does it –

Receipt Book

ELLEN G. WHITE
1827–1915

A nineteenth-century mystic, Ellen White advocated a vegetarian diet and profoundly influenced the eating habits of the Seventh-day Adventist church, whose prophet she became. She wrote prolifically on a variety of health matters.

In many families we find dyspeptics, and frequently the reason of this is the poor bread. The mistress of the house decides that it must not be thrown away, and they eat it. Is this the way to dispose of poor bread? Will you put it into the stomach to be converted into blood? Has the stomach power to make sour bread sweet? heavy bread light? moldy bread fresh? . . .

Many a wife and mother who has not had the right education and lacks skill in the cooking department, is daily presenting her family with ill-prepared food which is steadily and surely destroying the digestive organs, making a poor quality of blood, and frequently bringing on acute attacks of inflammatory disease and causing premature death. Many have been brought to their death by eating heavy sour bread. An instance was related to me of a hired girl who made a batch of sour, heavy bread. In order to get rid of it and conceal the matter, she threw it to a couple of very large hogs. Next morning the man of the house found his swine dead, and upon examining the trough, found pieces of this heavy bread. He made inquiries, and the girl acknowledged what she had done. She had not a thought of the effect of such bread upon the swine. If heavy, sour bread will kill swine, which can devour rattlesnakes, and almost every detestable thing, what effect will it have upon that tender organ, the human stomach?

Counsels on Diet and Foods

ELLA FARMAN PRATT
1837–1907

'Do you like brown bread, Marion?' asked Caddy, earnestly.

'Like brown bread?' she answered, folding a snowy towel over the pan, and placing it by the other sponges. 'Why, Caddy, didn't you know that intellectual people *always* liked brown bread? The papers said so only yesterday. My mental superiority, I will confide to you, young ladies, is chiefly due to the absence of the white loaf from the breakfast table . . . If I am not so brilliant as usual to-night, please to bear in mind that we've been out of brown bread for nearly two days.'

The Cooking Club of Tu-Whit Hollow

MARY WILKINS FREEMAN
1852–1930

Lucinda had always liked a bit of cold pork, some left-over dinner vegetables, some little savory relish, for supper, but now she ate a slice of bread-and-butter and a spoonful of sauce, and drank a glass of milk. Charlotte had decreed that that was better for her. Lucinda had not even her cup of tea since Charlotte reigned.

Lucinda had been fond of a rich cup-cake, which she had also enjoyed stirring up once a week for herself. She had taken an innocent pride in its excellence, and she had treated her few callers to it. She had like a slice of it between meals. But that was now all done away with; there was no cake baked in the house. 'That rich cake is not fit for you to eat, Aunt Lucinda,' Charlotte had said. 'I think we had better not have any more of it.' And poor Lucinda came gently down to her niece's views on diet, and put cup-cake and cold pork and vegetables away from her like devices of Satan. She concealed from herself her longing for them; and she felt the most sincere love and gratitude to Charlotte for her interest in her welfare.

'An Innocent Gamester'

ELIZABETH SEGAR
17th century

At her death, the novelist Sylvia Townsend Warner left a seventeenth-century manuscript household book by Elizabeth Segar to her literary executrix.

TO MAKE DYETT BREAD

Take 10 eggs both yolks and whites and beaten them in a wooden boule a quarter of an houre then put to them a pound of sugar and beat them well together half an houre longer then put to them one pound of fine flower and a few Aniseeds and beat them till the oven is hot as for a [*illegible*] then butter yr pans and set it unto them and shake it and afterward cut it in thin slices and dry it and keep it for use.

TO MAKE PLAGUE WATER

Take leaves of Celandine, rosemary, Rue, Sage, Mugwart, Wormwood, pimpernell, Stragon, Scabiouse, Agrimony, baume, Scordium, Centry, Cardus, Bettony, rosastlis, of each 2 handfulls, roots of Angelica, gentian, Tormentill (2 edvary), Lycorish, of each one ounce, Cutt ye hearbs, & bruise ye Roots, & Steep them 2 days, in a gallon of Spirit of wine, & a gallon of watter, then distill 6 quarts.

Hir Book

LADY LLANOVER
1802–96

*Few cookbooks are as unusual as the one Lady Llanover published in
1867, purportedly dictated to her by 'the Welsh hermit of the cell of
St. Gover'. It was the first cookbook dedicated to Welsh food and
recipes.*

The Hermit was very partial to mushrooms, and considered them not
only wholesome for persons in ordinary health, but so nutritious that he
believed them equal to meat, and questioned me closely as to the
improvement of their cultivation in the present age, but I did not distinguish myself by my answers, for I really could give no account of
them, excepting that rich persons had mushroom houses, where they
were produced by artificial heat in the winter, and that mushroom
spawn was generally purchased and was expensive, but I did *not know*
whether naturalists or horticulturalists had discovered any means of
cultivating them in the open ground, or securing the preservation of
mushrooms from one year to another in places where they spring up
spontaneously, though I had often heard surprise expressed at the abundance of mushrooms in some years and the absence of them in others,
in the same ground; and this being the sum and substance of my knowledge, I was taunted repeatedly, at the expense of my '*scientific friends,*'
who had not turned their attention to a natural production so beneficial
to rich and poor, and about the natural history and cultivation of which
so little (according to my report) appeared to be known; and I was
advised to offer a prize for new discoveries on the subject!

The First Principles of Good Cookery

CATHARINE E. BEECHER 1800–78
HARRIET BEECHER STOWE 1811–96

Harriet Beecher Stowe is famous for her anti-slavery novel, Uncle
Tom's Cabin. *Her sister Catharine Beecher was a teacher and a
pioneer home economist who also published* A Treatise on
Domestic Economy *and* Miss Beecher's Domestic Receipt Book.

There is no country where an ample, well-furnished table is more easily
spread, and for that reason, perhaps, none where the bounties of
Providence are more generally neglected. Considering that our
resources are greater than those of any other civilized people, our results
are comparatively poorer.

It is said that a list of summer vegetables which are exhibited on
New-York hotel-tables being shown to a French *artiste*, he declared that
to serve such a dinner properly would take till midnight. A traveler can
not but be struck with our national plenteousness, on returning from a
Continental tour, and going directly from the ship to a New-York hotel,
in the bounteous season of autumn. For months habituated to neat
little bits of chop or poultry, garnished with the inevitable cauliflower or
potato, which seemed to be the sole possibility after the reign of green
peas was over; to sit down all at once to such a carnival! to such ripe,
juicy tomatoes, raw or cooked; cucumbers in brittle slices; rich, yellow
sweet-potatoes; broad lima-beans, and beans of other and various
names; tempting ears of Indian-corn steaming in enormous piles; great
smoking tureens of the savory succotash, an Indian gift to the table for
which civilization need not blush; sliced egg-plant in delicate fritters;
and marrow-squashes, of creamy pulp and sweetness; a rich variety,
embarrassing to the appetite, and perplexing to the choice.

Verily, the thought must often occur that the vegetarian doctrine
preached in America leaves a man quite as much as he has capacity to
eat or enjoy, and that in the midst of such tantalizing abundance he has
really lost the apology, which elsewhere bears him out in preying upon
his less gifted and accomplished animal neighbors.

The American Woman's Home

MOLLIE KATZEN

Katzen has been called one of the five 'Women Who Changed the Way We Eat' and the inspirational Moosewood Cookbook, which she hand-lettered and illustrated, is one of the top ten bestselling cookbooks of all time. Its vegetarian recipes heralded a revolution in American eating habits. This recipe is typical of the 1970s.

Scheherezade Casserole

Ground soybeans with bulghar give this dish heartiness and a perfectly-balanced protein. Vegetables, spices and feta cheese lend a full and provocative flavor.

Soybeans need about 4 hours to soak.   6 servings
Preparation + Baking times = about 1½ hours   375° oven

¾ cup raw soybeans, soaked in lots of water for at least 4 hours

1 cup raw bulghar, soaked 15 minutes in 1 cup boiling water

2 medium green peppers, chopped

4 medium-sized fresh tomatoes, chopped

1½ cups chopped onion   2 cloves crushed garlic

¼ cup freshly-chopped parsley   salt, pepper, tabasco to taste

3 Tbs. tomato paste   1 tsp. ground cumin

1½ cups crumbled feta   1 tsp. basil

① Place soaked soybeans in the blender jar with 1½ cups water. Purée.
② Combine puréed soybeans and soaked bulghar.

③ Sauté the onions and garlic in a little oil, lightly-salted. When soft, add peppers. Sauté 5 minutes.

④ Combine all ingredients except feta. Place in a large, buttered casserole. Sprinkle feta on top.

⑤ Bake one hour at 375° (covered, first 45 minutes, uncovered, last 15)

The Moosewood Cookbook

LADY JEKYLL
1860–1937

*Lady Jekyll, who wrote the first cookery columns to be printed in
The Times, believed that cooking should always be suited to the
occasion and mood. Ruth Lowinsky later exploited the same idea to
amusing effect.*

A certain *maigre* luncheon on a sunny Friday of an early summer, now
far away and long ago, was vividly impressed on the mind of one of
the party of four who enjoyed it, partly because of the beauty of its
setting and the stimulating interest of the talk in that brief hour of
refection, but also because of the discovery that such very simple
things could be so much better than the elaborate and expensive
ones which often complicate the sweet uses of hospitality. The garden
room of an educational institution set amongst those lovely wooded
hills which dip to the sea near Dublin, a Jesuit father of great intellectual distinction and goodness, a nun with a 'divine plain face,' and
two searchers after truth – this the scene and the party. Never before
had newly-laid eggs scrambled so deliciously with young asparagus, or
pink-fleshed trout tasted so fresh in the company of tiny potatoes and
crisp lettuce. A wholemeal loaf and milk scones were there, with
home-made cream cheese; the first fruits of the bee-hive also, tasting
of the scent of lime trees in blossom, and the last fruits of the dairy in
golden butter. Woodland strawberries, harbingers of the summer, in
leaf-lined baskets, gave out their fugitive aroma, and finally a brown
jug of coffee freshly roasted and ground, hot and fragrant beyond all
previous experience, brought its valedictory blessing to a perfect
meal. How gross in comparison appeared the joints of butcher's meat,
the slaughtered game and poultry of daily life, until the great recon-
ciler, custom, should blunt afresh our susceptibilities! Since meatless
days are the rule of many at certain Church seasons, and of many
more at all seasons, some suggestions for making *maigre* menus more
generally acceptable to all may not come amiss; for did not Mary
Coleridge remind us in a pleasant volume of table talk that 'Self-

sacrifice is the noblest thing in the world, but to sacrifice other people, even for a noble thing, is as wrong as persecution.'

Kitchen Essays

LOUISA MAY ALCOTT
1832–88

Any housewife can imagine the emotions of Sister Hope, when she took possession of a large, dilapidated kitchen, containing an old stove and the peculiar stores out of which food was to be evolved for her little family of eleven. Cakes of maple sugar, dried peas and beans, barley and hominy, meal of all sorts, potatoes, and dried fruit. No milk, butter, cheese, tea, or meat, appeared. Even salt was considered a useless luxury and spice entirely forbidden by these lovers of Spartan simplicity. A ten years' experience of vegetarian vagaries had been good training for this new freak, and her sense of the ludicrous supported her through many trying scenes.

Unleavened bread, porridge, and water for breakfast; bread, vegetables, and water for dinner; bread, fruit, and water for supper was the bill of fare ordained by the elders. No teapot profaned that sacred stove, no gory steak cried aloud for vengeance from her chaste gridiron; and only a brave woman's taste, time, and temper were sacrificed on that domestic altar.

Silver Pitchers

HOLY FOOD

CAROLINE WALKER BYNUM

To religious women food was a way of controlling as well as renouncing both self and environment. But it was more. Food was flesh, and flesh was suffering and fertility. In renouncing ordinary food and directing their being toward the food that is Christ, women moved to God not merely by abandoning their flawed physicality but also by becoming the suffering and feeding humanity of the body on the cross, the food on the altar.

Holy Feast and Holy Fast

MARGERY KEMPE
c. 1373–after 1449

In between giving birth to fourteen children, Margery Kempe enjoyed visions, visited Julian of Norwich for spiritual guidance and made pilgrimages to Canterbury and the Holy Land. She was illiterate, but dictated what may well be the first autobiography in English. In this passage she is ordered to stop eating meat, though later the Lord ordered her to resume her carnivorous habits.

SHE SPEAKS WITH OUR LORD, WHO ORDERS HER TO ABSTAIN FROM FLESH-MEAT, AND TO CONTEMPLATE AND MEDITATE.

Then on the Friday before Christmas Day, as this creature was kneeling in a chapel of Saint John, within a Church of St. Margaret in N . . ., weeping wondrous sore, and asking mercy and forgiveness for her sins and trespasses, Our merciful Lord Christ Jesus, blessed may

He be, ravished her spirit and said unto her:—

'Daughter, why weepest thou so sore? I am coming to thee, Jesus Christ Who died on the cross, suffering bitter pains and passions for thee. I, the same God, forgive thee thy sins to the uttermost point, and thou shalt never come to Hell or Purgatory, but when thou shalt pass out of this world, within a twinkling of an eye, thou shalt have the bliss of Heaven, for I am the same God that hath brought thy sins to thy mind and made thee be shriven thereof . . . Also, My dearworthy daughter, thou must forsake that which thou lovest best in this world, and that is the eating of flesh. Instead of that flesh, thou shalt eat of My flesh and My blood, that is the Very Body of Christ in the Sacrament of the Altar. This is My will, daughter, that thou receive My Body every Sunday, and I shall flow so much grace into thee, that all the world shall marvel thereof. Thou shalt be eaten and gnawed by the people of the world as any rat gnaweth stockfish.

The Book of Margery Kempe

SIMONE WEIL
1909–43

In 1943, already ill with tuberculosis, Weil hastened her death by refusing food and medical treatment in order to proclaim her solidarity with the people of Occupied France.

It may be that vice, depravity and crime are nearly always . . . attempts to eat beauty, to eat what we should only look at. Eve began it. If she caused humanity to be lost by eating the fruit, the opposite attitude, looking at the fruit without eating it, should be what is required to save it.

Waiting on God, trans. by E. Craufurd

If I grow thin from labour in the fields, my flesh really becomes wheat. If that wheat is used for the host it becomes Christ's flesh. Anyone who labours with this intention should become a saint.

First and Last Notebooks, trans. by R. Rees

ELIZABETH BARRETT BROWNING
1806–61

My future will not copy fair my past
On any leaf but Heaven's. Be fully done
Supernal Will! I would not fain be one
Who, satisfying thirst and breaking fast,
Upon the fulness of the heart at last
Says no grace after meat. My wine has run
Indeed out of my cup, and there is none
To gather up the bread of my repast
Scattered and trampled; yet I find some good
In earth's green herbs, and streams that bubble up
Clear from the darkling ground, – content until
I sit with angels before better food: –
Dear Christ! When thy new vintage fills my cup,
This hand shall shake no more, nor that wine spill

'Past and Future'

JANE GRIGSON
1920–90

*Along with Elizabeth David and M.F.K. Fisher, Jane Grigson is
famed for her elegant prose. Most people know her through her
Observer food columns, which she wrote from 1968 until 1990.*

In the Middle Ages – and until recently in some parts – the cherry fair
was a great festival. People wandered about the orchards; the fruit was
picked and sold; there was dancing, drinking and making love (a few
years ago there were still some old people in our Wiltshire village with
birthdays nine months after Clyffe feast, which took place every year at
cherry time). The poignancy of colour and glory in lives which were
normally brutish had by the thirteenth century turned the fair into a
symbol of the passing moment:

This life, I see, is but a cherry fair.
All things pass and so must I algate.

Which is also, I suppose, the feeling behind Japanese cherry blossom festivities, when everyone goes out to picnic beneath the flowers – and reflect on the *neiges d'antan*.

The precious unkeepable cherry was the fruit of paradise, the glimpse and symbol of perfection. No wonder Mary longed for cherries when she was walking with Joseph and saw a laden cherry tree. She asked Joseph to reach some down, but he felt irritable and refused 'with words so unkind, Let them get thee cherries who got thee with child!' Then Jesus cried out from Mary's womb to the cherry tree. It leaned down one of its branches right to her hand. She called out like any girl at a cherry fair, 'See, Joseph, there are cherries for me!'

I wonder if Memling knew that carol when he painted his 'Mother and Child with two angels', now in the Uffizi: Jesus sits on Mary's knee, ivory pale against her rust-coloured robe, with a cherry clutched in one hand, symbol of the Heaven he had left behind. With the other hand, he stretches towards a fine red and yellow apple, held up by one of the angels and the symbol of man's fall by which death came to the world. Jesus leans towards his own death, taking on man's fate and redeeming him. The paradise cherry orchard is for a time forgotten.

Jane Grigson's Fruit Book

HILDEGARD OF BINGEN
1098–1179

There is little that the twelfth-century abbess Hildegard did not write about: medicine, natural history, music and theology. Some of her work is notable for its food imagery.

THE PARABLE OF THE FIRE AND THE BREAD

The will is like a fire baking every action in an oven. Bread is baked in order to feed people and strengthen them so that they can live. The will is the force behind the whole of the action. It grinds the action in a mill, it adds yeast and kneads it firmly and thus carefully prepares the action, like a loaf of bread which the will bakes to perfection in the heat of its zeal. In so doing it provides human beings with a better food than bread for the activities they do. For while food is taken into the human body and used up, the action of the will endures within the human being until the separation of the soul from the body. And although the action will vary greatly in childhood, in youth, in maturity and in the declining years, nevertheless the will directs it stage by stage and brings it to perfection.

Selected Writings
trans. by Mark Atherton

ISABEL ALLENDE

I remember the kitchen of a convent in Brussels, where I witnessed, with reverence, the mysterious comingling of yeast, flour and water. A nun, not wearing her habit, with the shoulders of a stevedore and delicate hands of a ballerina, arranged the dough in round and rectangular loaf pans, covered them with white cloths washed a thousand times and then washed again, and left them to rise beside a window, on a large medieval wood table. As she worked, at the far end of the kitchen the simple, daily miracle of flour and poetry ensued, the content of the pans took on life, and a slow and sensual process evolved beneath those white napkins that were discreet sheets covering the nakedness of the unbaked bread. The raw dough swelled with secret sighs, moved softly, pulsed like a woman's body in the surrender of love. The acid odor of the fermenting dough blended with the intense and vigorous breath of newly baked loaves. And I, sitting on a penitent's bench in a dark corner of that vast stone room, immersed in the warmth and fragrance of that mysterious process, wept, without knowing why.

Aphrodite

MARY TYLER PEABODY MANN
1807–87

Her famous cookbook, Christianity in the Kitchen, *warned: 'There's death in the pot.' And one of her cake recipes called for 20 eggs and a batter that had to be beaten for 3 hours.*

There is no more prolific, – indeed, there is no *such* prolific cause of bad morals as abuses of diet, – not merely by excessive drinking of injurious beverages, but excessive eating, and by eating unhealthful food. Compounds like wedding cake, suet plum-puddings, and rich turtle soup, are masses of indigestible material which should never find their way to any Christian table.

Christianity in the Kitchen

ALICE KIRK GRIERSON
1828–88

Recipes for this classic cake are to be found in many sources. Just as varied as the texts and the ingredients are the theories of its origin. One suggestion is that it originated in New England and travelled West with pioneers. This version is from the kitchen of Alice Kirk Grierson, wife of a colonel in the Civil War. Her cookbook contains approximately 600 recipes, of which over half are for desserts. There are thirteen recipes for lemon pie and nineteen for muffins.

SCRIPTURE CAKE

1 cup of butter	Judges 5, verse 25
3 cups of sugar	Jeremiah 6, verse 20
3½ cups of flour	1 Kings 4, verse 22
2 cups of raisins	1 Samuel 30, verse 12
2 cups of figs	1 Samuel 30, verse 12
1 cup of water	Genesis 24, verse 17
1 cup of almonds	Genesis 24, verse 17
6 eggs	Isaiah 10, verse 14
One tablespoon of honey	Exodus 16, verse 21
A pinch of salt	Leviticus 2, verse 31
Spices to taste	

Follow Solomon's advice for making good boys, and you will have a good cake.

Proverbs 13, verse 24

An Army Wife's Cookbook

EDNA FERBER
1885–1968

In our own household there was no celebration of the informal home ceremonies so often observed in Jewish families. The Passover, with its Sedar service, was marked in our house only by the appearance of the matzos or unleavened bread, symbolic of the hardships of the Jews in the wilderness. I devoured pounds of the crisp crumbling matzos with hunks of fresh butter and streams of honey, leaving a trail of crumbs all over the house, and thought very little, I am afraid, of the tragic significance of the food I was eating or of that weary heartsick band led by Moses out of Egypt to escape the Hitler of that day, one Pharaoh; or of how they baked and ate their unsalted unleavened bread because it was all they had, there in the wilderness. I still have matzoth (matzos, we always called them) in my house during the Passover, and just as thoughtlessly.

A Peculiar Treasure

CLEMENTINE PADDLEFORD
1900–67

There are two schools of thought regarding the pretzel's origin, but both start at the church. The crossed dough ends of the bread are said to represent the crossed arms of the priest or the acolyte at prayer. From this point forward pretzel authorities differ. (Don't smile, there are pretzel experts, and they take themselves quite seriously.) One story is that glazed hard pretzels encrusted with coarse salt were given out at monastery doors to passing pilgrims. The hole in the center had a functional purpose – pretzels could be strung on a pilgrim's staff.

A more charming theory is that the name pretzel is derived from the Latin 'pretiola' meaning a small reward, and the bread was made by the monks of southern Europe to give to those children who learned their prayers perfectly.

The art of pretzel making was brought to this country by the

Germans and Austrians. The first American pretzels were baked in home kitchens on open hearth fires. Then in 1861 came the first commercial pretzel bakery established in Lititz. Soon pretzels were baking in near-by Reading [Pennsylvania]. Soon every little Dutch hamlet had its pretzel maker.

How America Eats

PATRICIA STORACE

I have a palm-sized icon that I found one Easter on Corfu in the shop of an impulsive, affectionate woman named Mrs. Gift-of-God. The painting shows three angels dressed in ruby-colored caftans, sitting together at a round table covered with a beautiful sea-green tablecloth, just the color of the Aegean in certain lights and depths. You can tell they have come a long way; they have the slightly weary, relaxed posture of people who have arrived at their destination after a long flight, and their bare feet are propped on soft cushions. They look cheerfully hungry; on the table are three tiny forks and three golden goblets, the same gold as their wings and halos. They are talking together with delicacy and wit, judging from the inclinations of their heads and the appreciative smile of the angel on the right. It is obvious that the cool wine in their glowing goblets and the aromatic scent of their dinner cooling is inspiring them. I know they represent the angels who visited Abraham in the desert and that, theologically, they are supposed to prefigure the Holy Trinity, but I don't care. For me they are the angels of the table, presiding over one of the arts of peace, the arts in which the sensual and the spiritual, the physical and metaphysical love, are fused into one substance, far more difficult to accomplish than any of the arts of war.

My gastronomic guardians, who traveled with me throughout Greece, are the patron saints of the answered prayer, which every good meal is, and they remind me of one of the most important elements of

Greek cooking. If French cooking is an ongoing inquiry into the ultimate rules of cuisine and Italian cooking explores the nature of impulse and improvisation, Greek cuisine, with its combination of frugality and richness and its transformation of scarcity into plenty, is a demonstration of the miraculous. Think of the olive, a bony-looking tree with a fruit no bigger than a fingertip, which can be turned into pies, sauces, fuel, and even light itself.

In Greece, when you go to the herb and spice seller for a handful of bay leaves, what you ask for is Daphne, the name of the nymph who gave this flavor to the world, the legacy of her flight from Apollo and her transformation into the laurel tree. Greek life is thoroughly entangled with myth, but nowhere more intimately than in the kitchen, where someone wielding a wooden spoon is always sure to remind you that the Greeks like to say that their words for cooking and magic are related. And one of the most charming double entendres I know I learned when I was searching for a rolling pin, called a *plastis*, which is another name for the Creator of the Universe. I was delighted to think of God as a bread-maker, perhaps even a *pâtissier* – at last we had something in common.

'God as *Pâtissier*'

CASSANDRA AUSTEN
1739–1827

This recipe in verse may have been composed to order by Jane Austen's mother, Cassandra Leigh Austen, for the household book of a family friend, Martha Lloyd.

If the vicar you treat,
You must give him to eat,
A pudding to his affection,
And to make his repast,
By the canon of taste,
Be the present receipt your direction.

First take 2 lbs of bread,
Be the crumb only weigh'd
For crust the good housewife refuses.
The proportions you'll guess
May be made more or less
To the size the family chuses.

Then its sweetness to make;
Some currants you take,
And sugar, of each half a pound
Be not butter forgot.
And the quantity sought
Must the same with your currants be found.

Cloves and mace you will want,
With rose water I grant,
And more savoury things if well chosen.
Then to bind each ingredient,
You'll find it expedient,
Of eggs to put in half a dozen.

Some milk, don't refuse it,
But boil as you use it,
A proper hint for its maker.
And the whole when compleat,
With care recommend the baker.

In praise of this pudding,
I vouch it a good one,
Or should you suspect a fond word,
To every guest,
Perhaps it is best
Two puddings should smoke on the board.

Two puddings! – yet – no,
For if one will do
The other comes in out of season;
And these lines but obey,
Nor can anyone say,
That this pudding's without rhyme or reason.

'A Receipt for a Pudding'

BARBARA PYM
1913–80

A sudden anxious picture came into my mind – the two priests in the clergy house kitchen, trying to cook fillets of plaice or cod steaks. Perhaps in the end they would have to open a tin of sardines or spaghetti, unless they had decided to dine out. They might even have got a housekeeper by now. How wonderful it would be if Father Thames had interviewed and engaged Mr Bason, and he was even now preparing them a delicious sole véronique! I saw him at the kitchen table, peeling grapes. Of course I had no idea what he looked like – I just saw his fingers, long and sensitive as befitted an Anglo-Catholic fond of cooking, removing the pips.

A Glass of Blessings

TONI MORRISON

It was Stamp Paid who started it. Twenty days after Sethe got to 124 he came by and looked at the baby he had tied up in his nephew's jacket, looked at the mother he had handed a piece of fried eel to and, for some private reason of his own, went off with two buckets to a place near the river's edge that only he knew about where blackberries grew, tasting so good and happy that to eat them was like being in church. Just one of the berries and you felt anointed. He walked six miles to the riverbank; did a slide-run-slide down into a ravine made almost inaccessible by brush. He reached through brambles lined with blood-drawing thorns thick as knives that cut through his shirtsleeves and trousers. All the while suffering mosquitoes, bees, hornets, wasps and the meanest lady spiders in the state. Scratched, raked and bitten, he maneuvered through and took hold of each berry with fingertips so gentle not a single one was bruised. Late in the afternoon he got back to 124 and put two full buckets down on the porch. When Baby Suggs saw his shredded clothes, bleeding hands, welted face and neck she sat down laughing out loud.

Buglar, Howard, the woman in the bonnet and Sethe came to look and then laughed along with Baby Suggs at the sight of the sly, steely old black man: agent, fisherman, boatman, tracker, savior, spy, standing in broad daylight whipped finally by two pails of blackberries. Paying them no mind he took a berry and put it in the three-week-old Denver's mouth. The woman shrieked.

'She's too little for that, Stamp.'

'Bowels be soup.'

'Sickify her stomach.'

But the baby's thrilled eyes and smacking lips made them follow suit, sampling one at a time the berries that tasted like church. Finally Baby Suggs slapped the boys' hands away from the bucket and sent Stamp around to the pump to rinse himself. She had decided to do something with the fruit worthy of the man's labor and his love. That's how it began.

She made the pastry dough and thought she ought to tell Ella and John to stop on by because three pies, maybe four, were too much to keep for one's own. Sethe thought they might as well back it up with a couple of chickens. Stamp allowed that perch and catfish were jumping into the boat – didn't even have to drop a line.

From Denver's two thrilled eyes it grew to a feast for ninety people. 124 shook with their voices far into the night. Ninety people who ate so well, and laughed so much, it made them angry. They woke up the next morning and remembered the meal-fried perch that Stamp Paid handled with a hickory twig, holding his left palm out against the spit and pop of the boiling grease; the corn pudding made with cream; tired, overfed children asleep in the grass, tiny bones of roasted rabbit still in their hands – and got angry.

Baby Suggs' three (maybe four) pies grew to ten (maybe twelve). Sethe's two hens became five turkeys. The one block of ice brought all the way from Cincinnati – over which they poured mashed watermelon mixed with sugar and mint to make a punch – became a wagonload of ice cakes for a washtub full of strawberry shrug. 124, rocking with laughter, goodwill and food for ninety, made them angry. Too much, they thought. Where does she get it all, Baby Suggs, holy? Why is she and hers always the center of things? How come she always knows exactly what to do and when? Giving advice; passing messages; healing the sick, hiding fugitives, loving, cooking, cooking, loving, preaching, singing, dancing and loving everybody like it was her job and hers alone.

Now to take two buckets of blackberries and make ten, maybe twelve, pies; to have turkey enough for the whole town pretty near, new peas in September, fresh cream but no cow, ice *and* sugar, batter bread, bread pudding, raised bread, shortbread – it made them mad. Loaves and fishes were His powers – they did not belong to an ex-slave who had probably never carried one hundred pounds to the scale, or picked okra with a baby on her back.

Beloved

CATHERINE COTTON
17th century

Tucked away among Cotton's seventeenth-century medicinal and cookery recipes is this verse mocking Presbyterians. Another version can be found in the commonplace book of Henry Docker.

A RECEIPT HOW TO MAKE A RIGHT PRESBYTERIAN IN TWO DAYS
Take the herbes of hypocrasie and ambition of each two handfuls of ye flowers of formality two scruples of ye spirit of pride and malice two

drams each of the seeds of contention & stubbornness of each four ounces, of the cordial of reflection and lyes of each fifty ounces, of the root of moderation as small a quantity as you please.

Drink the cordial, chop the herbs, powder the seeds, slice the roots, bruse them alltogether in a morter of vainglory with pestles of contradiction & deceit, put them in a pan of [—] water to be infus'd over a brimstone fire of fained seal which is hypocrasie adding thereto a hundred ounces of ye syrup of self-conceit, covetousness & self-ends, when luke-warm let ye person that is to be made a presbyterian take ten spoonfulls night and morning, and when his mouth is full of this hellish compound let him make wry mouths and squeese out some tears of dissimulation.

This will do wonders and make the schismaticks maintain of [—], run down the church, delude the people, justise dissention, foment contention, & rebellion & call it all liberty of conscience.

'Her Booke', as quoted in *Eat My Words*

RUTH LOWINSKY
1892–1958

Painful though it must be for the expert cook to watch a delicious joint being ruined by a novice, his agony cannot compare with that of the victim who is himself the aforesaid joint. Let us hope that Saints Lorenzo of Rome and Juan de Prado, two patron saints of cooking, were lost in admiration of the skill with which they were roasted alive. Perhaps the following meal would be considered by them a foretaste of Paradise.

ICED AND CURRIED PRAWNS

*

FILET OSCAR

*

PETITS POTS DE CRÊME

Lovely Food

CONSTANCE SPRY 1886–1960
ROSEMARY HUME 1907–

People of sensitive and unadventurous palate or of delicate digestion might regard with apprehension dishes with such filibustering and satanic names [as devils, barbecues and marinades]. Yet the bark, if I may so express it, of barbecues and devils is generally fiercer than their bite. The truth is that with one or two exceptions the finished dish might be described as aromatic rather than peppery; even when the initial ingredients sound fiery the final dish often presents a spicy and agreeable flavour without any tongue-burning propensities. Take, for example, that best of Christmas-time dishes, devilled turkey bones, one of the high lights, it might be said, of this type of dish. The flesh, marinaded in a bath of hot-sounding liquid, ends up with an appetizing and agreeable flavour and certainty without any real fire. The mushrooms in a creamed devilled sauce, again, are quite bland and pleasing to a delicate palate.

The Constance Spry Cookery Book

JEAN RHYS
1890–1979

During World War I, the novelist Jean Rhys worked as a volunteer in a soldiers' canteen.

Now Sister Marie Augustine is leading me out of the dormitory, asking if I am ill, telling me that I must not disturb the others and though I am still shivering I wonder if she will take me behind the mysterious curtains to the place where she sleeps. But no. She seats me in a chair, vanishes, and after a while comes back with a cup of hot chocolate.

I said, 'I dreamed I was in Hell.'

'The dream is evil. Put it from your mind – never think of it again,' and she rubbed my cold hands to warm them.

She looks as usual, composed and neat, and I want to ask her if she gets up before dawn or hasn't been to bed at all.

'Drink your chocolate.'

Wide Sargasso Sea

ELISABETH LAMBERT ORTIZ
1915–2003

I have always thought of the 17th century legends of the colonial origin of Mexico's festival dish, *Mole Poblano de Guajolote* (Turkey in Chili Pepper and Chocolate Sauce), as charming, but thoroughly silly . . .

I believe the origin of the dish to be far less romantic than any of the legends. I am sure it existed before the Conquest, and since it contained chocolate was a royal dish. Chocolate was forbidden to women and among men was reserved for royalty, the military nobility, the higher ranks of the clergy and the most prominent of the merchants. The Aztec girls in the Convent would not have mentioned the dish since they lived in a world of women. I like to imagine that when the visit of Don Juan and the Archbishop was announced, the convent was in a simmer of excitement, eager to give the distinguished guests a very splendid meal. There were many Aztec girls in the Convents in addition to Indian servants, and it must surely have seemed to them that this was the occasion for a royal dish – the Viceroy being equated with their Emperor, and the Archbishop with their High Priest. What else but a dish with turkey, a native bird that the Aztecs had long domesticated, forbidden chocolate, chilis, with which they were entirely familiar, and tomatoes, another commonplace, but exotic to the nuns. Pooling memories, they could have pieced the recipe together with the nuns making their own contribution. I think perhaps instead of cloves and cinnamon, so recently brought by Spain from the Far East and at that time immensely popular in cooking, the original dish used allspice, native to the region; and *epazote*, a favourite local herb instead of coriander; and peanuts instead of almonds. Onions and garlic were common to both the Old World and the New, and would naturally be included. I cannot prove the authenticity of my version of this early post-Conquest serving of the famous *mole*, but at least it presents a logical solution to the problem of where the dish came from.

There is no doubt that after the Conquest the richly imaginative and varied kitchen of Indian Mexico fell into decline, so that even if the nuns did not invent the turkey *mole* they certainly saved the recipe from oblivion. I am grateful to them.

Petits Propos Culinaires

WILLA CATHER
1873–1947

On coming into the dining-room, Bishop Latour placed his candle-sticks over the fireplace, since there were already six upon the table, illuminating the brown soup-pot. After they had stood for a moment in prayer, Father Joseph lifted the cover and ladled the soup into the plates, a dark onion soup with *croûtons*. The Bishop tasted it critically and smiled at his companion. After the spoon had travelled to his lips a few times, he put it down and leaning back in his chair remarked—

'Think of it, *Blanchet*, in all this vast country between the Mississippi and the Pacific Ocean, there is probably not another human being who could make a soup like this.'

'Not unless he is a Frenchman,' said Father Joseph. He had tucked a napkin over the front of his cassock and was losing no time in reflection.

'I am not deprecating your individual talent, Joseph,' the Bishop continued, 'but, when one thinks of it, a soup like this is not the work of one man. It is the result of a constantly refined tradition. There are nearly a thousand years of history in this soup.'

Father Joseph frowned intently at the earthen pot in the middle of the table. His pale, near-sighted eyes had always the look of peering into distance. 'C'est ça, c'est vrai,' he murmured. 'But how,' he exclaimed as he filled the Bishop's plate again, 'how can a man make a proper soup without leeks, that king of vegetables? We cannot go on eating onions for ever.'

Death Comes for the Archbishop

HANNAH GLASSE
1708–70

To make a rich Seed Cake called the Nun's Cake

You must take four pounds of the finest flour, and three pounds of double-refined sugar beaten and sifted; mix them together, and dry them by the fire till you prepare the other materials; take four pounds of butter, beat it with your hand till it is soft like cream; then beat thirty-five eggs, leave out sixteen whites, strain off your eggs from the treads, and beat them and the butter together till all appears like butter; put in four or five spoonfuls of rose or orange-flower water, and beat again; then take your flour and sugar, with six ounces of carraway-seeds, and strew them in by degrees, beating it up all the time for two hours together; you may put in as much tincture of cinnamon or ambergris as you please; butter your hoop, and let it stand three hours in a moderate oven. You must observe always, in beating of butter, to do it with a cool hand, and beat it always one way in a deep earthen dish.

The Art of Cookery, Made Plain and Easy

ALICE THOMAS ELLIS
1932–2005

Aunt Irene really inclined to that simplest of all views: the one expressed so cogently in the book of Genesis, which explained everything with appealing clarity. This was the only view that explained, for instance, mayonnaise. It was patently absurd to suppose that mayonnaise had come about through random chance, that anyone could ever have been silly or brilliant enough to predict what would happen if he slowly trickled oil on to egg yolks and then gone ahead and tried it. An angel must have divulged that recipe and then explained what to do with the left-over whites. Meringues – there was another instance of the exercise of superhuman intelligence. To Aunt Irene the Ten Commandments seemed almost insignificant compared with the astonishing miracle of what you could do with an egg. As the angel had left in his fiery chariot he must have added, 'And don't forget omelettes, and cake and custard and soufflés and poaching and frying and boiling and baking. Oh, and they're frightfully good with anchovies. And you can use the shells to clarify soup – and don't forget to dig them in round the roots of your roses', the angelic tones fading into the ethereal distance.

The 27th Kingdom

CLEMENTINE PADDLEFORD
1900–67

One hot August I spent a week visiting a Tennessee camp meeting, the Taylor family's kinsfolk revival held near Brownsville, sixty miles north of Memphis. This meeting has been a family tradition for over one hundred years. Here the good eats came next to godliness.

The camp hummed with voices. There was the shrill shouting of children, merry-mouthed as young guinea hens, the scraping of deck chairs, the creak-squeak of swings. A calling of greetings. 'Well, if it isn't Cousin Bessie! When did you get in?'

There was the clatter of dishes. Came the good eating smells, all fittin' to stir the hunger of a stone man. Southern ham was frying, buttermilk biscuits were baking; rich simmerings gave off their varying scents as cooks lifted pot lids.

Late August, as in the olden times, when the crops are laid in, it's meeting time at the church. Here come the Tennessee Taylors from every part of the nation, to worship together, to eat fried chicken, to christen the year's crop of babies, to pay their respects to their dead.

Tabernacle is strictly a family affair with a few invited guests. Get invited three times and you are considered a 'fixture.' Averil Taylor, that's Mrs. Edmund Taylor, invited me to come and sample the camp-meeting cooking. Food served at Tabernacle is the talk of the countryside. Cooks there strive to outdo one another.

At the Edmund Taylor camp, 'Dick' runs the kitchen with a firm and batter-smeared hand. Dick's been coming to Tabernacle since she was nine years old. Her mother and grandmother had cooked here in their day.

'Dick's calling supper,' said Averil, cocking an ear. The long table for grownups was set for twenty places. In the lean-to off the kitchen the children's table packed them in ten strong.

Pan-fried steak for supper, and green beans, whipped potatoes, steak gravy. Of course, hot biscuits to make one more background for good gravy. Sliced tomatoes, big thick slices, the colour of Christmas, a spaghetti dish as an extra filler, and Dick's candied apples, corn on the cob, chess pie for dessert. Taylors on local farms bring their own hams, beef, lamb, and chicken for this occasion. They have freezers in town and drive in almost daily for fresh supplies. Each summer a special garden is planted to bear in late August: sweet corn, field peas, butter beans, turnip greens.

The last mouthful of chess pie, the last sip of coffee, the cow horn was tooting the signal for evening meeting.

The church on the rise seats three hundred people, and on this August night the place overflowed. Chairs were put up; Taylors sat on the porch, spread out on the lawn. Front rows were reserved for the little shavers. The drugstore set, the 12- to 18-year-olds, some forty-odd, sat on the platform. This was the choir. And everyone sang, whether he could 'hyst a hymn' or not.

The benediction, then gaiety took over. Hand-shaking on the lawn. 'Come to our camp, we're cutting a melon.' 'Come to our camp, we're having a sing.' 'Can't you drop in for a cake and coffee?' And the cakes they pass! Averil cut a melon.

Women gathered around to tell me who is who among the good Taylor cooks. They were eager to help me get recipes, believing there is nothing good to eat north of Washington. Nobody in our camp went to bed before three.

At six came the sound of the horn, a signal for rising. I skipped prayer meeting but was on hand for the big breakfast; pink-brown slices of ham afloat in red-eye gravy. There was beef hash undefiled, nothing in it but potatoes, beef and onions – not a catchall. Plateloads of whole-wheat muffins came by, and homemade blackberry jam . . .

After all at this pleasant revival there was more pie than piety.

How America Eats

JHUMPA LAHIRI

They discovered the first one in a cupboard above the stove, beside an unopened bottle of malt vinegar.

'Guess what I found.' Twinkle walked into the living room, lined from end to end with taped-up packing boxes, waving the vinegar in one hand and a white porcelain effigy of Christ, roughly the same size as the vinegar bottle, in the other.

Sanjeev looked up. He was kneeling on the floor, marking, with ripped bits of a Post-it, patches on the baseboard that needed to be retouched with paint. 'Throw it away.'

'Which?'

'Both.'

'But I can cook something with the vinegar. It's brand-new.'

'You've never cooked anything with vinegar.'

'I'll look something up. In one of those books we got for our wedding.'

Sanjeev turned back to the baseboard, to replace a Post-it scrap that had fallen to the floor. 'Check the expiration. And at the very least get rid of that idiotic statue.'

'But it could be worth something. Who knows?' She turned it upside down, then stroked, with her index finger, the minuscule frozen folds of its robes. 'It's pretty.'

'We're not Christian,' Sanjeev said. Lately he had begun noticing the need to state the obvious to Twinkle. The day before he had to tell her that if she dragged her end of the bureau instead of lifting it, the parquet floor would scratch.

She shrugged. 'No, we're not Christian. We're good little Hindus.' She planted a kiss on top of Christ's head, then placed the statue on top of the fireplace mantel, which needed, Sanjeev observed, to be dusted.

By the end of the week the mantel had still not been dusted; it had, however, come to serve as the display shelf for a sizable collection of Christian paraphernalia. There was a 3-D postcard of Saint Francis done in four colors, which Twinkle had found taped to the back of the medicine cabinet, and a wooden cross key chain, which Sanjeev had stepped on with bare feet as he was installing extra shelving in Twinkle's study. There was a framed paint-by-number of the three wise men, against a black velvet background, tucked in the linen closet. There was also a tile trivet depicting a blond, unbearded Jesus, delivering a sermon on a mountaintop, left in one of the drawers of the built-in china cabinet in the dining-room.

'Do you think the previous owners were born-agains?' asked Twinkle, making room the next day for a small plastic snow-filled dome containing a miniature Nativity scene, found behind the pipes of the kitchen sink . . .

'Did you sweep the attic?' he asked Twinkle later as she was folding paper napkins and wedging them by their plates. The attic was the only part of the house they had not yet given an initial cleaning.

'Not yet. I will, I promise. I hope this tastes good,' she said, planting the steaming pot on top of the Jesus trivet. There was a loaf of Italian bread in a little basket, and iceberg lettuce and grated carrots tossed with bottled dressing and croutons, and glasses of red wine. She was not terribly ambitious in the kitchen. She bought preroasted chickens from the supermarket and served them with potato salad prepared who knew when, sold in little plastic containers. Indian food, she complained, was a bother;

she detested chopping garlic, and peeling ginger, and could not operate a blender, and so it was Sanjeev who, on weekends, seasoned mustard oil with cinnamon sticks and cloves in order to produce a proper curry.

He had to admit, though, that whatever it was that she had cooked today, it was unusually tasty, attractive even, with bright white cubes of fish, and flecks of parsley, and fresh tomatoes gleaming in the dark brown-red broth.

'How did you make it?'

'I made it up.'

'What did you do?'

'I just put some things into the pot and added the malt vinegar at the end.'

'How much vinegar?'

She shrugged, ripping off some bread and plunging it into her bowl.

'What do you mean you don't know? You should write it down. What if you need to make it again, for a party or something?'

'I'll remember,' she said. She covered the bread basket with a dish-towel that had, he suddenly noticed, the Ten Commandments printed on it. She flashed him a smile, giving his knee a little squeeze under the table. 'Face it. This house is blessed.'

'This Blessed House'

MEAGRE RATIONS

JOAN WYNDHAM

Joan Wyndham grew up at Clouds, a Victorian country house with forty bedrooms and a kitchen so far from the dining room that a miniature railway track was built to carry food from one place to the other. Wyndham later opened Oxford's first espresso bar, ran a hippy restaurant on London's Portobello Road, and cooked at major pop festivals.

Saturday 14th September

Everybody was in the shelter by now, and one by one we began talking about food until we had worked ourselves up into a kind of gastric frenzy. We each made up our ideal menu, and recited it amid groans of thwarted appetite and sighs of appreciation. 'Entrecote minute!', 'Irish stew!', 'Cheese omelette!' echoed among the steel girders that held up the roof. Soon we had all sunk into a state of exhausted lethargy, long silences broken only by an occasional mutter of 'roast beef and Yorkshire pudding' or 'treacle sponge and custard'. Some late arrivals aroused us to a new peak by bringing their lunch in from De Cock's, and eating it with champings and loud swallowing noises.

Love Lessons

MARIA CORELLI

*During the Second World War, when Corelli was hiding in a grotto
above Picinisco, in southern Italy, she recorded her dreams, some of
which, unsurprisingly, featured food.*

One evening, Auntie Eva, Anne, Lewis and I are discussing where we
can eat. Eva has come from Via Tronto, where she lives, especially to eat
with us. Finally we decide to go to a restaurant nearby, in via Babuino.
We eat well and there is also meat. We decide we will eat here also
tomorrow for lunch . . . Lewis asks for some jam because he has some
bread left, and I ask for some butter, so we eat butter and jam together.
Then the waiter brings us some raspberries with cream and sugar. What
a joy! They are in a large glass bowl and are a beautiful colour. He also
brings us some little plates of dark glass to eat them on. We are very
happy. But we look at the time and see that it is nearly curfew time.
Fortunately we are near home but it is already 10.25. Then it occurs to
me that Eva has to pass the night in a bookshop and will probably be
hungry during the night. So I prepare some more raspberries on other
plates for Eva. I pour out the cream and sugar. I am having a lovely
time – they are so beautifully red and make me think back to other days.
But the minutes are passing. Lewis says 'Be quick, you can't play about
with curfew – they take it seriously.' Yes, yes – but just two more raspberries, there, there, they look so nice and just a little more cream and
sugar otherwise they don't taste good. Now they are ready to give to
Eva. But now it is twenty to eleven – ten minutes late! . . . Suddenly on
the path in front of me three men appear – two soldiers and one plain
clothes man. The latter has a gun in his hand and he raises it and
shoots. Instinctively I put my hand over my heart for protection and fall
to the ground with a shout. The glass plate of raspberries is smashed to
pieces and I lie motionless.

In Love and War

RUTH SCHWERTFEGER

Food parcels enabled many of the prisoners in Terezín to survive.
The Danish and Czech Jews received the most food parcels, the
Dutch the fewest.

Food, memories of it, missing it, craving it, dreaming of it, in short, the obsession with food colours all the Theresienstadt memoirs. Schneider had this to say, when asked what women talked about during internment: 'You know, the main topic of conversation was food, the most beautiful recipes that anybody could think of, and also a hot bath as soon as the war was over.' Cernyak-Spatz, a surviver of Theresienstadt, added: 'The funny thing was that many of us were of an age group that had never been to cookery classes, but we had the wildest imagination about what we would cook. I don't think I ever became so good a cook as I was with my mouth.'

The Women of Theresienstadt

MINA PACHTER
d. 1944

Hitler styled Terezín, or Theresienstadt, a 'paradise ghetto' where
prisoners were allowed to engage in cultural and artistic activities. Yet
prisoners there, as elsewhere, regularly died of starvation. Many of
the women in Terezín coped with their hunger by remembering what
they ate before the war, and one of them, Mina Pachter, gathered
together their recipes. Shortly before she herself died of starvation,
Pachter entrusted the manuscript to a friend in the camp, with
instructions that should he survive, he must find her daughter in
Palestine and give it to her. But without an address, it was twenty-
five years before the collection made its way to Anny Stern, then
living in New York.

RICH CHOCOLATE CAKE

Beat 10 decagrams butter, 10 decagrams sugar, 4 egg yolks, 14 decagrams softened chocolate. Fold in 4 [egg whites stiffly beaten to] snow, 3 decagrams flour. Bake a thin layer in a cake pan. [Pour] the rest [of the batter] on a baking sheet, [bake] and make crumbs [from it]. In cake pan always put a layer [of] cream, a layer [of] crumbs. Top with glaze or cream. Cream: 14 decagrams choc. with 5 decagrams sugar, 2 spoons water. Mix over fire. Fold in ½ liter whipped heavy cream.

COLD STUFFED EGGS PÄCHTER

Hard boil 10 eggs, cut them in half. Remove yolks and press them through a sieve. Add 5 decagrams butter, 2 anchovies pressed through a sieve, a little mustard, 3–4 drops Maggi [liquid seasoning], ⅛ liter whipped heavy cream, parsley, lemon juice. Now put eggs on a platter. Pour [liquid] aspic over. Before [pouring on the aspic] let fantasy run free and the eggs are garnished with ham, [smoked] salmon, caviar, capers. One can put the eggs into paper cuffs and serve them with hot sliced rolls.

WAR DESSERT

7 boiled grated potatoes, 5–6 spoons sugar, 2 spoons flour, 1 spoon cocoa, 2 spoons dry milk, 1 spoon [illegible], 1 knife point [pinch] [illegible]. Bake slowly.

TORTE (VERY GOOD)

4 large raw grated potatoes or carrots, 4 large tablespoons rolled oats, 3 tablespoons coffee substitute, 5 tablespoons sugar, a pinch baking soda, 1 packet gingerbread spice powder, a little flavoring. Fill with cream and glaze.

In Memory's Kitchen: A Legacy from the Women of Terezín

RUTH SCHWERTFEGER

It was a big day for Heidi. She asked me to accompany her to the post office. She was really happy and could not believe that she now was one of the fortunate people getting a parcel. Sardines, dates and figs from Portugal! Her face was shining and we hurried back to the barrack, where I discreetly allowed her to enjoy her treasure undisturbed. But what happened? 'Heidi' opened it, took out the contents and beaming with joy proceeded to share her only parcel with the twenty-five women in the room.

Heidi was later transported, and died in Auschwitz.

The Women of Theresienstadt

ANNE FRANK
1929–45

Anne Frank's diary is remarkably full of references to foods: those she tired of eating, those she wished she could eat, and the rituals surrounding her meals in hiding.

Monday, 3 April, 1944

Dear Kitty,

Contrary to my usual custom, I will for once write more fully about food because it has become a very difficult and important matter, not only here in the 'Secret Annexe' but in the whole of Holland, all Europe, and even beyond.

In the twenty-one months that we've spent here we have been through a good many 'food cycles' – you'll understand what that means in a minute. When I talk of 'food cycles' I mean periods in which one has nothing else to eat but one particular dish or kind of vegetable. We had nothing but endive for a long time, day in, day out, endive with sand, endive without sand, stew with endive, boiled or *en casserole*; then it was spinach, and after that followed kohlrabi, salsify, cucumbers, tomatoes, sauerkraut, etc., etc.

For instance, it's really disagreeable to eat a lot of sauerkraut for lunch and supper every day, but you do it if you're hungry. However, we have the most delightful period of all now, because we don't get any fresh vegetables at all. Our weekly menu for supper consists of kidney beans, pea soup, potatoes with dumplings, potato-chalet and, by the grace of God, occasionally turnip tops or rotten carrots, and then the kidney beans once again. We eat potatoes at every meal, beginning with breakfast, because of the bread shortage. We make our soup from kidney or haricot beans, potatoes, Julienne soup in packets, French beans in packets, kidney beans in packets. Everything contains beans, not to mention the bread!

In the evening we always have potatoes with gravy substitute and – thank goodness we've still got it – beetroot salad. I must still tell you about the dumplings, which we make out of government flour, water and yeast. They are so sticky and tough, they lie like stones in one's stomach – ah, well!

The great attraction each week is a slice of liver sausage, and jam on dry bread. But we're still alive, and quite often we even enjoy our poor meals.

The Diary of a Young Girl
trans. by B.M. Mooyaart-Doubleday

GERTRUD SALOMON
1875–?

Barley, Barley is the motto,
Tomorrow we will eat risotto.
Barley, barley till we burst,
After Pharaoh, Matzoh first.
Soft in coffee, good for dunking,
And after Haman, hamantaschen.

And now we eat, it tastes so fine,
Barley after Hitler's time!

'Barley 1945'

COLETTE
1873–1954

To Renée Hamon

Paris, November 4, 1940

Mon petit corsaire, enclosed you'll find a check for 500 francs. With this you will get a sack of potatoes, add a chaplet of garlic and a few onions, and ship the whole thing by train, collect. Collect, because that's the faster way. And if you use a crate instead of a sack, it would be even more sure of arriving . . .

Excuse me for asking you to do this. But the battle for potatoes is truly rough here in Paris. It's unbelievable. And eggs!

Paris, November 16, 1940

. . . I'm assured that the provisions you are sending will have a hard time getting through, even in a crate. Risk one anyway. And declare its contents on the outside of the package. That is, write 'apples and chestnuts.' Perhaps it would be better to be even more precise and say 'fruit apples.'

Paris, December 12, 1940

Quick, quick, a line to praise the beautiful package! I'll write presently at length, but let me just acknowledge that everything has arrived. The pink potatoes, and above all the GARLIC! Here it is absolutely not to be found. Two francs for half a clove, and even so it's not to be had. So you'll realize what a treasure trove you have sent me. And the reddish-brown onions! And the princely apples! You are a love of a little pirate – and to cap it all, the herbs!

Paris, December 25, 1940

Bon noël à mon petit corsaire! It will be a Christmas that cannot be very merry or good. What endurance we are still going to need . . . Here in Paris, no more woolens, nor any oranges for the past eight days. There remain a few pears at *sixteen* francs each, and beautiful apples at ten to twelve francs – always apiece. Everything else has been carried off by our 'guests.' I only hope they don't do the same with your precious packages . . .

Letters
trans. by Robert Phelps

RAYNES MINNS

Fruit, like vegetables, was distributed according to supply, but was so scarce that an hour's queuing for a pound of cooking apples was thought to be worthwhile. For many people fresh fruit became a luxurious memory. Once again it was a matter of growing your own or making the most of what you could get. One Hampstead woman with four small children and not enough money to make ends meet remembers: 'Our blackcurrant bush was a treasure. We used to have a few – about five each – for lunch sometimes, and collect blackberries on the Heath for fruit pies, and with the glut of plums we could make puddings that even our billetted refugees liked.' A Manchester housewife remembers one of the rare arrivals of oranges: 'Somehow, some oranges arrived and I carefully cut the rinds and sugared them and made strips of sweets, quite a delicacy, and later a friend with whom we had shared them, asked us to tea and produced jellies in little cups from a packet she had kept as a treat. We made a bit of jam by going out of the city to pick blackberries and we had gooseberries in the garden, and also a few apple trees.'

One lady remembers to her astonishment watching a monkey toying with a banana at the zoo. She hovered, filled with moral righteousness, outraged complaints on the tip of her tongue, only to realise the animal had been given a potato wrapped in a more seductive skin. Another family who managed to get hold of a banana, after showing it to everyone and meticulously sharing it out, could not bear to part with the skin. They arranged it on the pavement and watched, from behind their curtains, the reactions of passers-by.

Bombers and Mash

MARGUERITE PATTEN

Marguerite Patten worked for the Ministry of Food during the Second World War and until the end of rationing in 1954. She was also the regular cookery expert in the BBC's first television magazine programme, Design for Women.

Over the years I have been asked repeatedly to describe whale meat. Nowadays, we would be horrified at the thought of using these magnificent and protected mammals for food, but in 1946 we were anxious to have more generous helpings of meat so the Government were ready to persuade us to avail ourselves of this unrationed 'bonus', which became better known in 1947. Whale meat looked like a cross between liver and beef, with a firm texture. Because the raw meat had a strong and very unpleasant smell of fish and stale oil, I loathed handling whale meat to create recipes or to use in my demonstrations to the public. When cooked, the smell was not apparent.

The Ministry of Food's *Food and Nutrition* booklet for September 1947 included advice on preparing and cooking whale meat: 'Tests were made in our Experimental Kitchens using the best cuts of whale meat, which was bought in its frozen state, thawed out slowly and treated as ordinary beef steak. It was found that although the raw meat looked somewhat unattractive and is not very satisfactorily grilled or cooked as a joint, most people cannot distinguish it from beef steak when it is finely cut before cooking or mixed with strong flavours.'

Marguerite Patten's Post-war Kitchen

ETHEL RAGLAN
1857–1940

In the days of which I am writing, when ill fortune befell the master he could still count on receiving faithful and devoted service; and this recalls to my memory a little story of an incident that occurred one Christmas recently, which seems to illustrate the different attitude adopted now. The servants were highly indignant because their mistress could not afford to provide them with a turkey, but gave them a chicken instead!

'It is not what we have been accustomed to!' was the burden of their complaint. 'And we must ask you to accept our notice.'

I recollect yet another case where a servant gave the following reason for handing in her notice: 'Because you do not give me green vegetables every evening for supper! And I have such a delicate h'appetite!'

Memories of Three Reigns

EMILY DICKINSON
1830–86

The reclusive nineteenth-century poet used to lower a basket from her bedroom window to the children playing below, who would reach inside to find iced gingerbread.

> God gave a loaf to every bird,
> But just a crumb to me;
> I dare not eat it, though I starve, –
> My poignant luxury
> To own it, touch it, prove the feat
> That made the pellet mine, –

Too happy in my sparrow chance
For ampler coveting.

It might be famine all around,
I could not miss an ear,
Such plenty smiles upon my board,
My garner shows so fair.
I wonder how the rich may feel, –
An Indiaman – an Earl?
I deem that I with but a crumb
Am sovereign of them all.

The Complete Poems

JANE WELSH CARLYLE
1801–66

March 1843

Oh, I must tell you, for my uncle's benefit, a domestic catastrophe that occurred last week! One day, after dinner, I heard Helen lighting the fire, which had gone out, in the room above, with perfectly unexampled vengeance; every stroke of the poker seemed an individual effort of concentrated rage. What ails the creature now? I said to myself. Who has incurred her sudden displeasure? or is it the red herring she had for dinner which has disagreed with her stomach? (for in the morning, you must know, when I was ordering the dinner, she had asked, might *she* have a red herring? 'her heart had been set upon it a good while back:' and, of course, so modest a petition received an unhesitating affirmative). On her return to the subterranean, the same hubbub wild arose from below, which had just been trying my nerves from above; and when she brought up the tea-tray, she clanked it on the lobby-table, as if she were minded to demolish the whole concern at one fell stroke. I looked into her face inquiringly as she entered the room, and seeing it black as midnight (*morally*, that is), I said very coolly, 'A little less

noise, if you please; you are getting rather loud upon us.' She cast up her
eyes with the look of a martyr at the stake, as much as to say, 'Well, if I
must be quiet, I must; but you little know my wrongs.' By-and-by
Geraldine went to the kitchen for some reason; she is oftener in the
kitchen in one day than I am in a month, but that is irrelevant. 'Where
is the cat?' said she to Helen; 'I have not seen her all night.' She takes
a wonderful, most superfluous charge of the cat, as of everything else in
this establishment. 'The cat!' said Helen grimly, 'I have all but killed
her.' 'How?' said Geraldine. 'With the besom,' replied the other. 'Why?
for goodness' sake.' 'Why!' repeated Helen, bursting out into new rage;
'why indeed? Because she ate my red herring! I set it all ready on the
end of the dresser, and she ran away with it, and ate it every morsel to
the tail – such an unheard of thing for the brute to do. Oh, if I could
have got hold of her, she should not have got off with her life!' 'And
have you had no dinner?' asked Geraldine. 'Oh yes, I had mutton
enough, but I had just set my heart on a red herring.' Which was the
most deserving of having a besom taken to her, the cat or the woman?

Letters

MRS GASKELL
1810–65

TEA FOR CARLO

In a few minutes tea was brought. Very delicate was the china, very old
the plate, very thin the bread and butter, and very small the lumps of
sugar. Sugar was evidently Mrs. Jamieson's favourite economy. I question
if the little filigree sugar-tongs, made something like scissors, could
have opened themselves wide enough to take up an honest, vulgar,
good-sized piece; and when I tried to seize two little minnikin pieces at
once, so as not to be detected in too many returns to the sugar-basin,
they absolutely dropped one, with a little sharp clatter, quite in a mali-
cious and unnatural manner. But before this happened we had a slight
disappointment. In the little silver jug was cream, in the larger one was

milk. As soon as Mr. Mulliner came in, Carlo began to beg, which was a thing our manners forbade us to do, though I am sure we were just as hungry, and Mrs. Jamieson said she was certain we would excuse her if she gave her poor dumb Carlo his tea first. She accordingly mixed a saucerful for him, and put it down for him to lap; and then she told us how intelligent and sensible the dear little fellow was; he knew cream quite well, and constantly refused tea with only milk in it: so the milk was left for us; but we silently thought we were quite as intelligent and sensible as Carlo, and felt as if insult were added to injury when we were called upon to admire the gratitude evinced by his wagging his tail for the cream which should have been ours.

Cranford

PEARL BUCK
1892–1973

The Nobel Prize winner grew up in China, and always preferred Chinese food to that of the United States.

Wang Lung and his family had come from a country where if men starve it is because there is no food, since the land cannot bear under a relentless heaven. Silver in the hand was worth little because it could buy nothing where nothing was.

Here in the city there was food everywhere. The cobbled streets of the fish market were lined with great baskets of big silver fish, caught in the night out of the teeming river; with tubs of small shining fish, dipped out of a net cast over a pool; with heaps of yellow crabs, squirming and nipping in peevish astonishment; with writhing eels for gourmands at the feasts. At the grain markets there were such baskets of grain that a man might step into them and sink and smother and none know it who did not see it; white rice and brown, and dark yellow wheat and pale gold wheat, and yellow soy-beans and red beans and green broad beans, and canary-coloured millet, and grey sesame. And at the meat markets whole hogs hung by their necks, split open the length of their great bodies to show the red meat and the layers of goodly fat, the skin soft and thick and white. And in duck-shops hung, row upon row, over the ceilings and in the doors, the brown baked ducks that had been turned slowly on a spit before coals, and the white salted ducks, and the strings of duck giblets; and so with the shops that sold geese and pheasant and every kind of fowl.

As for the vegetables, there was everything which the hand of man could coax from the soil; glittering red radishes and white, hollow lotus root and taro, green cabbages and celery, curling bean sprouts and brown chestnuts and garnishes of fragrant cress. There was nothing which the appetite of man might desire that was not to be found upon the streets of the markets of that city. And going hither and thither were the vendors of sweets and fruits and nuts and of hot delicacies of sweet potatoes browned in sweet oils and little delicately spiced balls of pork wrapped in dough and steamed, and sugar cakes made from glutinous rice; and the children of the city ran out to the vendors of these things with their hands full of pennies and they bought and they ate until their skins glistened with sugar and oil.

Yes, one would say that in this city there could be none who starved.

Still, every morning a little after dawn Wang Lung and his family came out of their hut and with their bowls and chopsticks they made a small group in a long procession of people, each issuing from his hut, shivering in clothes too thin for the damp river fog, walking curved against the chill morning wind in the public kitchens, where for a penny a man may buy a bowl of thin rice gruel. And with all Wang Lung's pulling and running before his rickshaw and with all O-lan's begging, they never could gain enough to cook rice daily in their own hut.

The Good Earth

EDNA FERBER
1885–1968

This extract from the author's novel, Fanny Herself, *is based on a childhood experience shared with her sister Esther.*

Fanny and Bella met, giggling, in the vestibule.

'Come on over to my house for a minute,' Bella suggested. 'I want to show you something.' The Weinberg house, a great comfortable well-built home, with encircling veranda and a well-cared-for lawn, was just across the way. They skipped across the street and in at the back door. The big sunny kitchen was deserted. The house seemed very quiet and hushed. Over it hung the delicious fragrance of freshly baked pastry. Bella, a rather baleful look in her eyes, led the way to the butler's pantry that was as large as the average kitchen. And there, ranged on platters and baking boards and on snowy-white napkins, was that which made Tantalus's feast seem a dry and barren snack. The Weinbergs had baked.

It is the custom in the households of Atonement Day fasters of the old school to begin the evening meal, after twenty-four hours of abstinence, with coffee and freshly baked coffee cake of every variety. It was a lead-pipe blow at one's digestion, but delicious beyond imagining. Bella's mother was a famous cook, and her two maids followed in the ways of their mistress. There were to be sisters and brothers and out-of-town relatives as guests at the evening meal, and Mrs. Weinberg had outdone herself.

'Oh!' exclaimed Fanny in a sort of agony and delight.

'Take some,' said Bella, the temptress.

The pantry was as fragrant as a garden with spices and fruit scents and the melting delectable perfume of brown, freshly baked dough, sugar-coated. There was one giant platter devoted wholly to round plump cakes with puffy edges, in the center of each a sunken pool that was pure plum, bearing on its bosom a snowy sifting of powdered sugar. There were others whose centers were apricot, molten gold in the sunlight. There were speckled expanses of cheese kuchen, the golden-brown surface showing rich cracks through which one caught glimpses of the lemon-yellow cheese beneath. There were cakes with jelly; cinnamon kuchen, and cunning cakes with almond slices nestling side by side. And there was freshly baked bread; twisted loaf with poppy seed freckling its braid, its sides glistening with the butter that had been swabbed on just before it had been thrust into the oven.

Fanny Brandeis gazed, hypnotized. As she gazed Bella selected a plum tart and bit into it – bit generously, so that her white little teeth met in the very middle of the oozing red-brown juice and one heard a little squish as they closed on the luscious fruit. At the sound Fanny quivered all through her plump and starved little body.

'Have one,' said Bella, generously. 'Go on. Nobody'll ever know. Anyway, we've fasted long enough for our age. I could fast till supper time if I wanted to, but I don't want to.' She swallowed the last morsel of the plum tart and selected another – apricot this time – and opened her moist red lips. But just before she bit into it she selected its counterpart (the Inquisition could have used Bella's talents) and held it out to Fanny. Fanny shook her head slightly. Her hand came up involuntarily. Her eyes were fastened on Bella's face.

'Go on!' Bella urged. 'Take it. They're grand! M-m-m-m!' The first bite of apricot vanished between her sharp white teeth. Fanny shut her eyes as if in pain. She was fighting the great fight of her life. She was to meet other temptations, and perhaps more glittering ones, in her lifetime, but to her dying day she was never to forget that first battle between the flesh and the spirit, there in the sugar-scented pantry – and the spirit won. As Bella's lips closed upon the second bite of apricot tart, the while her eye roved over the almond cakes and her hand still held the sweet out to Fanny, that young lady turned sharply and marched blindly out of the house, down the back steps, across the street and into the temple.

Fanny Herself

ALESSANDRA ARACHI

This story begins with three meatballs in tomato sauce. Three veal meatballs, vomited into the toilet in my bathroom, with the door wide open.

'Anorexia' would be the diagnosis. My father would never have believed it – my father, who did not even live long enough to see the end of this story. A textbook story. To find a similar one, you've only to open a book on medicine, the modern branch that studies the mind, and reveals that it's possible for someone to die simply because food has become the enemy.

Eating had always given me pleasure. Whipped cream and ice lollies, but also tortellini, chips and chocolate. I was a lively little girl, a sporty and cheerful teenager . . .

It was my father who suggested the diet. My mother spirited away, into the kitchen cupboard, all the biscuits I'd loved as a child. I began heroically bearing my cross against food and I felt immediately adult, deciding just like that to stand firm against greed . . . In less than a month my brain succeeded in transforming a piece of bread into a dangerous concoction of sugar; oil into an indigestible stream of fat. I was suspicious of anything that was edible, all the while devoting my every thought to food, the whole day long . . .

More than ever, in those days, I loved watching others eat . . . I'd stand at the stove for hours, cooking elaborate meals, rich in calories. My eyes and my hands would busy themselves with the food and arrange it with care on the trays. I forced whoever was around to swallow it all, right down to the last crumb. Me? I wouldn't lick even a spoon.

Briciole
trans. by Jill Foulston

MARIA GRAMMATICO
MARY TAYLOR SIMETI

Her father's early death and the family's poverty forced Maria Grammatico into a cloistered orphanage in her native Sicily. She sometimes spent all day beating eggs and sugar together to make the pastries sold to support the convent. At twenty-two, she left to make her way in the world, taking with her only the recipes she'd memorised – nothing was written down in the convent – and the experience of making marzipan sweets, pastries and preserves according to centuries-old traditions. The shop she founded is now a recognised stop on any gastronomic tour of Sicily.

Once this Maria Franchini and I, we got hold of an old burner and a canister of gas, the one they used to heat up the milk for the priest, to make him a cappuccino when he had finished hearing our confessions. We hid this burner in the closet behind the bathroom, and one day when we had pasta with cauliflower, some cauliflower was left over. So Maria said, 'Let's make cauliflower fritters.' So we stole a little flour, just enough to make a batter for these fritters, and we took a pan and a little oil from the kitchen. Other times we'd make a salad, we'd steal a tomato, for example, and a sardine and we'd make ourselves a salad. We had to eat, didn't we? Growing girls made to fast like that! So that's what we did. Then one day Titì came and spied on us while we were at it. The nun came and she took everything that we had and she threw it down the toilet . . .

We got into the habit, Maria and I: we'd steal a tomato, we'd steal half a sardine, or a little bit of cheese, and then we would go up onto the terrace when we got out of church, after prayers. In the summer we'd go up onto the terrace. 'Where have those pumpkinheads got to now?' – which meant they were looking for us, and we'd hide ourselves and start eating. A slice of cheese. Can you imagine? That's what we stole, a slice of cheese. Bread we never stole, they gave us half a kilo a day, more than we wanted. We wanted something different. The food was always the same: beans, cauliflower, beans, cauliflower, and then sometimes they'd

give us peas. You know the kind? The dried split peas? They always
stuck to the pot and burned. The stink was enough to kill you. Down
the toilet! Phooey! We managed to survive, though, that's for sure.

Bitter Almonds: Recollections and Recipes from a Sicilian Girlhood

MARLENA DE BLASI

*An established food writer, Marlena had her own restaurant in
Missouri when she travelled to Venice with friends. There she met a
'blueberry-eyed stranger' in a small cafe and shortly thereafter
dropped everything in the USA to go and live with him in the
Venetian lagoon. Today, the two run gastronomic tours in Tuscany
and Umbria.*

The next evening the stranger stands by the stove like the Duke of
Montefeltro, in purple silk boxers. Bringing out a balance, he measures 125 grams of pasta, for each of us. I am going to marry a Venetian
J. Alfred Prufrock who measures out his supper in grams! He pours
tomato purée into a small, thin, beat-up old pan rather than one of my
little copper beauties. He adds salt and big pinches of dried herbs that
he kept in a tin on top of the stove. '*Aglio, peperoncino, e prezzemolo.*
Garlic, chili, and parsley,' he says, as though he believes it. The pasta
is good, and I tell him so, but I am still hungry.

Three hours later I am hollow with that hunger and so, when
Fernando falls asleep, I creep out of bed and cook a whole pound of fat,
thick spaghetti. I drench it with butter scented with a few drops of the
twenty-five-year-old balsamic vinegar that I'd carried, coddled like a
Fabergé egg, from Spilamberto to Saint Louis to Venice. I grate a wedge
of Parmesan over the pasta until my hand gets tired and then ornament
the silky, steamy mass with long grindings of pepper. I raise the shutters
in the dining room to let in moonlight and midnight breezes, light a
candle, and pour wine. Serving myself over and over again, I devour the
pasta, I absorb it, smelling, tasting, chewing, feeling the comfort of it

explode again and again. Revenge flutters, and so I twirl it rebelliously, round and round on my fork exactly the way Fernando told me not to twirl it. Finally Lucullus has dined with Lucullus.

A Thousand Days in Venice

M.F.K. FISHER
1908–92

There was one person . . . who was a part of my education and who refuted all my tentative rules for fortunate wolf-dodging, and did it with such grace that I often think of her half-doubtingly, as if she were a dream.

Her name was Sue. She was delicate bodily . . . not ill, but never well the way most people are well. She flitted like a night moth through all her days, bemazed by the ardors of sunlight but conducting herself with wary sureness; so that she seldom banged against shut doors or hit her thin bones on sharp table corners.

She was, as far as anyone knew, completely alone. It was impossible to think of her in any more passionate contact with other humans than the occasional suppers she gave for them. The fact that once she must have been young did not change her present remoteness: you could not see her any warmer at seventeen than at seventy.

But her withdrawn impersonal attitude did not make her any less delicately robust. She loved to eat, and she apparently loved, now and then, to eat with other people. Her suppers were legendary. Of course, it depended on who was telling about them: sometimes they were merely strange, or even laughable, and sometimes they sounded like something from a Southern California Twelfth Night, with strange games and witchlike feastings.

Sue lived in a little weatherbeaten house on a big weatherbeaten cliff. At first when you entered it, the house seemed almost empty, but soon you realized that like all dwellings of old lonely people, it was stuffed with a thousand relics of the fuller years. There were incredibly dingy and lump-filled cushions that Whistler had sat on, and a Phyfe chair that had one stormy night been kicked into kindling wood by Oscar Wilde. It was held together with rubber bands, and naturally was not to be used as a chair, but rather as a casually treated but important altar.

When you went to her house, you ate by one candle, no matter whether you were two or eight at table. Of course this seemed intensely romantic to young Americans, but it was because she could afford neither more candles nor electricity.

The walls, covered with third-rate etchings by first-rate men, and a few first-rate ones by the almost unknown Sue, emerged gradually from the dingy darkness. There was an underlying smell, delicate as early death, of age and decay.

The main smell, though, was a good one. It never had the forthright energy of braised meat (although I remember one time, when I may have looked a little peaked, that Sue went against her custom and put a tiny morsel of cooked liver on my plate, and said, 'Now, I want you to try to eat *all* of this!' It was no bigger than a dollar, and I made it into at least twelve bites, in a kind of awe).

There was always the exciting, mysterious perfume of bruised herbs, plucked fresh and cool from the tangle of weeds around the shack. Sue put them into a salad.

Then there was usually sage, which she used like a Turk or Armenian in practically everything that went into her pot. She gathered it in the hills, and dried it in bunches above her stove, and in spite of gastronomical scouts who wail now that California sage all has a taste of turpentine, hers never did. She knew only about a hundred kinds, she confessed quietly; someone had told her that the hills behind the village held at least fifty more.

Sue had only a few plates, and no knives. You ate everything from one large Spode soup-plate, when you went there, but it never seemed mussy. And knives were unnecessary, because there was nothing to cut.

As I remember now, her whole cuisine was Oriental. There were the little bowls of chopped fresh and cooked leaves. There were the fresh and dried herbs, which she had gathered from the fields. There was the common bowl of rice (or potatoes that Sue had probably stolen the night before from some patch up the canyon). There was tea, always. There was, occasionally, a fresh egg, which also was stolen, no doubt, and which Sue always put in the teapot to heat through and then broke over the biggest dish of food.

I have never eaten such strange things as there in her dark smelly room, with the waves roaring at the foot of the cliff and Whistler's maroon-taffeta pillow bruising its soft way into the small of my back. People said that Sue robbed garbage pails at night. She did not, of course. But she did flit about, picking leaves from other gardens than her own and wandering like the Lolly Willowes of Laguna along the cliff-tops and the beaches looking in the night light for sea-spinach and pink ice-plant.

The salads and stews she made from these little shy weeds were indeed peculiar, but she blended and cooked them so skillfully that they never lost their fresh salt crispness. She put them together with thought and gratitude, and never seemed to realize that her cuisine was one of intense romantic strangeness to everyone but herself. I doubt if she spent more than fifty dollars a year on what she and her entranced guests ate, but from the gracious abstracted way she gave you a soup dish full of sliced cactus leaves and lemon-berries and dried crumbled kelp, it might as well have been stuffed ortolans. Moreover, it was good.

I doubt very much if anybody but Sue could make it good. Few other humans know the secret of herbs as she did . . . or if they know them, can use them so nonchalantly.

But anyone in the world, with intelligence and spirit and the knowledge that it must be done, can live with her inspired oblivion to the ugliness of poverty. It is not that she wandered at night hunting for leaves and berries; it is that she cared enough to invite her friends to share them with her, and could serve them, to herself alone or to a dozen guests, with the sureness that she was right.

Sue had neither health nor companionship to comfort her and warm her, but she nourished herself and many other people for many years,

with the quiet assumption that man's need for food is not a grim obsession, repulsive, disturbing, but a dignified and even enjoyable function.
Her nourishment was of more than the flesh, not because of its strangeness, but because of her own calm.

How to Cook a Wolf

JONI MITCHELL

Come to the dinner gong
The table is laden high
Fat bellies and hungry little ones
Tuck your napkins in
And take your share

Some get the gravy
And some get the gristle
Some get the marrow bone
And some get nothing
Though there's plenty to spare

I took my share down by the sea
Paper plates and Javex bottles on the tide
Seagulls come down
And they squawk at me
Down where the water-skiers glide

'Banquet'

MISSED MEALS, COMFORT FOOD

JEANETTE WINTERSON

Do you ever think of your childhood?

I think of it when I smell porridge. Sometimes after I've been by the docks I walk into town and use my nose tracking fresh bread and bacon. Always, passing a particular house, that sits like the others in a sort of row, and is the same as them, I smell the slow smell of oats. Sweet but with an edge of salt. Thick like a blanket. I don't know who lives in the house, who is responsible, but I imagine the yellow fire and the black pot. At home we used a copper pot that I polished, loving to polish anything that would keep a shine. My mother made porridge, leaving the oats overnight by the old fire. Then in the morning when her bellows work had sent the sparks shooting up the chimney, she burned the oats brown at the sides, so that the sides were like brown paper lining the pot and the inside slopped white over the edge.

We trod on a flag floor but in the winter she put down hay and the hay and the oats made us smell like a manger.

Most of my friends ate hot bread in the mornings.

The Passion

CONSTANCE SPRY 1886–1960
ROSEMARY HUME 1907–

Many years ago there used to be in the middle of the town of Derby a little house with a front door rather high up in the wall, and outside it a stone platform approached by a flight of stone steps. On the platform stood a large table covered in a snowy sheet on which were arranged high piles of crumpets, pikelets, and muffins. The whole was presided over by a wrinkled old woman enveloped in a gathered apron and wearing a white bonnet.

In spite of my extreme youth – for I used to be pushed there in a 'mail-cart' – I still remember the delicious smell of baking, the general sense of snowy whiteness, and my excitement in carrying the purchases home, and ever since I have wanted to be able to achieve such beautifully made crumpets and muffins; but I never have . . .

When during the war I found myself spending a great deal of time in the kitchen I was fired with a wish to make muffins, though I cannot think where I hoped to find butter to put on them. I had some good American books and found lots of recipes made with all manner of ingredients, nuts and fruit, eggs and sugar, but they were not at all what I wanted. I was after the muffin of the muffin-man, the floury, yeasty affair that has to be properly toasted and buttered before it is eaten. I do not suppose I have ever got them to quite the point of perfection of those the old lady sold outside her funny little house.

The Constance Spry Cookery Book

NIGELLA LAWSON

If Delia Smith taught us how to cook, Nigella has ensured that we know how to eat. She and Elizabeth Robins Pennell might have seen eye to eye on greed.

If you've got that lust for something soft and sweet, for babyfied comfort food, you might as well go flat out for it. Eating alone, I make what I remember my mother making for herself, bread and milk, in a large, cream china pudding basin. Put some torn-up pieces of white bread in a bowl, sprinkle over some sugar, and then pour in some hot milk. Eat, in an

armchair, bowl on lap. If you keep vanilla sugar in the house, use that, but
fiddle no further; this is not a dish that lends itself to great refinements.

How to Eat

JOHANNA SPYRI
1827–1901

'I think we might have something to eat . . .' said the grandfather, 'what
do you think?'

Heidi in the excitement of bed-making had forgotten everything
else; but now when she began to think about food she felt terribly
hungry, for she had had nothing to eat since the piece of bread and little
cup of thin coffee that had been her breakfast early that morning before
starting on her long, hot journey. So she answered without hesitation,
'Yes, I think so too.'

'Let us go down then, as we both think alike,' said the old man, and he
followed the child down the ladder. Then he went up to the hearth,
pushed the big kettle aside, and drew forward the little one that was hanging on the chain, and seating himself on the round-topped, three-legged
stool before the fire, blew it up into a clear bright flame. The kettle soon
began to boil, and meanwhile the old man held a large piece of cheese on
a long iron fork over the fire, turning it round and round till it was toasted
a nice golden yellow colour on each side. Heidi watched all that was going
on with eager curiosity. Suddenly some new idea seemed to come into her
head, for she turned and ran to the cupboard, and then began going busily
backwards and forwards. Presently the grandfather got up and came to the
table with a jug and the cheese, and there he saw it already tidily laid with
the round loaf and two plates and two knives each in its right place; for
Heidi had taken exact note that morning of all that there was in the cupboard, and she knew which things would be wanted for their meal.

'Ah, that's right,' said the grandfather, 'I am glad to see that you
have some ideas of your own,' and as he spoke he laid the toasted cheese
on a layer of bread, 'but there is still something missing.'

Heidi looked at the jug that was steaming away invitingly, and ran quickly back to the cupboard. At first she could only see a small bowl left on the shelf, but she was not long in perplexity, for a moment later she caught sight of two glasses further back, and without an instant's loss of time she returned with these and the bowl and put them down on the table.

'Good, I see you know how to set about things; but what will you do for a seat?' The grandfather himself was sitting on the only chair in the room. Heidi flew to the hearth, and dragging the three-legged stool up to the table, sat herself down upon it.

'Well, you have managed to find a seat for yourself, I see, only rather a low one I am afraid,' said the grandfather, 'but you would not be tall enough to reach the table even if you sat in my chair; the first thing now, however, is to have something to eat, so come along.'

With that he stood up, filled the bowl with milk, and placing it on the chair, pushed it in front of Heidi on her little three-legged stool, so that she now had a table to herself. Then he brought her a large slice of bread and a piece of the golden cheese, and told her to eat. After which he went and sat down on the corner of the table and began his own meal. Heidi lifted the bowl with both hands and drank without pause till it was empty, for the thirst of all her long hot journey had returned upon her. Then she drew a deep breath – in the eagerness of her thirst she had not stopped to breathe – and put down the bowl.

'Was the milk nice?' asked her grandfather.

'I never drank any so good before,' answered Heidi.

Heidi

SYLVIA THOMPSON

I hugely enjoyed the neighborhood of our apartment. It was in the dignified seventh *arrondissement*, very quiet, very family. Usually after school from my autobus stop on the Seine, I would walk down the rue

Jean Nicot to the big open air market on the rue St. Dominique. I would buy a treat of some cheese or sausage or pastry to hold me until dinner (I was still a growing girl). It was there at the *confiserie* I discovered *pain d'épice*. Then, it was exotica. Now, it seems I've seen long thin cellophane-wrapped loaves of the Burgundian honey bread on the counters of grocery stores everywhere.

But none have tasted the same as that *pain d'épice* from the rue St. Dominique. I always kept some in my school bag and snitched hunks to give me moral support while the sleek brunette geography professor sat on the edge of the long dais in the ancient Sorbonne amphitheater, slim legs crossed, chalk bouncing in one hand, rattling off elevations of the Alpes Cotiennes and the depths of the Plaine d'Aquitaine in her high-pitched voice, no notes in sight. One morning's lecture, in fact, I ate an entire *pain d'épice* out of nervousness trying desperately to copy down all her facts, and it was a couple of months before I could face *pain d'épice* again.

Pain d'épice has been a tradition in Burgundy since the fourteenth century. Traditional recipes call for rye flour. But just because something is traditional doesn't make it matchless. A whole lot of indifferent cooks can get something going for a very long time and make you believe it's marvelous just because they say so. I have been making *pain d'épice* on and off for more than thirty years, and I have come to believe that the lovely light tang of rye flour clouds the delicate flavor of the spices and honey, so I use untraditional white flour. And finally, after all these years, I've made a bread that tastes the way those little loaves did out of my school bag in the *Salle Richelieu*.

I might add that *pain d'épice* is not to everyone's taste. If you are a honey fancier, you'll like it. *Perhaps* you'll like it, it's a bit of an acquired taste. But there are those of us who think one or two thin slices of *pain d'épice* in the afternoon, slathered with sweet butter, sipped with black China tea, can cure all the ills to which flesh is heir.

Feasts and Friends

JULIA CHILD 1912–2004
SIMONE BECK 1904–91
LOUISETTE BERTHOLLE

She dreamed of becoming a spy when the Second World War broke out, but instead Julia Child went on to publish what was in 1961 regarded as the definitive work on French cuisine for English speakers: Mastering the Art of French Cooking. *The first of three volumes, it was ten years in the making, written and researched with the help of Simone Beck and Louisette Bertholle. Soon afterwards, the American public began a long television love affair with Julia Child, a 6′ 2″ domestic goddess with a wobbly voice. This self-confessed 'natural ham' demystified French cuisine for millions of Americans rather in the way that Fanny Cradock brought haute cuisine to the British during the same period. In an effort to allay public fear of the fat used in French cooking, she noted: 'You don't see all those big fat people over there that you see lumbering around here at Disneyland'. She herself never became overweight, and ended every show with the words, 'Bon Appetit!'*

The memory of a good French *pâté* can haunt you for years. Fortunately they are easy to make, and you can even develop your own special *pâté maison*. Do not expect a top-notch mixture to be inexpensive, however, for it will contain ground pork, pork fat, and usually veal, as well as cognac, port, or Madeira, spices, strips or cubes of other meats, game, or live, and often truffles. If the mixture is cooked and served cold in its baking dish it is called either a *terrine* or a *pâté*. If it is molded in a pastry crust, it is a *pâté en croûte*. A boned chicken, turkey, or duck filled with the same type of mixture is a galantine. *Pâtés* and *terrines* will keep for about 10 days under refrigeration; they are fine to have on hand for cold impromptu meals, since all you need to serve with them are a salad and French bread.

Mastering the Art of French Cooking

MRS ROBERT HENREY
1906–2004

Madeleine Henrey enjoyed success as a mid-century writer of auto-biography. She was born in France, but married an Englishman and wrote in English for an English audience. Her first book, A Farm in Normandy, set the tone for future evocations of rural life abroad.

Besides looking after the house in which we lodged my grandmother was the keeper of a garden which was a veritable paradise. A lovely road of yellow earth led to it beside a high wall, at the end of which was an ogival door, thick, sculptured with medieval designs, and barded with decorative ironwork. When we stopped in front of this door we were overcome, Granny and I, by the silence we had made for ourselves, for all along the road the wheelbarrow had creaked and now its noisy wheel was stilled at our feet. Impressed and a little frightened, Granny would lift up her black apron and fetch out a key from a pocket in her under-skirts. My heart beat at the sight of this, so eager was I to penetrate into the garden, but Granny would first stoop down and, nodding her old head, examine with great suspicion the state of the lock to see if anybody had tampered with it since her last coming. Then, making some incomprehensible remark, she would insert the key into the hole and try to turn it with both hands. The rusty lock resisted, a spider came running out, and just as I was certain that we were going to be kept out for ever the lock turned, the door opened scratchily against the gravel, just a few inches before sticking, and a great wave of sweet smells rushed into our nostrils.

We pushed against the door with all our might. Since the previous week the herbs, the flowers, and the weeds had sprung up in the path and made a luxuriant barrier. We now went back to fetch the wheelbarrow. All round us the bees and insects buzzed and sang in the hot, dry air. Purple irises, tall, thick, and beautiful, reaching to the level of my eyes, headily scented arum lilies, red currant bushes from which hung strings of rubies, peaches resting their velvet cheeks against the hot wall, greeted me, causing me to run from one to the other. At every new discovery I would call Granny and she, hurrying up, would screw up her face, purse her lips, and exclaim 'Heu!' as if she were just as surprised as I. Indeed, that is why Granny and I got on so well together. She was always expressing the most candid surprise. The magnificent strawberries and peaches, red currants, and greengages all about us seemingly filled her with perplexity as if she were trying to decide how to turn them all into jam. She said: 'We would need a magic cauldron for all this. I have an idea. Let's first have something to eat.'

A small tool-house stood against the garden wall. The windowpanes were broken, and inside the table and chairs were covered with spiders' webs; but we had it clean in no time and my grandmother, plunging her wrinkled hands into a black basket which she carried about with her on all important occasions (she had brought it to Paris when she came to see us), brought out a beautiful white napkin, smelling of soapy wash being dried in the sun, and laying it on the table placed on it a long French bread, into which she stuck her pointed knife, a goat's cheese, and a bottle of black coffee.

I was longing for the bread: Granny was thinking about the coffee. Like a witch in a fairy-story she was soon gathering dry sticks to make a fire, and now I understood why there were always so many saucepans in her wheelbarrow. When the coffee was hot she brought it into the summer-house. Then she took the bread, removed the knife from it, and holding the golden crust against her black dress made the sign of the cross upon it. She cut several large slices. Then it was the turn of the goat's cheese, hard and blue. I was deliriously happy, but soon, finding that I was tired of sitting down, I took a final slice of bread and ran out into the garden, where I picked some greengages and strawberries for dessert . . .

At four o'clock we had to leave this paradise. The wheelbarrow was full of fruit and dry wood. Its wooden wheel sang over the yellow road. The black basket was strung round me and was so large I could hardly see where I was going, but I never felt under my feet the cobbles of the bridge across the Loire. I moved ethereally, my mouth daubed in the juice of sun-ripened fruit.

The Little Madeleine

CLEMENTINE PADDLEFORD
1900–67

Sudden sweet the memory of late April, prairie grasses leaning with the wind. At this time the peach put forth her bitter tinted pink, the red bud empurpled the wooded stretch, and plum thickets burst into a starry shower of white that drew the bees from miles away. With delight we watched the small green fruit enlarge, watched the green take on shades of yellow, then burnished red and under the heat of a Kansas summer turn to winy purple. Picking time had come!

Sand plums we put to many uses. They were canned and preserved, made into tender dumplings, into pies, tucked into tarts. The sand-plum jelly was made, at least three-dozen glasses by my mother, to serve with meat and game.

Plumtime was July; then the thicket in the pasture draw yielded plums by the bushel . . . A mile further down would be another great thicket. Every family had all the wild plums they could use. If your grandmother came from New York State as Grandmother Paddleford did, the plums were combined with raisins and used for pie and cobblers. But women transplanted from the South made plum spread for Sunday breakfast biscuits. Holiday fare was sometimes prairie chicken or roast pork accompanied by sand-plum jelly, its sharp acid way going just right with these meats . . .

The beach plums found rooted in the dunes along the eastern coast in Cape Cod, Long Island, New Jersey, are similar in appearance and flavor to the sand plums of the west. Since sand plums are but extinct, use beach plums if you can find a bush and the fruit is yours to make my grandmother's jelly . . . We use pectin – but she didn't.

Threshers' dinner was the acid test of housewifery in our community. Mother won her cooking spurs at threshing time with fresh sand-plum pie. If the thresher broke down, as it often did, and didn't reach our house on the expected day, we ate the pies and baked fresh ones on the morrow. Better even than plum pie was a steamed roly-poly, the dough tinted through with the red juices of the fruit. Served with it was a steaming hot sauce of the spiced dark juice. We could never get enough.

A Flower for My Mother

LAURA INGALLS WILDER
1867–1957

The days were growing shorter and the nights were cooler. One night Jack Frost passed by, and in the morning there were bright colors here and there among the green leaves of the Big Woods. Then all the leaves stopped being green. They were yellow and scarlet and crimson and golden and brown.

Along the rail fence the sumac held up its dark red cones of berries above bright flame-colored leaves. Acorns were falling from the oaks, and Laura and Mary made little acorn cups and saucers for the playhouses. Walnuts and hickory nuts were dropping to the ground in the Big Woods, and squirrels were scampering busily everywhere, gathering their winter's store of nuts and hiding them away in hollow trees.

Laura and Mary went with Ma to gather walnuts and hickory nuts and hazelnuts. They spread them in the sun to dry, then they beat off the dried outer hulls and stored the nuts in the attic for winter.

It was fun to gather the large round walnuts and the smaller hickory nuts, and the little hazelnuts that grew in bunches on the bushes. The soft outer hulls of the walnuts were full of a brown juice that stained their hands, but the hazelnut hulls smelled good and tasted good, too, when Laura used her teeth to pry a nut loose.

Everyone was busy now, for all the garden vegetables must be stored away. Laura and Mary helped, picking up the dusty potatoes after Pa had dug them from the ground, and pulling the long yellow carrots and the round, purple-topped turnips, and they helped Ma cook the pumpkin for pumpkin pies.

With the butcher knife Ma cut the big, orange-colored pumpkins into halves. She cleaned the seeds out of the center and cut the pumpkin into long slices, from which she pared the rind. Laura helped her cut the slices into cubes.

Ma put the cubes into the big iron pot on the stove, poured in some water, and then watched while the pumpkin slowly boiled down, all day long. All the water and the juice must be boiled away, and the pumpkin must never burn.

The pumpkin was a thick, dark, good-smelling mass in the kettle. It did not boil like water, but bubbles came up in it and suddenly exploded, leaving holes that closed quickly. Every time a bubble exploded, the rich, hot, pumpkin smell came out.

Laura stood on a chair and watched the pumpkin for Ma, and stirred it with a wooden paddle. She held the paddle in both hands and stirred carefully, because if the pumpkin burned there wouldn't be any pumpkin pies.

For dinner they ate the stewed pumpkin with their bread. They made it into pretty shapes on their plates. It was a beautiful color, and smoothed and molded so prettily with their knives. Ma never allowed them to play with their food at table; they must always eat nicely everything that was set before them, leaving nothing on their plates. But she did let them make the rich brown, stewed pumpkin into pretty shapes before they ate it.

Little House in the Big Woods

ELISABETH LUARD

Like Dorothy Hartley and Patience Gray, Luard seasons her offer-ings with folklore, legend, local history and memories.

The embers of a wood fire are the best place to cook the last old pota-toes of the year. I remember the bonfire my grandfather would light at dusk on a cold November evening – my grandmother knew it was to burn up the dry leaves and debris of summer, but we children knew dif-ferently. When the fire burned down, we were allowed to tuck potatoes into the hot ash at the edge. It was our reward for a day's raking fallen leaves and dead branches in the garden. We would crouch, scarlet faces turned to the flames, icy night wind cold on the backs of our necks, until long past suppertime. At last we would poke out our very own 'tattie', charred and crisp outside, soft and sweet within. My grand-mother looked the other way when we thieved a pat of butter and a little salt from the larder. An unbeatable dish.

The Old World Kitchen

ANNE TYLER

For supper they had Rose's pot roast, a salad with Macon's dressing, and baked potatoes. Baked potatoes had always been their favorite food. They had learned to fix them as children, and even after they were big enough to cook a balanced meal they used to exist solely on baked potatoes whenever Alicia left them to their own devices. There was something about the smell of a roasting Idaho that was cozy, and also, well, *conservative*, was the way Macon put it to himself. He thought back on years and years of winter evenings: the kitchen windows black out-side, the corners furry with gathering darkness, the four of them seated at the chipped enamel table meticulously filling scooped out potato skins with butter. You let the butter melt in the skins while you mashed and seasoned the floury insides; the skins were saved till last. It was almost a ritual. He recalled once, during one of their mother's longer absences, her friend Eliza had served them what she called potato boats – restuffed, not a bit like the genuine article. The children, with pinched, fastidious expressions, had emptied the stuffing and proceeded as usual with the skins, pretending to overlook her mistake. The pepper should be freshly ground. Paprika was acceptable, but only if it was American. Hungarian paprika had too distinctive a taste. Personally, Macon could do without paprika altogether.

The Accidental Tourist

KATIE BROWN
20th century

The Georgia Writers' Project looked at the persistence of African artistic and linguistic traditions and their influence on American culture. Here one woman describes what her grandmother remembers eating.

Yes'm, I membuh muh gran too. Belali he frum Africa but muh gran she come by Bahamas. She speak funny wuds we didn know. She say 'mosojo' an sometime 'sojo' wen she mean pot. Fuh watuh she say 'deloe' an fuh fyuh she say 'diffy.' She tell us, 'Tak sojo off diffy.' . . .

She make funny flat cake she call 'saraka.' She make um same day ebry yeah, an it big day. Wen dey finish, she call us in, all duh chillun, an put in hans in flat cake an we eats it. Yes'm, I membuh how she make it. She wash rice, an po off all duh watuh. She let wet rice sit all night, an in mawnin rice is all swell. She tak dat rice an put it in wooden mawtuh, an beat it tuh paste wid wooden pestle. She add honey, sometime shuguh, an make it in flat cake wid uh hans. 'Saraka' she call un.

as interviewed for *Drums and Shadows*

MONICA ALI

The rice was perfect. Fluffy white grains, each one separate from its neighbour. In the rainy season, back home, when the land had given way to water and the buffaloes grew webbed feet, when the hens took to the roofs, when marooned goats teetered on minuscule islands, when the women splashed across on the raised walkway to the cooking hut and found they could no longer kindle a dung-and-husk fire and looked to their reserves, when the rain rang louder than cow bells, rice was the means, the giver of life. Precooked, it congealed and made itself glue. Or fashioned itself into hard lumps that only worked loose inside the stomach, the better to bloat the innards and make even the children lie down and groan with satisfaction. Even then it was good. This rice was superb. Just the rice would be enough for her. But fresh coriander made her swoon for the chicken. The deeply oily aubergine beckoned lasciviously. She wanted to stick her tongue in the velvety dal.

Brick Lane

JULIE SAHNI

Writing about *thandai* brings back sweet memories of my childhood in Kanpur. Summer vacation was always a very special time of the year; that was when various candies and pickles were prepared and different spice blends ground and mixed. Every day a fresh beverage was made especially for us while we played in the yard with the sun beating down. The most flavorful of all these was a cardamom-scented almond drink called *thandai*. It is a specialty of Uttar Pradesh and its preparation was, I remember, a long drawn-out process. First, different nuts and seeds were carefully measured. Then each was cleaned and blanched. Then the nuts were mixed and ground to a paste, with a little milk or water, on an Indian stone grinder. This paste was then blended into milk, sweetened with sugar, and poured into tall glasses filled with crushed ice.

Classic Indian Cooking

KATE CHOPIN
1850–1904

'But you look tired,' [Robert] added, solicitously. 'Would you like a cup of bouillon? Shall I stir you a toddy? Let me mix you a toddy with a drop of Angostura.'

She acceded to the suggestion of bouillon, which was grateful and acceptable. He went himself to the kitchen, which was a building apart from the cottages and lying to the rear of the house. And he himself brought her the golden-brown bouillon, in a dainty Sèvres cup, with a flaky cracker or two on the saucer.

The Awakening

GWEN RAVERAT
1885–1957

The regular round of formal dinner-parties was very important in Cambridge . . . We children used to huddle on the stairs in our night-gowns to watch the formal procession going from the drawing-room to the dining-room, led by my father with the principal lady on his arm, while my mother brought up the rear, on the arm of the most important gentleman. After they had all swept grandly by, we could dash down and warm ourselves by the drawing-room fire, before taking up our sta-tions by the serving-hatch to help finish up the good things as they came out. The strident roar of conversation pointed by the clatter of knives and forks came through the hatch in bursts, cut off suddenly when it was closed.

Dinner was at 7.45, and there were eight, nine, or even ten courses: I have some of the menus. Such dinners needed good organization, especially as they were all prepared and served by our own ordinary three servants, with very little extra help, beyond a waitress. Some people had special dishes sent in from the college kitchens, but my mother considered that extravagant. Here is a dinner given by my parents on 31st October 1885, when Sir William and Lady Thomson (the Kelvins) came to stay. This is clearly rather a grand dinner.

Clear Soup
Brill and Lobster Sauce
Chicken Cutlets and Rice Balls
Oyster Patties
Mutton, Potatoes, Artichokes, Beets
Partridges and Salad
Caramel Pudding
Pears and Whipped Cream }
Cheese Ramequins }
Cheese Straws
Ice
Grapes, Walnuts, Chocolates and Pears

But on 1st April 1885, there were only four people at dinner: my mother, my father, Edmund Gosse and Dew Smith, and yet they had:

Tomato Soup
Fried Smelts and Drawn Butter Sauce
Mushrooms on Toast
Roast Beef, Cauliflower and Potatoes
Apple Charlotte
Toasted Cheese
Dessert: Candied Peel, Oranges, Peanuts, Raisins and Ginger

I know this because after dinner my mother left the three men alone and came into the drawing-room and wrote it all down in a letter to her sister. This was five months before I was born; she was twenty-three, and she clearly felt very grand and grown-up, with three servants of her own.

Period Piece

SARAH WATERS

Have you ever tasted a Whitstable oyster? If you have, you will remember it. Some quirk of the Kentish coastline makes Whitstable natives – as they are properly called – the largest and the juiciest, the savouriest yet the subtlest, oysters in the whole of England. Whitstable oysters are, quite rightly, famous. The French, who are known for their sensitive palates, regularly cross the Channel for them; they are shipped, in barrels of ice, to the dining-tables of Hamburg and Berlin. Why, the King himself, I heard, makes special trips to Whitstable with Mrs Keppel, to eat oyster suppers in a private hotel; and as for the old Queen – she dined on a native a day (or so they say) till the day she died . . .

Like Molly Malone in the old ballad, I was a fishmonger, because my parents were. They kept the restaurant, and the rooms above it: I was raised an oyster-girl, and steeped in all the flavours of the trade. My first few childish steps I took around vats of sleeping natives and barrels of ice; before I was ever given a piece of chalk and a slate, I was handed an oyster-knife and instructed in its use; while I was still lisping out my alphabet at the schoolmaster's knee, I could name you the contents of an oyster-cook's kitchen – could sample fish with a blindfold on, and tell you their variety. Whitstable was all the world to me, Astley's Parlour my own particular country, oyster-juice my medium. Although I didn't long believe the story told to me by Mother – that they had found me as a baby in an oyster-shell, and a greedy customer had almost eaten me for lunch – for eighteen years I never doubted my own oysterish sympathies, never looked far beyond my father's kitchen for occupation, or for love.

It was a curious kind of life, mine, even by Whitstable standards; but it was not a disagreeable or even a terribly hard one. Our working day began at seven, and ended twelve hours later; and through all those hours my duties were the same. While Mother cooked, and Alice and my father served, I sat upon a high school at the side of a vat of natives, and scrubbed, and rinsed, and plied the oyster-knife. Some people like their oysters raw; and for them your job is easiest, for you have merely to pick out a dozen natives from the barrel, swill the brine from them, and place them, with a piece of parsley or cress, upon a plate. But for those who took their oysters stewed or fried – or baked, or scalloped, or put in a pie – my labours were more delicate. Then I must open each oyster, and beard it, and transfer it to Mother's cooking-pot with all of its savoury flesh intact, and none of its liquor spilled or tainted. Since a supper-plate will hold a dozen fish; since oyster-teas are cheap; and since our Parlour was a busy one, with room for fifty customers at once – well, you may calculate for yourself the vast numbers of oysters which passed, each day, beneath my prising knife; and you might imagine, too, the redness and the soreness and the sheer salty soddenness of my fingers at the close of every afternoon. Even now, two decades and more since I put aside my oyster-knife and quit my father's kitchen for ever, I feel a ghostly, sympathetic twinge in my wrist and finger-joints at the sight of a fishmonger's barrel, or the sound of an oyster-man's cry; and still, sometimes, I believe I can catch the scent of liquor and brine beneath my thumb-nail, and in the creases of my palm.

Tipping the Velvet

MARIA CORELLI

In the summer of 1944, Maria Corelli began a letter from Rome to her parents in Sussex. In it, she explained her long silence and outlined what had happened to her since the beginning of the Second World War. With the approach of the Germans, she and her husband, both singers, had fled Rome with their friend, the celebrated Jewish opera singer Sigbert, and made their way to southern Italy.

We shall never forget one tea party with Giuseppe and Jean (who have a large Café in Edinburgh) when Jean made biscuits, scones and homemade doughnuts that were all squidgy and melted in your mouth. The memory of this helped us later in many unfortunate moments. One of the most beautiful things in our life in Picinisco were the evenings when Sigbert sang, accompanied by Mrs Berent . . . He sang wonderfully – night after night – going through piece after piece in his extensive repertoire . . . Afterwards we would go up on the balcony and eat grapes in the dark . . .

In Love and War

GRACE NICHOLS

In London
every now and then
I get this craving
for my mother's food
I leave art galleries
in search of plantains
saltfish/sweet potatoes

I need this link

I need this touch
of home
swinging my bag
like a beacon
against the cold

'Like a Beacon'

WORKS OF ART

CLEMENTINE PADDLEFORD
1900–1967

I can close my eyes and still see that picture luncheon – a pastel in pinks.
And when the dish was ready – the rich brown of baked chickens
contrasting so pleasantly with the rosy pink of ham. And then the rice
was ready – shell pink, each grain separate. What finer color scheme, the
rice banked around the sauce-laved birds, a silver tray for a picture frame.
It was a dish as romantic in its conception as the Pastorale of Corot.

How America Eats

SUE HUBBARD

All day the juice dripped
like liquid time, fuschia
against the white, enamel rim,
clear as claret, if patient
and not hurried with a wooden spoon
disturbing the fruity sump.

Past dog roses denuded already
to hairy crimson hips, a scrub
of dock and battered aluminium
trough, over earth pock-marked with
hoof-prints that trapped wellingtons
and reached above your knees,

down into the valley's steep
throat, with plastic bags
and kitchen bowls we tumbled
to pick the last late fruit,
competing with blow flies
and the first bruising of frost.

Now that bleeding muslin seems
a life away. The slow erasure
of memory clouds like impure jelly,
the picture fading as the filming
of an ageing eye. Do you even
remember that pungent yeasty smell?

Here in this empty house these things
seep back, disturbing the silence.
Outside leaves choke the gutters
as sparrows compose themselves
on city wires against
the deep flush of a Rothko sky.

'Making Jelly'

DELLA LUTES
1872–1942

In honor of cherry pie a special eulogy should be written, one not
restricted to the limitations of page or space. The sensitive hand of a
Gaugin is required to portray the bowl – a bowl of Old Staffordshire in
flowing blue, into whose heavenly depths the luscious crimson of juicy
fruit was pitted. And only the epicure in taste and touch can gauge for
you the exact amount of sugar which will temper the acid and still
leave free just the right tartness to tingle the palate and tease the
tongue.

My mother, however, knew her cherry pie. She compounded a mixture of flour, lard, and water, rolled it into a nicety of depth, neatly fitted it to a tin, and filled it not quite to the top with cherries reeking of crimson juice. A second crust embellished with an embroidered scroll was laid over the top, pinched down around the edges to melt with its mate, and the whole brought to a state of consummate perfection in an oven of slow-baking temperature. Served, not warm, never chilled, but just *fresh*, a cherry pie like this without doubt one of the items in those Olympic feasts which gave rise to the phrase 'foods for the gods.'

The Country Kitchen

MARGARET COSTA
1917–99

The Four Seasons (1970) encouraged seasonal and unpretentious cooking. Its author, Costa, was the cookery writer for the Sunday Times *magazine; she also contributed the column 'London at Table' to* Gourmet. *With her third husband, she ran a restaurant, Lacy's; when it failed, the couple lost their money and were thought at one point to have been living in their car.*

The age of French colonialism is over, but French food, the gentle omelette above all, still conquers the world. There is no civilized country where one cannot find an omelette, the simplest and best of all French dishes.

More than any other uncomplicated and economical dish, the omelette has a prestige all its own. Remember Hélène, Gertrude Stein's cook, who disliked Matisse? When Miss Stein told her that he was staying for dinner she would reply: 'In that case I will not make an omelette but fry the eggs. It takes the same number of eggs and the same amount of butter, but it shows less respect and he will understand.'

There are many legends about the origins of the omelette and many myths about how it should be made. Strange secrets are ascribed to La Mère Poulard of Mont St Michel. But all she said herself was 'Je casse de bons oeufs dans une terrine, je les bats bien, je mets un bon morceau de beurre dans la poële, j'y jette les oeufs et je remue constamment.'

Margaret Costa's Four Seasons Cookery Book

ALICE B. TOKLAS
1877–1967

Gertrude Stein's lover and cook was born in San Francisco to a middle-class Jewish family. Her book of some 300 recipes was first published when she was 77.

One day when Picasso was to lunch with us I decorated a fish in a way that I thought would amuse him. I chose a fine striped bass and cooked it according to a theory of my grandmother who had no experience in cooking and who rarely saw her kitchen but who had endless theories about cooking as well as about many other things. She contended that a fish having lived its life in water, once caught, should have no further contact with the element in which it had been born and raised. She recommended that it be roasted or poached in wine or cream or butter. So I made a *court-bouillon* of dry white wine with whole peppers, salt, a laurel leaf, a sprig of thyme, a blade of mace, an onion with a clove stuck in it, a carrot, a leek and a bouquet of *fines herbes*. This was gently boiled in the fish-kettle for ½ hour and then put aside to cool. Then the fish was placed on the rack, the fish-kettle covered and slowly brought to a boil and the fish poached for 20 minutes. Taken from the fire it was left to cool in the *court-bouillon*. It was then carefully drained, dried and placed on the fish platter. A short time before serving it I covered the fish with an ordinary mayonnaise and, using a pastry tube, decorated it with a red mayonnaise, not coloured with catsup – horror of horrors – but with tomato paste. Then I made a design with sieved hard-boiled eggs, the whites and the yolks apart, with truffles and with finely chopped *fines herbes*. I was proud of my *chef d'oeuvre* when it was served and Picasso exclaimed at its beauty. But, said he, should it not rather have been made in honour of Matisse than of me.

The Alice B. Toklas Cook Book

GILLIAN RILEY

A recent correspondence in the *Times Literary Supplement* raised the subject of the old woman cooking eggs in the painting by Velasquez in the National Gallery of Scotland in Edinburgh.

Perplexed and distressed at the suggestion by Alejandro Oliveros that the old woman in the Velasquez painting might be attempting to poach her eggs in acidulated water, I turned to Spain's leading food historians, Alicia Rios and Manuel Martinez Llopis, for comfort and enlightenment. They expounded to me the honourable role of the fried egg in the gastronomy of Spain. The old woman is instructing the boy in the art of frying eggs, one of the basic skills of olive oil cookery. They can be prepared '*sin puntilla, con puntilla, y abuñuelados*', with or without a crisp, golden, lacey edging to the white, or deep fried at a very high heat. This last is a high-risk procedure which would indeed produce a shower of 'sputtering sparks', and has been known to destroy many a kitchen. The non-lace treatment, however, uses oil at a low temperature, where careful basting would give a gently rounded, opaque egg, without splashes. My sources explained that the old woman is flicking moderately hot oil around the edges of the eggs with a wooden spoon to achieve a lacey frill, like that on the skirts of a *traje de Sevillana*.

Cookery books of the period make no mention at all of methods of poaching eggs, a technique that is quite alien to the spirit of Spanish cooking. It is hard to imagine Velasquez choosing to illustrate any other way of preparing eggs, though an equally respectable alternative might have been Don Quixote's Saturday night supper of '*duelos y quebrantos*',

'lamentation and mourning', which may have been bacon and eggs, or
a more sophisticated version of eggs scrambled with *tocino* and *chorizos*,
the ingredients of which are lovingly recorded by Meléndez in one of his
kitchen still lives.

The Wilder Shores of Gastronomy

ELLA FARMAN PRATT
1837–1907

Mrs. Halliday had cut the ham. The slices were placed in boiling water,
and boiled until they were thoroughly cooked. Then they were put in a
frying-pan and browned nicely. After that, Marion fried some eggs to
'look like pictures.' She didn't 'turn' them, but carefully dripped gravy
over them, until they were done. These eggs she laid upon the slices of
ham, the golden centers shining through the pearly settings; and the
ham was so pink where it was not brown, and so brown where it was not
pink – truly, Marion's platter was like a bit of painting, and the pretty
cook of fourteen was as proud of it as she could be.

The Cooking Club of Tu-Whit Hollow

LOUISA MAY ALCOTT
1832–88

'It's time for lunch, girls, and I brought mine along with me, it's so
much jollier to eat in sisterhood. Let's club together, and have a revel,'
said Kate, producing a bag of oranges, and several big, plummy buns.

'We've got sardines, crackers, and cheese,' said Bess, clearing off a
table with all speed.

'Wait a bit, and I'll add my share,' cried Polly, and catching up her
cloak, she ran off to the grocery store near by.

'You'll be shocked at our performances, Miss Shaw, but you can call
it a pic-nic, and never tell what dreadful things you saw us do,' said

Rebecca, polishing a paint knife by rubbing it up and down in a pot of ivy, while Kate spread forth the feast in several odd plates and a flat shell or two.

'Let us have coffee to finish off with; put on the pot, Bess, and skim the milk,' added Becky, as she produced cups, mugs, and a queer little vase, to supply drinking vessels for the party.

'Here's nuts, a pot of jam, and some cake. Fan likes sweet things, and we want to be elegant when we have company,' said Polly, flying in again, and depositing her share on the table.

'Now, then, fall to, ladies, and help yourselves. Never mind if the china don't hold out; take the sardines by their little tails, and wipe your fingers on my brown-paper napkins,' said Kate, setting the example with such a relish that the others followed it in a gale of merriment.

Fanny had been to many elegant lunches, but never enjoyed one more than that droll pic-nic in the studio; for there was a freedom about it that was charming, an artistic flavour to every thing, and such a spirit of good-will and gaiety, that she felt at home at once. As they ate, the others talked, and she listened, finding it as interesting as any romance to hear these young women discuss their plans, ambitions, successes and defeats. It was a new world to her, and they seemed a different race of creatures from the girls whose lives were spent in dress, gossip, pleasure, or *ennui*. They were girls still, full of spirits, fun, and youth; but below the light-heartedness each cherished a purpose, which seemed to ennoble her womanhood, to give her a certain power, a sustaining satisfaction, a daily stimulus, that led her on to daily effort, and in time to some success in circumstance or character, which was worth all the patience, hope, and labour of her life.

An Old-Fashioned Girl

ELISABETH VIGÉE-LE BRUN
1755–1842

Elisabeth Vigée-Le Brun, famous for her portraits of Marie-Antoinette and other members of the French royal family, executed over 900 works during her lifetime.

I will now give you, my dear friend, the exact account of the most brilliant supper I ever gave in the days when people were always talking about my luxurious and magnificent mode of life.

One afternoon, while taking my rest before receiving a dozen or so persons I had invited, I got my brother to read aloud to me several pages of the *Travels of Anarcharsis*. When he came to the passage describing the way to make several Grecian sauces, he suggested that I should have them prepared for table that evening. I sent immediately for my cook and gave her the necessary instructions for the preparation of a certain sauce for the fowl and of another for the eel. As I was expecting some very beautiful women, I thought it a good idea to dress everybody in Grecian costumes, in order to have a surprise ready for M. de Vaudreuil and M. Boutin, who were not expected till ten o'clock . . .

The hour was getting late and I had had little time to think about myself; but as I always wore a white dress like a tunic (what is called a blouse nowadays) I needed only to put a veil and a chaplet of flowers on my head. I took particular care with my daughter and Mme de Bonneuil, who was as beautiful as an angel. Both were ravishing to the sight, carrying a very light ancient vase and getting ready to serve us with drink. At half-past nine the preparations were completed. When we were all in our places, the effect of the table was so novel and picturesque that we took turns in getting up and going to look at those who remained seated . . .

Besides the two dishes I have already told you of, we had a cake made of honey and currants, and two dishes of vegetables. It is true that we drank a bottle of old Cyprus wine which had been given me for a present. That was all the excess. Nevertheless, we remained at table a very long time. Lebrun recited several odes of Anacreon which he had translated. I do not believe I have ever spent a more amusing evening.

M. Boutin and M. de Vaudreuil were so delighted with the evening that they talked about it to all their acquaintances next day. Some ladies of the Court begged me to repeat the fun. I refused for various reasons, whereat several of the ladies took offence. The report soon got abroad that I had spent twenty thousand francs on the entertainment. The King mentioned it jokingly to the Marquis de Cubières, who luckily happened to have been one of the company and convinced His Majesty of the nonsense of such a suggestion.

Nevertheless, the cost, which was kept as modest as twenty thousand at Versailles, rose to forty thousand at Rome. At Vienna, Baroness Strogonoff told me that I had spent sixty thousand on my Grecian supper. At Petersburg it was settled at last at eighty thousand. And the truth is, it cost me fifteen francs.

Memoirs
trans. by Siân Evans

CECILIA BEAUX
1855–1942

Cecilia Beaux studied in Paris in 1888–9 and was considered by her contemporaries the most distinguished woman portrait painter in America. Her sitters included Mrs Theodore Roosevelt, Georges Clemenceau and Admiral Lord Beatty.

The hotel in the place faced the whole scene of Concarneau; the fortress in the distance, the sea and the quays, prickling with masts, and ruddy with the sails of the fishing fleet, at anchor, or tied up to their dock. Lights were beginning to show from lantern and lamp-post and moving spots of white – or what one called white – were present everywhere in the circulating crowds. The hotel was warm and populous; dinner was served; our friends hastened to meet us; every window contained a spectacle. Every line and movement of the *bonnes* who served us at the table was a detaining composition. Even the thoroughly bourgeois appointments of the dining-room, where no trace of primitive beauty could be seen, outside of Madame and the servants, was toned and massed by the not too generous lighting. The quality of generosity was in the unctuous exhalations of the cuisine, the steaming soup tureen (we had a tureen at home), the great fish lying brown and rich on its huge platter, which easily accommodated head, tail, and every natural accessory, and the subtle underlying constant of cheese, knotty apples, and wine.

Background with Figures

SOR JUANA INÉS DE LA CRUZ
1648–95

Gila, so tart
that rather than give
the taste buds sweetmeats,
you pucker them up:
    I'll paint you to the tune
of Saint John of Lima.
There's a lime to sharpen
the tartness in you.

    Amber and myrrh
anoint your hair –
small wonder then,
it's so bittersweet.

    Jasmine once wanted
to tint your brow
but what prevailed
was lemon flower.

    It was ink that gave
your eyebrows color:
that's why they reek
of vitriol and gallnuts.

With your olive eyes
a seasoning comes,
made to order for them:
oregano and salt.

A winepress sought
to stain your cheeks
but you're such a child,
the wine proved too green.

The liveliest scarlet
enlivens your mouth—
lovely to look at,
bitter to taste.

The white of your neck
is such pure driven snow,
it's like lemon rind covered
with crusted salt.

Your hands might be dipped
in curdled milk,
which during the night
turns good and sour.

The gold of your buskin
attracts all eyes,
but then they must swallow
the bitter pill inside.

And if this portrait
isn't acid enough,
just add a dash
of your natural gall.

A Sor Juana Anthology
trans. by Alan S. Trueblood

GUADELUPE RIVERA
MARIE-PIERRE COLLE

The stepdaughter of Frida Kahlo recalls the artist's way with food.

As the days passed, my already warm relationship with Frida grew deeper. I went home from the Law School for lunch every morning at about the time that Frida, who by then had finished painting for the day, was busy preparing the midday meal. On some days, my father would come back to the Blue House for lunch, but on other days Frida would send a basket of food over to his studio at San Angel.

The preparation of this box lunch was a ritual in itself. The blue pewter dinner pail was divided into compartments, each of which contained one of 'Dieguito's' ('Little Diego's') favorite dishes. Frida would add freshly made tortillas and bread that was still warm and fragrant from the oven. She saved the fruits for last, using them with fresh-cut flowers to provide an ornamental touch. When Eulalia had brought tasty pulque from Ixtapalapa, '*la niña Fridita*' would include it in an earthenware jar. For a covering Frida chose colorfully embroidered white napkins that featured floral themes and whimsical birds. Occasionally there was lettering, too, that spoke of love, with expressions like '*Felicidades mi amor.*'

When Frida felt bored and lonely she would carry the pail herself. Arriving at my father's studio, she would busy herself setting up a little table in some out-of-the-way corner. She would then share the contents of the basket with the Master. I always thought this was proof of the affection that Diego and Frida felt.

Toward the middle of the month, as my birthday drew near, I decided that the best way to celebrate was by inviting some of my university friends to dinner – in particular my boyfriend Luis Echeverría, who was at that time a leader of the student political movement and who later became president of Mexico . . . thanks to the wonderful food prepared by the lady of the house – especially the old family recipes – my birthday was a success.

Frida made a superb stew of pork, liver, and kidneys in a sauce of pulque and serrano chiles. My grandmother Isabel had invented this dish and made it for the peasants who worked in her father's fields in Zapotlán el Grande, in the state of Jalisco, the ancestral seat of the Preciado and Marín families. The rest of the recipes for that dinner came from the same area: *jocoque* soup, macaroni with spinach sauce, chicken with nut sauce. For dessert there were guavas and doughnuts and a special quince paste with almond cookies.

Frida's Fiestas

DARRA GOLDSTEIN

Legend has it that Catherine planned a visit to her consort, Count Potemkin, at a time when no sturgeon was to be had in all of Moscow. Potemkin, never one to give up easily, sought out a cunning fishmonger who supplied him with enough fish for the soup. But it cost him dearly. In exchange for the sturgeon, Potemkin relinquished a painting he had recently purchased for 10,000 rubles. But when Catherine the Great is coming for dinner, what else can one do?

A Taste of Russia

EDITH TEMPLETON

Edith Templeton spent much of her childhood in a castle in Bohemia and began publishing short stories in the New Yorker *in the 1950s. The Surprise of Cremona (1954) is a highly irreverent account of her journey through northern Italy.*

That night, at the Padovana, I start dinner with a salad of *finocchi*. This is a round, whitish-green, fascinating vegetable, wrapped up in layers of itself which overlap like the tiles of a roof. At the top it sprouts four pale, reeded stems which bear dark green leaves, delicate, like feathers made up of needles, reminiscent of the foliage of wild asparagus. Only the round part is eaten, boiled or raw, sliced, with oil and vinegar. It has a cool, clean, nutty flavour.

After I have finished the salad, the *padrone* appears, rolling a trolley towards me. He comes, I see, I am conquered. On the trolley there is a composite dish. It is called *bollito misto*, and is the counterpart of its better-known brother the *fritto misto*. Whereas the *fritto misto* is all golden, dry, crinkled, and crisp, the *bollito* is silvery smooth and watery. Who shall say which of the two is more glorious? They must be taken according to one's mood, like the Sun and the Moon.

The *padrone* carves me a slice of broiled tongue, a sliver of boiled chicken, a chunk of boiled beef, half of a boiled calf's knuckle, and a round of a large boiled sausage. There are two sauces to go with it, the *salsa verde* and the *salsa rossa*. Intelligent as he is, he does not ask me which of the two I prefer. He knows I shall want both.

The green sauce is an enticing mixture of aromatic herbs, smoothed with oil and sharpened with vinegar. The red sauce is of an evenly thick consistency and cannot be analysed easily. Here is the recipe as told me by the *padrone*:

'Chop a shallot and fry in oil till it blushes. Add fresh tomatoes and minced carrots and butter and simmer for about twenty minutes. Add minced fresh red peppers and simmer for another ten minutes.'

For those who cannot be captivated by either of the two sauces there is another still more picturesque choice, called the Mustard of Cremona.

This is a dish of fruit candied in syrup, to which a dash of pepper and mustard powder has been added. It serves as sweet spice to the mild meats and sets them on fire, in a cool and lovely way, like moonlight burning on water. The fruit is luminously transparent, like semi-precious stones. I am given a plateful. There are several cherries, unevenly rounded like antique corals; a green pear of the size of a walnut, with the black pips shining like onyx; a larger pear of the colour of rose-quartz; a green fig clouded like a flawed emerald, a curved strip of pumpkin, reddish brown and veined like chrysopase, and the half of an apricot which could have been carved out of a topaz. They are almost too splendid to be eaten. Before starting, I ponder over their many-hued flamboyance, and come to the conclusion that the colours of the Mustard of Cremona are those found in Veronese's paintings. It is an exceedingly *raffiné* dish, a Baroque dish, sweet, full-bodied, glowing and tingling. Life is beautiful.

The Surprise of Cremona

EXOTIC TASTES

HANNAH GLASSE
1708–70

A *Frenchman* in his own country will dress a fine dinner of twenty dishes, and all genteel and pretty, for the expence he will put an *English* lord to for dressing one dish. But then there is the little petty profit. I have heard of a cook that used six pounds of butter to fry twelve eggs; when every body knows (that understands cooking) that half a pound is full enough, or more than need be used: but then it would not be *French*. So much is the blind folly of this age, that they would rather be imposed on by a *French* booby, than give encouragement to a good *English* cook!

The Art of Cookery, Made Plain and Easy

MRS GASKELL
1810–65

A FRENCH BREAKFAST

If we were French we should have a cup of *café-au-lait* and a piece of bread brought into our bedrooms every morning; but, in deference to us as strangers, a tray (without a napkin) with sugar, a copper pan containing the boiling milk just taken off the kitchen fire, and the white covered jug of bright strong coffee, is put on the dining-room table. Also, in deference to our English luxury, there is a plate of butter; our French friends never take butter, and not always bread, at this early breakfast. But where is the bread? I look round, and at last see a basket, about a yard high, standing on the ground near the fireplace; it is of dimensions just sufficient to hold a roll of bread a yard long and more, and about as thick as a man's wrist. It looks like a veritable staff of life. None of our French friends think of completing their toilette for this early breakfast, which indeed, as I have said, they would have taken in their bedrooms, if we had not been here . . .

Madame is always at home, and dressed with delicate neatness, by eleven o'clock, the time of our '*second déjeuner*,' or what we should call lunch in England. This breakfast consists generally of cold meat, a *rechauffé* of some *entrée* or dressed vegetables of the day before, an omelette, bread, wine, and a pot of *confitures*. For us our kind hostess has tea; but I can see that this is not their ordinary custom. It is curious to see how little butter is eaten in a French family; they, however, make up for this by the much greater use of it in cookery; for vegetables form a dish by themselves, always requiring either gravy, butter, or oil in their preparation.

French Life

JULIA CHILD 1912–2004
SIMONE BECK 1904–91
LOUISETTE BERTHOLLE

Cassoulet is a rich combination of beans baked with meats, as much a part of southwestern France as Boston baked beans are of New England. The composition of a *cassoulet* is, in typical French fashion, the subject of infinite dispute, so much so that if you have read or heard about *cassoulet* and never tasted it, you come to expect a kind of rare ambrosia rather than the nourishing country fare it actually is. As *cassoulet* is native to a relatively large region of France, each part of which has its own special-ties, arguments about what should go into this famous dish seem based on local traditions. *Toulousains* insist that it must include among its meats preserved goose, *confit d'oie*, or it is not a real *cassoulet*. After all, some-thing must be done with all the geese which housed the *foie gras*, and *cassoulet* is a natural solution in the Toulouse area. Then there are those who declare the *cassoulet* was born in Castelnaudary, and originally contained only beans, pork, and sausages. A heretical few suggest the *cassoulet* was not a French invention at all, but an adaption from the Arab *fava* bean and mutton stew. And so on, with variations and dogmatisms rampant. Fortunately all the talk can be regarded as so much historical background, for an extremely good *cassoulet* can be made anywhere out of beans and whatever of its traditional meats are available: goose, game, pork, sausages, lamb, mutton. The important item is flavor, which comes largely from the liquid the beans and meats are cooked in. And truth to tell, despite all the to-do about preserved goose, once it is cooked with the beans you may find difficulty in distinguishing goose from pork.

Mastering the Art of French Cooking

MICHÈLE ROBERTS

French cakes, Léonie mused: aren't as good when they come out of the oven as English cakes. No currants and raisins. No icing. No hundreds and thousands or anything.

French cooking, Victorine asserted: is the best in the world!

Her blue eyes narrowed to marble chips. She pushed back a long fair curl with one hand. She whacked butter and eggs with her wooden spoon.

Suet pudding with slabs of butter and white sugar, Léonie recited: fried eggs and bacon, fish and chips, kippers, marmalade, proper tea, Eccles cakes.

Thérèse flicked a piece of muddy potato peel across the table.

Everyone knows that English food is terrible, she stated: soggy boiled vegetables in white sauce, overcooked meat, I don't know how your mother could stand it, having to go and eat stuff like that. She stopped being really French, everyone says so. The English are just heathens, aren't they Victorine?

Daughters of the House

SYBIL KAPOOR

There are certain aspects of British cookery that never cease to fascinate me, and one of these is the extraordinary ability we have to gather up the delicate flavours of our countryside and transform them into exquisite dishes. Sweet-scented violets, primroses, cowslips, lime blossom, elderflowers and roses have been picked by British cooks since time immemorial and converted into fragrant messes. But while primroses, cowslips and lime blossom have slipped from common usage, the elderflower has remained popular.

It is one of those subtle flavourings that makes a dish taste quintessentially British. What Frenchman would dream of adding elderflower to his rhubarb compote? What American would add a dash of elderflower cordial to his spritzer? And surely no Italian would churn a gooseberry and elderflower sorbet? Yet as far as the British are concerned, elderflowers, with their sweet scent of Muscat grapes, add an indefinable charm to countless dishes from cooling drinks to creamy custards.

Simply British

SUSAN FERRIER
1782–1854

'An English breakfast,' glancing with contempt at the eggs, muffins, toast, preserves, &c. &c. he had collected round him, 'is really a most insipid meal: if I did not make a rule of rising early and taking regular exercise, I doubt very much if I should be able to swallow a mouthful – there's nothing to whet the appetite here; and it's the same every where; as Yellowchops says, our breakfasts are a disgrace to England. One would think the whole nation was upon a regimen of tea and toast – from the Land's End to Berwick-on-Tweed, nothing but tea and toast! Your ladyship must really acknowledge the prodigious advantage the Scotch possess over us in that respect.'

'I thought the breakfasts, like everything else in Scotland, extremely disgusting,' replied her ladyship, with indignation.

'Ha! well, that really amazes me. The people I give up – they are dirty and greedy; the country, too, is a perfect mass of rubbish; and the dinners not fit for dogs – the cookery, I mean; as to the materials, they are admirable. But the breakfasts! that's what redeems the land – and every country has its own peculiar excellence. In Argyleshire you have the Lochfine herring – fat, luscious, and delicious, just out of the water, falling to pieces with its own richness – melting away like butter in your mouth. In Aberdeenshire you have the Finnan haddo', with a flavour all its own, vastly relishing – just salt enough to be *piquant*, without parching you up with thirst. In Perthshire there is the Tay salmon, kippered, crisp, and juicy – a very magnificent morsel – a *leetle* heavy, but that's easily counteracted by a tea-spoonful of the Athole whisky. In other places you have the exquisite mutton of the country, made into hams of a most delicate flavour; flour scones, soft and white; oat-cake, thin and crisp; marmalade and jams of every description; and—'

Marriage

FANNY TROLLOPE
1780–1863

In relating all I know of America, I surely must not omit so important a feature as the cooking. There are sundry anomalies in the mode of serving even a first-rate table; but as these are altogether matters of custom, they by no means indicate either indifference or neglect in this important business; and whether castors are placed on the table or on the side-board; whether soup, fish, patties, and salad be eaten in orthodox order or not, signifies but little. I am hardly capable, I fear, of giving a very erudite critique on the subject; general observations therefore must suffice. The ordinary mode of living is abundant, but not delicate. They consume an extraordinary quantity of bacon. Ham and beef-steaks appear morning, noon, and night. In eating, they mix things together with the strangest incongruity imaginable. I have seen eggs and oysters eaten together; the sempiternal ham with apple-sauce; beef-steak with stewed peaches; and salt fish with onions. The bread is everywhere excellent, but they rarely enjoy it themselves, as they insist upon eating horrible half-baked hot rolls both morning and evening. The butter is tolerable; but they have seldom such cream as every little dairy produces in England; in fact, the cows are very roughly kept, com-pared with our's. Common vegetables are abundant and very fine. I never saw sea-cale, or cauliflowers, and either from the want of summer rain, or the want of care, the harvest of green vegetables is much sooner over than with us. They eat the Indian corn in a great variety of forms; sometimes it is dressed green, and eaten like peas; sometimes it is broken to pieces when dry, boiled plain, and brought to table like rice; this dish is called hominy. The flour of it is made into at least a dozen different sorts of cakes; but in my opinion all bad. This flour, mixed in the pro-portion of one-third, with fine wheat, makes by far the best bread I ever tasted.

I never saw turbot, salmon, or fresh cod; but the rock and shad are excellent. There is a great want of skill in the composition of sauces; not only with fish, but with every thing. They use very few made dishes, and I never saw any that would be approved by our savants. They have an excellent wild duck, called the Canvass Back, which, if delicately served, would surpass the black cock; but the game is very inferior to our's; they have no hares, and I never saw a pheasant. They seldom indulge in second courses, with all their ingenious temptations to the eating a second dinner; but almost every table has its dessert, (invariably pro-nounced desart) which is placed on the table before the cloth is removed, and consists of pastry, preserved fruits, and creams. They are 'extravagantly fond,' to use their own phrase, of puddings, pies, and all kinds of 'sweets,' particularly the ladies; but are by no means such con-noisseurs in soups and ragoûts as the gastronomes of Europe. Almost every one drinks water at table, and by a strange contradiction, in the country where hard drinking is more prevalent than in any other, there is less wine taken at dinner; ladies rarely exceed one glass, and the great

majority of females never take any. In fact, the hard drinking, so univer-
sally acknowledged, does not take place at jovial dinners, but, to speak
plain English, in solitary dram-drinking. Coffee is not served immediately after dinner, but makes part of the serious matter of tea-drinking,
which comes some hours later. Mixed dinner parties of ladies and gentlemen are very rare, and unless several foreigners are present, but little
conversation passes at table. It certainly does not, in my opinion, add to
the well ordering a dinner table, to set the gentlemen at one end of it,
and the ladies at the other; but it is very rarely that you find it otherwise.

Domestic Manners of the Americans

FIROOZEH DUMAS

*Her family's move from Iran to California in the early 1970s inspired
Firoozeh Dumas's* Funny in Farsi.

My father and his younger brother, Nematollah, share many interests,
none stronger than the love of new foods. Some experience a foreign
land through museums or historical sights, but for our family, America
was to be experienced through the taste buds. Every day, Kazem and
Nematollah, like cavemen headed for the hunt, would drive to the
local supermarket, returning with cans and boxes of mysterious
American products. They picked foods for the pictures on the containers, inadvertently proving that American marketing is sometimes better
than American cooking. Since Iranian flavors are quite different from
the flavors found in American convenience foods, most of the purchases ended up in the trash can.

In Iran, meal preparation took up half of each day, starting early in
the morning with my mother telling our servant, Zahra, which vegetables to clean and cut. The vegetables were either grown in our garden
or had been purchased the day before. The ingredients in our meals
were limited to what was in season. Summer meant eggplant or okra
stew, fresh tomatoes, and tiny cucumbers that I would peel and salt.

Winter meant celery or rhubarb stew, cilantro, parsley, fenugreek, and my favorite fruit, sweet lemon, which is a thin-skinned, aromatic citrus not found in America. There was no such thing as canned, frozen, or fast food. Everything, except for bread, which was purchased daily, was made from scratch. Eating meant having to wait for hours for all the ingredients to blend together just right. When the meal was finally ready, we all sat together and savored the sensuous experience of a delicious Persian meal. Upscale restaurants in America, calling themselves 'innovative and gourmet,' prepare food the way we used to. In Iran, it was simply how everybody ate . . .

After several weeks of trying every TV dinner, canned good, and cereal, my father and uncle concluded that the only ready-made American foods worth buying were canned chili, ice cream, and Chips Ahoy cookies. The rest, they concluded, was too salty, too sweet, or just plain bad.

They next set out to explore the unknown territory of American fast food. We lived near a strip mall well supplied with restaurants, all of which took a similar high-grease approach to cooking. Starting at one end, we ate our way through the mall, skipping only a hot dog place called Der Wienerschnitzel. The name was unpronounceable and we had no interest in dogs, hot or otherwise.

After weeks of research, we concluded that Kentucky Fried Chicken was the best thing we had tasted in America, followed by Baskin-Robbins, every last one of its flavors. No one was made happier by our foray into eating prepared foods than my mother, who, lacking both Iranian ingredients and Zahra, had a very difficult time cooking in America. The Colonel's secret recipe had set my mother free.

Funny in Farsi

AMY TAN

The linked stories in The Joy Luck Club *lifted the lid on Chinese-American mother-daughter relationships. Here, one of the daughters brings her boyfriend home for supper, with disastrous results.*

He had brought a bottle of French wine, something he did not know my parents could not appreciate. My parents did not even own wine-glasses. And then he also made the mistake of drinking not one but two frosted glasses full, while everybody else had a half-inch 'just for taste.'

When I offered Rich a fork, he insisted on using the slippery ivory chopsticks. He held them splayed like the knock-kneed legs of an ostrich while picking up a large chunk of sauce-coated eggplant. Halfway between his plate and his open mouth, the chunk fell on his crisp white shirt and then slid into his crotch. It took several minutes to get Shoshana to stop shrieking with laughter.

And then he had helped himself to big portions of the shrimp and snow peas, not realizing he should have taken only a polite spoonful, until everybody had had a morsel.

He had declined the sautéed new greens, the tender and expensive leaves of bean plants plucked before the sprouts turn into beans. And Shoshana refused to eat them also, pointing to Rich: 'He didn't eat them! He didn't eat them!'

He thought he was being polite by refusing seconds, when he should have followed my father's example, who made a big show of taking small portions of seconds, thirds, and even fourths, always saying he could not resist another bite of something or other, and then groaning that he was so full he thought he would burst.

But the worst was when Rich criticized my mother's cooking, and he didn't even know what he had done. As is the Chinese cook's custom, my mother always made disparaging remarks about her own cooking. That night she chose to direct it toward her famous steamed pork and preserved vegetable dish, which she always served with special pride.

'Ai! This dish not salty enough, no flavor,' she complained, after tasting a small bite. 'It is too bad to eat.'

This was our family's cue to eat some and proclaim it the best she had ever made. But before we could do so, Rich said, 'You know, all it needs is a little soy sauce.' And he proceeded to pour a riverful of the salty black stuff on the platter, right before my mother's horrified eyes.

And even though I was hoping throughout the dinner that my mother would somehow see Rich's kindness, his sense of humour and boyish charm, I knew he had failed miserably in her eyes.

Rich obviously had had a different opinion on how the evening had gone. When we got home that night, after we put Shoshana to bed, he said modestly, 'Well. I think we hit it off *A-o-kay*.' He had the look of a dalmatian, panting, loyal, waiting to be petted.

'Uh-hmm,' I said. I was putting on an old nightgown, a hint that I was not feeling amorous. I was still shuddering, remembering how Rich had firmly shaken both my parents' hands with that same easy familiarity he used with nervous new clients. 'Linda, Tim,' he said, 'we'll see you again soon, I'm sure.' My parents' names are Lindo and Tin Jong, and nobody, except a few older family friends, ever calls them by their first names.

'So what did she say when you told her?' And I knew he was referring to our getting married. I had told Rich earlier that I would tell my mother first and let her break the news to my father.

'I never had a chance,' I said, which was true. How could I have told my mother I was getting married, when at every possible moment we were alone, she seemed to remark on how much expensive wine Rich liked to drink, or how pale and ill he looked, or how sad Shoshana seemed to be.

Rich was smiling. 'How long does it take to say, Mom, Dad, I'm getting married?'

'You don't understand. You don't understand my mother.'

Rich shook his head. 'Whew! You can say that again. Her English was *so* bad. You know, when she was talking about that dead guy

showing up on *Dynasty*, I thought she was talking about something
that happened in China a long time ago.'

The Joy Luck Club

M.R. LOVRIC

In the Pasha's dining room I was placed between Hobhouse and Byron,
who laid his two large pistols on the table before he sat down. He
glanced around. Yes, everyone was looking at him.

Turbanned slaves encircled us, bearing platters. Lying in beds of
scented rice were whole blackened lambs with their little heads nodding
gently. There were ragouts of flamingo flesh swimming with oil and
sprinkled with cardamon seeds. There were whole fish with cabochon
emeralds where the eyes should have been. The eyes were served separately impaled upon little sticks with fresh herbs between them. There
were suggestively curved and swarthy vegetables stuffed with raisins
and minced meat. There were whole platters of cherries and more of
white peaches topped by black passion fruit, already slashed across the
middle so that the vivid seeds spilled onto the pale peach flesh below.
Silver jugs of pomegranate juice were poured into our glass goblets.

Carnevale

ELISABETH VIGÉE-LE BRUN
1755–1842

I must not forget to tell you how I painted two diplomats, who in spite
of being copper-coloured had splendid heads. In 1788 ambassadors were
sent to Paris by the Emperor Tippoo-Sahib. I saw these Indians at the
Opéra, and they appeared to me so unusually picturesque that I wished
to paint their portraits. Having informed them of my desire, I learnt that
they would never consent to be painted except at the request of the

King, so I obtained this favour from His Majesty . . .

Mme de Bonneuil, to whom I had spoken of my sittings, wanted very much to meet these ambassadors. They invited us both to dinner, and we accepted the invitation out of sheer curiosity. Entering the dining-room, we were somewhat surprised to find the dinner served on the floor, and we were thus obliged to do as they did, lying almost flat round the low table. They offered us with their hands what they took from the dishes, one of which contained a fricasse of sheep's feet with white sauce, very spicy, while the other held a sort of ragout. As you can imagine, it was a sad meal. We loathed watching them use their bronzed hands in the place of spoons.

Memoirs
trans. by Gerard Shelley

MADHUR JAFFREY

Indian food has long been popular in Britain, but Delhi-born Jaffrey taught the British to cook it for themselves, rather as Elizabeth David did with Mediterranean foods.

One of my fondest memories of school in Delhi is of the lunches that we all brought from our homes, ensconced in multitiered lunch boxes. My stainless steel lunch box used to dangle from my bicycle handlebar as I rode at great speed to school every morning, my ribboned pigtails fluttering behind me. The smells emanating from it sustained me as I dodged exhaust-spewing buses and, later, as I struggled with mind-numbing algebra. When the lunch bell finally set us free, my friends and I would assemble under a shady *neem* tree if it was summer or on a sunny verandah if it was winter. My mouth would begin to water even before we opened up our lunch boxes. It so happened that all my friends were of differing faiths and all came originally from different regions of the country. Even though we were all Indian, we had hardly any culinary traditions in common. Eating always filled us with a sense of adventure and discovery as we could not always anticipate what the others might bring.

My Punjabi friend was of the Sikh faith. She often brought large, round *parathas* made with wheat and *ghee* produced on her family farm. These were sometimes stuffed with tart pomegranate seeds and sometimes with cauliflower. We ate them with a sweet-and-sour, homemade turnip pickle.

Another friend was a Muslim from Uttar Pradesh, known to bring beef cooked with spinach, all deliciously flavoured with chilies, cardamon, and cloves. Many of us were Hindus and not supposed to eat beef. So we just pretended not to know what it was. Our fingers would work busily around the tender meat that covered the bones and our cheeks would hollow as we sucked up the spicy marrow from the marrow bones. But we never asked what we were eating. The food was far too good for that. On the other hand, whenever my father went boar hunting and we cooked that meat at home, I never took it to school. I knew it would offend my Muslim friends.

Another member of our gang was a Jain from Gujerat. Jains are vegetarians, some of them so orthodox as to refrain from eating beets and tomatoes because their colour reminds them of blood, and root vegetables because in pulling them out of the earth some innocent insect might have to lose its life. This friend occasionally brought the most delicious pancakes – *pooras* – made out of pulses.

One of us came from Kashmir, India's northernmost state. As she thrilled us with tales about tobogganing – the rest of us had never seen snow – she would unpack morel mushrooms from Kashmiri forests, cooked with tomatoes and peas and flavoured with asafetida. This friend was a Hindu, of course. Only Kashmiri Hindus cook with asafetida. And they do not cook with garlic. Kashmiri Muslims cook with garlic and frown upon asafetida. I found all this much easier to follow than algebra.

We had a South Indian friend too, a Syrian Christian from Kerala. She often brought *idlis*, slightly sour, steamed rice cakes that we ate with *sambar*, a pulse, and fresh vegetable stew.

I, a Delhi Hindu, tried to dazzle my friends with quail and partridge that my father shot regularly and that our cook prepared with onions, ginger, cinnamon, black pepper, and yogurt.

Indian Cooking

MARGARET MEAD
1901–78

In 1942 the anthropologist Margaret Mead assumed the role of Executive Secretary of the National Research Council's Committee on Food Habits based in Washington, D.C. In this extract she outlines the committee's findings on the value of particular foods to different national groups. Her autobiography, Blackberry Winter, *is fairly reticent on personal issues, but it does discuss some of the foods she ate during fieldwork.*

November 19, 1942

FOOD AND MORALE
Appendix I – Foods specially valued by different national background groups

The Committee wishes to divide foods particularly valued by different national background groups into two classes:

I. Condiments which give the food preparation its distinctive character.
II. Staple meats, cereals, vegetables, etc. which are highly valued by particular groups.

Group I we would classify as essential to morale and recommend that every effort be made, when regional and local distribution plans are perfected and when a point system for condiments is devised, to provide a supply of the distinctive condiments in the areas where different national background groups are concentrated.

Group II, specially valued staples and holiday foods, fall into a somewhat different class. They are foods whose presence enhances morale.

The deprivation of many familiar foods can be reduced by the occasional presence, especially at holiday time, of the highly valued foods. The list is presented here as background material for use in future planning, especially in planning for special holiday relaxations of rationing, or allocation plans for urban areas, or areas of temporary concentration of populations with foreign food habits.

Group I
Condiments

Italians:	hard cheese, salad oil with some olive oil for flavor, tomato paste
Czechs:	dill, poppy seeds, mushrooms
Poles:	dill, poppy seeds, dried mushrooms
Hungarians:	onions, paprika, saffron
Greeks:	olive oil, pine nuts
Chinese:	soy sauce, bean sprouts, fresh ginger roots
Mexicans:	chili, peppers
Porto Ricans:	chili peppers, saffron
Scandinavians:	caraway seeds
Jews:	pickles, poppy seeds
Syrians:	grape leaves, olive oil, nutmeg, ginger

Group II
Specially valued staples – A

Italians:	wine, greens, salads like romaine and escarole, cooked ones like broccoli, Italian bread, 'pasta'
Poles:	sour rye bread, sour cream, buckwheat groats and barley, cucumbers, noodles
Czechs:	Sour rye bread, pork, sauerkraut, dumplings, beer, goose
Hungarians:	sour rye bread, wine, 'bacon', dried fruits
Greeks:	whole wheat for boiling, lamb, matzoon (sour milk), dried fruits (figs, raisins, dates) eggplant, olives
Chinese:	rice, water chestnuts, tea

Mexicans:	beans, cornmeal, chocolate
Porto Ricans:	rice beans, dried codfish, coffee, mangoes, bananas(?) tomatoes
West Indians:	rice beans, (see above)
Germans:	beer sausage, cheese, sauerkraut, rye bread, coffee
Scandinavians:	coffee, beer, goat cheese, fish, dark hard bread, smoked meat and fish, pork, potatoes, brandy, salt pork
Jews:	chicken, noodles, sour cream and cottage cheese, dried fruits, bread: rye rolls, twist, matzoth, tea, butter, barley
Irish:	tea, beer, cabbage, ham, potatoes, corned beef
French Canadians:	ham, salt pork, split peas, beans, tea, chocolate
Syrians:	lamb, meat, wheat, pignolia nuts, coffee

Group II
Holiday Dishes – B

Italians:	Friday, fish; lamb or kid at Easter, eggs in blood and chocolate cake at Easter, meat on Sunday, 'pasta' on Thursday and Saturday
Czechs:	*Christmas*: sucking pig, or pig's head, 'Vannochki', boiled carp
	Easter: pascal lamb, eggs
	St. Wenceslas' Day (Sept. 28) and St. Martin's Day (Nov. 14) goose or duck
Poles:	*Christmas*: roast pork
	Easter: lamb, eggs
	St. Martin's Day: duck
	Sunday: meat (pork or fowl), 'babka' (yeast cake)
Hungarians:	grapes in autumn, goulash, eggs for Easter
Jews:	chicken and noodles on Friday nights, stuffed fish; poppy seed cakes ('Hamantaschen' – literally 'hats of Haman') for *Purim*; matzoth, horseradish, lamb bone, wine for *Passover*; honey, potato flour, for

sponge cake, nuts; also the whole gamut of 'Passover groceries' – milk and other dairy products, prepared under special ritual conditions.

Scandinavians: *Christmas*: roast goose, pork rib, special spiced and yeast cakes with anise, cardamon seed, nuts, citron, angelica

Martin Luther's Day (Nov. 11): goose

Prepared for the National Research Council Committee on Food Habits

ENCARNACIÓN PINEDO
1848–1902

HELADOS DE TUBEROSAS

Tuberose Ice

Put an ounce of tuberoses in a vase, having removed the leaves of the plant. Pour six quarts of water on top, in which you have already dissolved twelve ounces of sugar over the fire, but so that it is only lukewarm, without letting it boil or get too warm. Leave the flowers in the infusion for four hours, stirring the vase from time to time. Then pass the mixture through a very fine linen and put it in the ice-cream freezer to make the ice.

Encarnación's Kitchen
trans. by Dan Strechl

PATIENCE GRAY
1917–2005

KAKI PERSIMMON

Another oriental intruder, a tree of great splendour in winter. The fruits, pale green when they first appear, turn to burning gold and remain on the tree long after its leaves have fallen. The landscape of the Tiber Valley is illuminated by them and so are the narrower valleys between Naples and Benevento in late autumn. They falsely recall the Golden Apples of the Hesperides.

A favourite winter fruit, eaten when very ripe, the sign being the cracking of the delicate skin. The Japanese sculptor, Inoué Yukichi, told me that in Japan they are left on the bough until there is a heavy frost, the soft luscious pulp becomes frozen, and they are eaten on the spot, iced.

Honey from a Weed

DARRA GOLDSTEIN

We stayed for a few days in the village of Velistsikhe, which seems to belong to an old and almost forgotten world, with its narrow streets fronted on all sides by high stone walls plastered with mud. Throughout the Kahketian countryside are similar village compounds. On every promontory or rise the ruins of citadels and fortresses stand over the populace below. Our hosts in Velistsikhe were Bichiko and Dodo and their daughter Tamriko . . . Although it was nearly midnight, we immediately sat down to tea with an assortment of Dodo's wonderful homemade preserves: whole peaches suspended in sugar syrup, with a suggestion of cinnamon and clove; crunchy slices of spiced watermelon rind; aromatic rose-petal jam shimmering in its bowl; and the favourite Georgian green walnut preserve, lush and ambrosial.

The next morning we rose early to watch Dodo make bread in the *toné* [clay oven]. After starting a fire with dried grape vines, she brought out the dough she had mixed the night before. Soon a neighbor appeared to help with the baking. Unlike Dodo, who wore a light, sleeveless frock, seemingly indifferent to the hazards of baking, the neighbor was dressed entirely in black, from the scarf reaching halfway down her forehead to the fingerless gloves she wore to protect her hands from the oven's intense heat. Now the activity began, a series of rhythmic movements as the women worked in harmony, shaping the loaves, slapping them onto the sides of the oven, spearing them once they'd turned crusty and brown, then turning them out onto a board to cool. Their graceful, repetitive motions were mesmerizing, as were the smells of wood smoke and fresh bread. But Bichiko was eager to show us his orchard, so while the breadbaking continued, we dashed off to pick fresh fruits for breakfast. Bichiko's plot lay on the outskirts of town, a brief car ride away, in a public area set aside for individual gardens. While some of the gardens seemed overgrown or haphazard, Bichiko's was a model of tidiness, with virtually every square foot under intensive cultivation. Here grew several varieties of peaches, apricots, plums, and summer apples, as well as red and white grapes and tomatoes. Bichiko beamed and pointed as we harvested buckets full of sweet plums, rosy peaches, and apricots with the dew still clinging to them. Racing back in time to enjoy the bread still warm from the oven, we savored homemade yogurt, cheese, and olives along with our fruit . . .

This Kakhetian breakfast highlighted all that is best about the way Georgians eat – their excitement over seasonal produce, the absolute freshness of their food, the simplicity of much of its preparation. But splendid as the meal was, the memory that remains with me most vividly is of two bent old women working so skillfully around the *toné*. In another setting, these women might have seemed unremarkable, but here, intent upon a task that generations of Georgians had performed before them, they became models of grace, priestesses tending a sacred fire. The force of the *toné*'s heat was staggering – pure and elemental.

With the craggy mountains looming in the distance, the spirit of Prometheus seemed surely alive.

The Georgian Feast

WILLA CATHER
1873–1947

In the midst of winter in the Great Plains of America, the Narrator of My Ántonia *first samples the mysterious taste of wild mushrooms from central Europe.*

She threw the package into the stove, but I bit off a corner of one of the chips I held in my hand, and chewed it tentatively. I never forgot the strange taste; though it was many years before I knew that those little brown shavings, which the Shimerdas had brought so far and treasured so jealously, were dried mushrooms. They had been gathered, probably, in some deep Bohemian forest.

My Ántonia

SARAH QUIGLEY

The Domanskis are a Polish immigrant family living in San Francisco, where they run a comedy club called The Sausage.

A they arrived at the door of the house, the street lights came on. 'Make a wish,' said Bella, stepping aside for Mr Domanski to unlock the door.

'I wish—' said Lena. But there was too much to say.

'I know what I wish for,' said Bella, shutting her eyes tight for a moment and stumbling over the mat.

'My wish is that Ma will have made us *hundreds* and *thousands* of donuts,' said Davey greedily. And then they were in the room.

The *paczki* were there all right, lying on a tray in pasty splendour, lightly snowed over with flour. Beside them on the bench stood the sunflower oil and the salt and the sugar, all in a neat row. But the kitchen was empty . . .

It was like a scene from the mystery of the *Marie Celeste*: no sign of life, and the ship's captain nowhere to be seen.

The meat loaf browned and then blackened in its dish. Still they sat and waited, and then Mr Domanski lost patience. 'We will eat,' he said. 'We are as hungry as hunters after our big day.' He carved the loaf and shining rounds of egg fell cleanly onto the plates. 'Eat, drink, and loosen your belt!' he said, pouring himself a tiny measure of vodka to celebrate not only Epiphany but the fact that he was home with his family instead of at The Sausage . . .

Lena ate the roasted onions and the potatoes from around the side of the dish. She could detect but tried to ignore the taste of beef and pork fat. Every now and then she glanced longingly over at the far better second course: the fat round circles of yeasty dough, ready to be cooked, still rising.

'Could you fetch some water, Lena?' asked Mr Domanski. 'A jug for the table, please.' . . .

Lena wiped the onion grease away from her mouth and went to the kitchen. Her foot skidded on the linoleum, she fell against the bench, and her elbow caught the baking tray. Donuts leapt through the air like flying saucers: some fell to the floor and promptly sank.

'Elephant feet!' said Bella from the dining table.

'I slipped,' said Lena with dignity. 'I was not *clumsy*.' She bent to pick up the donuts, and also the piece of paper that had made her slip in the first place. 'It's a note from Ma,' she said. And as she looked at the handwriting she began to shake, so much that she had to sit down on the floor amongst the fallen donuts.

'What is it?' said Mr Domanski sharply. He came over and snatched the note out of Lena's hand, not politely at all. For a minute there was complete silence in the room: the only sounds were the bright hum of the fluorescent light, and Bella's stomach giving a loud gurgle. Then Mr Domanski went back to his chair and sat down, so heavily that it seemed as if he weighed twice as much as usual, and the chair cracked underneath him.

'Where's Ma?' said Bella. 'What does she say?'

'She has gone,' said Mr Domanski simply. He picked up a discarded crust of bread and mechanically began to chase the stray breadcrumbs around his plate. Neatly, he shovelled up the crumbs and the grease and placed them in his mouth.

'Gone?' said Bella with alarm in her voice. 'Gone where?'

'She has returned to Poland,' said Mr Domanski. Although his teeth were covered with parsley, he retained a strange dignity. 'It is Our fault, he said, as if he were royalty. 'We have not made her happy.' Without another word he left the room and they heard the front door bang.

Bella began to cry, Davey kicked the table leg repeatedly with his foot, and Lena sat completely still on the floor. She pressed her back against the kitchen cupboard which was where she last remembered her mother. The flat hardness against her shoulder blades helped a little.

'She might come back,' she offered. 'If we wrote to her.'

No one spoke. The rhythmic banging of Davey's food continued. Tiredly, Lena got to her feet and gathered the donuts up off the floor. There was no dust on them, no hairs or specks, and this was hardly surprising as the floor had probably been cleaned several times that day. Yes, the donuts were pristine but they had lost their lightness.

'What next?' said Lena to herself. What was the right thing to do, she wondered, when your mother had left the dinner in the oven and gone to Poland?

Shot

MIKI

March 30, 2004

RAMPS

Ah, spring, season of dirt-cheap asparagus and tasty Girl Scout Cookies. And ramps, which I tried yesterday for the first time. Ramps are wild leeks native to these parts (and the occasion of many ramps festivals) and taste somewhere between leeks and garlics, with a sort of grassiness that puts me in mind of green peppers. I followed this recipe for ramps with pasta, except that I added cream, because, um, I add cream to almost anything I can get away with.

Those of you not in these parts can find ramps at this site, which also sells fiddlehead ferns (never had them but would very much like to) and morels (oh, yum . . .).

Theory of the Daily weblog

GERTRUDE STEIN
1874–1946

A tripartite work of word clusters sometimes called poetry, Tender Buttons *shows the influence of cubism on Stein's writing. It includes an entire section on food. Read aloud, it soon assumes both sense and rhythm.*

ROASTBEEF

In the inside there is sleeping, in the outside there is reddening, in the morning there is meaning, in the evening there is feeling. In the evening there is feeling. In feeling anything is resting, in feeling anything is mounting, in feeling there is resignation, in feeling there is recognition, in feeling there is recurrence and entirely mistaken there is pinching. All the standards have steamers and all the curtains have bed linen and all the yellow has discrimination and all the circle has circling. This makes sand . . .

Please be the beef, please beef, pleasure is not wailing. Please beef, please be carved clear, please be a case of consideration.

EGGS

Kind height, kind in the right stomach with a little sudden mill.

Cunning shawl, cunning shawl to be steady.

In white in white handkerchiefs with little dots in a white belt all shadows are singular they are singular and procured and relieved.

No that is not the cows shame and a precocious sound, it is a bite.

Cut up alone the paved way which is harm. Harm is old boat and a likely dash.

RHUBARB

Rhubarb is susan not susan not seat in bunch toys not wild and laughable not in little places not in neglect and vegetable not in fold coal age not please.

CUSTARD

Custard is this. It has aches, aches when. Not to be. Not to be narrowly. This makes a whole little hill.

It is better than a little thing that has mellow real mellow. It is better than lakes whole lakes, it is better than seeding.

CELERY

Celery tastes tastes where in curled lashes and little bits and mostly in remains.

A green acre is so selfish and so pure and so enlivened.

PASTRY

Cutting shade, cool spades and little last beds, make violet, violet when.

SALAD

It is a winning cake.

SALAD DRESSING AND AN ARTICHOKE

Please pale hot, please cover rose, please acre in the red stranger, please butter all the beef-steak with regular feel faces.

Tender Buttons

URSULA K. LᴱGUIN

In this 1969 classic of science fiction, the inhabitants of the lost world Winter – the Gethenians – live in a world based on genderless interrelations and enjoy a diet free of mammalian-based products.

I had dinner at my island and at Fourth Hour striking on the gongs of Remny Tower I was at the Palace ready for supper. Karhiders eat four solid meals a day, breakfast, lunch, dinner, supper, along with a lot of adventitious nibbling and gobbling in between. There are no large meat-animals on Winter, and no mammalian products, milk, butter or cheese; the only high-protein, high-carbohydrate foods are the various kinds of eggs, fish, nuts, and the Hainish grains. A lowgrade diet for a bitter climate, and one must refuel often. I had got used to eating, as it seemed, every few minutes. It wasn't until later in that year that I discovered the Gethenians have perfected the technique not only of perpetually stuffing, but also of indefinitely starving.

The Left Hand of Darkness

CLAUDIA RODEN

When I visited the old Ghetto of Venice and asked a rabbi about Venetian Jewish cooking, he directed me to the Casa di Riposo Israelitico (Jewish old people's home), where they also serve meals to tourists during Jewish holidays. One of the ladies in charge of the cooking answered my question by pointing to the three synagogues (scole) that stood together in the piazza – the *spaniola*, the *levantina* and the *tedesca*. They represented, she said, the different styles (a fourth one was Italian) that make up the Venetian Jewish style.

The coexistence in the ghetto bore fruit in the kitchen. The *levantini* brought riso pilaf and risi colle uette (rice with raisins, eaten cold, as in Istanbul today). The Iberian *ponentini* introduced salt-cod dishes, frittate (vegetable omelettes), almondy sweets, orange cakes, flans, and chocolate cakes. The *levantini* and *ponentini* introduced the range of spices and aromatics that they dealt in. The Arab combination of pine nuts and raisins came both with the Sicilians and the *levantini*.

The *tedeschi* introduced goose and duck, beef sausages and goose salame, pesce in gelatina (jellied fish) and polpettine di pesce (gefilte fish), penini de vedelo in gelatina (calf's-foot jelly) and knaidlach, which became 'cugoli.' An example of the interweaving of cultures is pastizzo di polenta, with raisins and pine nuts. Another is the burriche – little pies halfway between Portuguese empanadas and Turkish borekas but with fillings unique to Italy, such as fish with hard-boiled egg; or anchovies and capers with fried eggplant and zucchini; or pumpkin with crushed amaretti and chopped crystallized citrus peel. A bakery in the old ghetto sells the old Jewish pastries, and at Passover you can find pane azzimo (matzos) hand-made in the old ways, with holes or with a lattice design.

The Book of Jewish Food

ISABELLA BEETON
1836–65

The bread in the south of Spain is delicious: it is white as snow, close as cake, and yet very light; the flavour is most admirable, for the wheat is good and pure, and the bread well kneaded. The way they make this bread is as follows:- From large round panniers filled with wheat they take out a handful at a time, sorting it most carefully and expeditiously, and throwing every defective grain into another basket. This done, the wheat is ground between two circular stones, as it was ground in Egypt 2,000 years ago, the requisite rotary motion being given by a blindfolded mule, which paces round and round with untiring patience, a bell being attached to his neck, which, as long as he is in movement, tinkles on; and when it stops, he is urged to his duty by the shout of '*Arre, mula*,' from some one within hearing. When ground, the wheat is sifted through three sieves, the last of these being so fine that only the pure flour can pass through it: this is of a pale apricot-colour. The bread is made in the evening. It is mixed with only sufficient water, with a little salt in it, to make it into dough: a very small quantity of leaven, or fermenting mixture, is added. The Scripture says, 'A little leaven leaveneth the whole lump;' but in England, to avoid the trouble of kneading, many put as much leaven or yeast in one batch of household bread as in Spain would last them a week for the six or eight donkey-loads of bread they send every night from their oven. The dough made, it is put into sacks, and carried on the donkeys' backs to the oven in the centre of the village, so as to bake it immediately it is kneaded. On arriving there, the dough is divided into portions weighing 3 lbs. each. Two long narrow wooden tables on trestles are then placed down the room; and now a curious sight may be seen. About twenty men (bakers) come in and range themselves on one side of the tables. A lump of dough is handed to the nearest, which he commences kneading and knocking about with all his might for about 3 or 4 minutes, and then passes it on to his neighbour, who does the same; and so on successively until all have kneaded it, when it becomes as soft as new putty, and ready for the oven. Of course, as soon as the first baker has handed the first lump to his neighbour, another is given to him, and so on till the whole quantity of dough is successively kneaded by them all. The bakers' wives and daughters shape the loaves for the oven, and some of them are very small, and they are baked immediately. The ovens are very large, and not heated by fires *under* them; but a quantity of twigs of the herbs of sweet marjoram and thyme, which cover the hills in great profusion, are put in the oven and ignited. They heat the oven to any extent required; and, as the bread gets baked, the oven gets gradually colder; so the bread is never burned. They knead the bread in Spain with such force, that the palm of the hand and the second joints of the fingers of the bakers are covered with corns; and it so affects the chest, that they cannot work more than two hours at a time.

Mrs Beeton's Book of Household Management

FANNY CRADOCK
1909–93

Although, thanks to the assistance of our good friends, we have supplied you with a complete list of the recommended establishments in Barcelona, we would like to fling just one more of our own pet restaurants in as a suggestion. Finisterre is a place to go to in summer when luncheon begins in the afternoon heat and pursues its leisurely way until five-thirty.

On the occasion of our first post-war visit in 1948 we had been recommended to Finisterre by some Spanish friends. We had come into Spain by car for a one day initial exploration, and were casting about before deciding to move in from France. We were very hot, very cross, very hungry. Finisterre received us. We sat in a tiny awning-shaded patio, took one look at the un-priced bath-sheet menu and sent wild telegrams across the table to one another, (we were four). These were of the 'damn-the-consequences' type, and the 'if we run out of money we'll go straight back so what does it matter if we have come to the most expensive restaurant in town' genre.

We began with Gaspacho. This variable ice-cold soup – a crude mélange of breadcrumbs, garlic, onions and oil among the peasants – can be a dream of delight if it is well made. It was, and the accompanying side dishes of diced pimentoes (red, green and yellow), of diced cucumber, diced tomatoes and diced fried crôutons made together a most refreshing prelude which we washed down with white wine and ate with enormous crescents of white bread and iced roses of creamy butter. A Paella followed, dressed with whole lobster claws, mussels and baby octopus, and stuffed with bits of chicken, sausage, vegetables, etc. We stodged and drank our fill. We continued with sharp cheeses, finished with Cremas Planchadas, drank quarts of black coffee and liberal potations of brandy. Then we surreptitiously slid pesetas under the table to Johnnie and waited for the pay off. It was £4 for 4 persons! That was when we decided to return to Spain.

Holiday in Barcelona and the Balearics

MARGARET COSTA
1917–99

From mid-December to late January the streets of Seville are hung with gold. The brilliant globes of the bitter oranges shine from the trees that line the *avenidas*. Outside the city the gipsies have gathered to cut down the golden fruit in the leafy orange groves. Men pick; women pack. The Moors, who loved them for the beauty of the tall trees and darkly glowing fruit and the exquisite perfume of their flowers, far stronger and sweeter than that of sweet orange blossom, first brought the bitter oranges to Spain. They have long been prized for their use in perfumery but in Spanish cooking they are used hardly at all – simply, I believe, to remove any muddy or unpleasant flavour from the flesh of wild ducks which are rubbed well, inside and out, with the cut surface of a Seville orange before roasting.

There are many references to Seville oranges in old English cookery books. But by a quirk of fate it is Scotland that has put Seville oranges on the gastronomic map and given us a delicacy for which we are respected all over the world. Marmalade has been made with bitter oranges in Scotland since the beginning of the eighteenth century.

Margaret Costa's Four Seasons Cookery Book

DIANA KENNEDY

Known as 'the high priestess of Mexican cooking', British-born Kennedy first went to Mexico in 1957 to marry a foreign correspondent for the New York Times. *Her books celebrate the traditional and festive foods of local pueblos and towns, and are responsible for revolutionising the concept of Mexican food internationally.*

Of all the jellies I have eaten, there are only two that I consider sublime: red currant and guava – well, perhaps crab apple as a third. After all, there is never enough time to eat everything, so you have to choose, and why not pick out the best?

At home in England there was only a small quantity of red currant jelly made, mainly because the birds got to the currants first, despite the netting over the bushes, and partly because of the work involved. It was a laborious job to remove the currants from their stringy bunched stems, and after all that, there was so little to show for it. We used to eat the jelly in the fall with roast lamb or use it as a glaze over a fruit tart, and very occasionally with scones at teatime.

Guava jelly provided another treat, and to my sister and me it was a very exotic one. Mother's oldest sister, Aunt Maud, lived for many years in Jamaica and every other year would make a trip home. To us at the time she was a rather glamorous figure; although short and dumpy, she was very handsome in her big floppy hats and chic dresses of the finest materials. Her greying hair was slightly tinged with lavender and a delicate perfume always wafted after her – that is, when she wasn't smoking one of her flat Turkish cigarettes. When she visited us the whole household deferred to her – she had quite a regal presence – and total quiet reigned while she had her afternoon nap, followed by her maté tea, before gathering up anyone she could get hold of to play bridge for the rest of the evening. We would go to the railway station to meet her, and it was quite a sight to see her walking along the platform with soft colorful baskets crammed full of goodies from Jamaica. She always somehow managed to preserve some huge and delicious Bombay mangoes in the ship's cold room. There were large bags of cashew nuts, large floppy panama hats, and tins of guava jelly . . . Aunt Maud's visits started off my passion for cashews and guava jelly, so little wonder that when I first arrived in Mexico and saw real guavas my enthusiasm knew no bounds. I started to make guava jelly galore, for friends and acquaintances alike, whether they wanted it or not.

Nothing Fancy

SYBILLE BEDFORD
1911–2006

The service at X's is as regular as the lighting and the wine. To sit in the penumbra with nothing but death and Santo Tomás to occupy one's mind is unnerving. My cries rend the shadows for something to eat.

'Where is that *Terrine* we ordered? It must be ready.'

'It is ready. But the Prawns-and-Rice are not.'

'But we are having the *Terrine* first.'

'Yes, the *Terrine* comes first, but the Prawns are not ready.'

'We are not going to eat them at the same time. Please bring us the *Terrine* now.'

'Señora: we must wait for the Prawns. Then you will eat the *Terrine* first.'

'I mean first now, not first then.'

'Yes, Señora, first. First in a little while.'

'*Will you please bring the* Terrine *at once.*'

'At your taste, Señora. I shall run to tell the chef to hurry up the Prawns.'

We wait. Then the *Terrine* is brought over from the sideboard in the Stygian corner where it had been reposing, and here on its heels are the Prawns, sizzling. So much is clear now, everything is allowed to take its time but once your dinner is on its breathless way, there must be no pause. The custom must have ruined tempers and digestions. It is unfathomable, and it is bedrock.

A Visit to Don Otavio

REGRETTABLE MEALS

LAURIE COLWIN
1944–92

One of the most engaging food writers, Colwin occasionally cooked and served at a centre for homeless women in New York city.

There is something triumphant about a really disgusting meal. It lingers in the memory with a lurid glow, just as something exalted is remembered with a kind of mellow brilliance. I am not thinking of kitchen disasters – chewy pasta, burnt brownies, curdled sauces: these can happen to anyone. I am thinking about meals that are positively loathsome from soup to nuts, although one is not usually fortunate enough to get either soup or nuts.

Bad food abounds in restaurants, but somehow a bad meal in a restaurant and a bad home-cooked meal are not the same: after all, the restaurant did not invite you to dinner.

My mother believes that people who can't cook should rely on filet mignon and boiled potatoes with parsley, and that they should be on excellent terms with an expensive bakery. But if everyone did that, there would be fewer horrible meals and the rich, complicated tapestry that is the human experience would be the poorer for it.

My life has been much enriched by ghastly meals, two of the awfulest of which took place in London. I am a great champion of English food, but what I was given at these dinners was neither English nor food so far as I could tell.

Once upon a time my old friend Richard Davies took me to a dinner party in Shepherd's Bush, a seedy part of town, at the flat of one of his oldest friends.

'What is he like?' I asked.

'He's a genius,' Richard said. 'He has vast powers of abstract thought.'
I did not think this was a good sign.

'How nice,' I said. 'Can he cook?'

'I don't know,' Richard said. 'In all these years, I've never had a meal
at his house. He's a Scot, and they're very mean.'

When the English say 'mean,' they mean 'cheap.'

Our host met us at the door. He was a glum, geniusy-looking person and
he led us into a large, bare room with a table set for six. There were no
smells or sounds of anything being cooked. Two other guests sat in chairs,
looking as if they wished there were an hors d'oeuvre. There was none.

'I don't think there will be enough to go around,' our host said, as if
we were responsible for being so many. Usually, this is not the sort of
thing a guest likes to hear but in the end we were grateful that it turned
out to be true.

We drank some fairly crummy wine, and then when we were practically gnawing on each other's arms, we were led to the table. The host
placed a rather small casserole in the center. We peered at it hopefully.
The host lifted the lid. 'No peeking,' he said.

Usually when you lift the lid of a casserole that has come straight
from the oven, some fragrant steam escapes. This did not happen,
although it did not immediately occur to me that this casserole had not
come straight from the oven, but had been sitting around outside the
oven getting lukewarm and possibly breeding salmonella.

Here is what we had: the casserole contained a layer of partially
cooked rice, a layer of pineapple rings and a layer of breakfast sausages,
all of which was cooked in a liquid of some sort or other. Each person
received one pineapple ring, one sausage and a large heap of crunchy
rice. We ate in perfect silence, first in shock, then in amazement, and
then in gratitude that not only was there not enough to go around, but
that nothing else was forthcoming. That was the entire meal.

Later as Richard and I sat in the Pizza Express finishing off a second
pie, I said: 'Is that some sort of Scottish dish we had tonight?'

'No,' said Richard. 'It is a genius dish.'

*

Several years later on another trip to London, Richard and I were invited to a dinner party in Hampstead. Our host and hostess lived in a beautiful old house but they had taken out all the old fittings and the place had been redesigned in postindustrial futuristic.

At the door, our hostess spoke these dread words: 'I'm trying this recipe out on you. I've never made it before. It's a medieval recipe. It looked very interesting.'

Somehow I have never felt that 'interesting' is an encouraging word when applied to food.

In the kitchen were two enormous and slightly crooked pies.

'How pretty,' I said. 'What kind are they?'

'They're medieval fish pies,' she said. 'A variation on starry gazey pie.' Starry gazey pie is one in which the crust is slit so that the whole baked eels within can poke their nasty little heads out and look at the pie crust stars with which the top is supposed to be festooned.

'Oh,' I said, swallowing hard. 'In what way do they vary?'

'Well, I couldn't get eel,' said my hostess. 'So I got squid. It has squid, flounder, apples, onions, lots of cinnamon and something called gallingale. It's kind of like frankincense.'

'I see,' I said.

Home Cooking

VIRGINIA WOOLF
1882–1941

A DINNER AT OXBRIDGE

Here was my soup. Dinner was being served in the great dining-hall. Far from being spring it was in fact an evening in October. Everybody was assembled in the big dining-room. Dinner was ready. Here was the soup. It was a plain gravy soup. There was nothing to stir the fancy in that. One could have seen through the transparent liquid any pattern that there might have been on the plate itself. But there was no pattern. The plate was plain. Next came beef with its attendant greens and potatoes –

a homely trinity, suggesting the rumps of cattle in a muddy market, and sprouts curled and yellowed at the edge, and bargaining and cheapening, and women with string bags on Monday morning. There was no reason to complain of human nature's daily food, seeing that the supply was sufficient and coal-miners doubtless were sitting down to less. Prunes and custard followed. And if anyone complains that prunes, even when mitigated by custard, are an uncharitable vegetable (fruit they are not), stringy as a miner's heart and exuding a fluid such as might run in misers' veins who have denied themselves wine and warmth for eighty years and yet not given to the poor, he should reflect that there are people whose charity embraces even the prune. Biscuits and cheese came next, and here the water-jug was liberally passed round, for it is the nature of biscuits to be dry, and these were biscuits to the core. That was all. The meal was over.

A Room of One's Own

LORNA SAGE
1943–2001

Sage spent her career at the University of East Anglia, but it was her extraordinary account of a strange upbringing in north Wales, Bad Blood, *that brought her critical acclaim and public notice. Here she describes her mother's attitude to food and cooking.*

She just wished – out loud, quite often – that the housework would do itself. In the same spirit she cursed cooking and as she dumped our plates in front of us on the eating end of the table she would announce that we could take it or leave it, and that she wished we could all live on pills. In the beginning it was mostly stew, shreds of grey, nameless meat and lumps of carrot and turnip floating in salty water, with a surface shimmer of yellow fat. This was what I had at school, too, so there was nothing special about it, except for the spice of her revulsion. But as the days of rationing receded, and you could buy a joint of lamb or even a chicken for Sunday dinner (roasting chickens were rare birds back then) her fear of food grew and grew. All meat had to be made safe by boiling, or by simmering it in a lake of spitting fat in the oven for hours, and even then it was dangerously full of knots of choking gristle and shards and spikes of bone, which she'd warn us against with a shudder. She herself could seldom bear to eat any of this nasty stuff, although occasionally she would daintily dissect a sliver on her plate and observe – which was true – that even the boneless bits were tough and stringy.

You might have mistaken her for an aspiring vegetarian, but in fact the thought that we were eating the very lambs that went bleating to market in Dad's trucks didn't move her at all. She didn't care for farm animals. And if anything, she thought vegetables even more danger-ous and difficult to subdue. They had to be cooked all morning, particularly green ones like sprouts, which got very salty and stuck to the pan as their water boiled away, and came out in a yellow mush. Potatoes got the same treatment and her ritual Sunday lunchtime cry, as she lifted the saucepan lid – 'They've gone to nothing!' – became a family joke, an immortal line that later converged magically in my mind with the smartest 1950s intellectual slogans. *Gone to nothing* was wonderfully Absurd, a phrase of existentialist and sub-Beckettian power. As for my mother, she should be so lucky was her meaning – if only those wretched roots full of eyes *would* go to nothing! But no, there was a grey sludge left at the bottom of the pan (we never needed to mash our potatoes) which had after all to be spooned resignedly on to our plates.

Bad Blood

EDITH WHARTON
1862–1937

She had expected to view the company through a bower of orchids
and eat pretty-coloured entrées in ruffled papers. Instead, there was
only a low centre-dish of ferns, and plain roasted and broiled meat that
one could recognize – as if they'd been dyspeptics on a diet! With all the
hints in the Sunday papers, she thought it dull of Mrs. Fairford not to
have picked up something newer; and as the evening progressed she
began to suspect that it wasn't a real 'dinner party,' and that they had
just asked her in to share what they had when they were alone.

The Custom of the Country

DOROTHY WORDSWORTH
1771–1855

Friday, September 2nd

We lost sight of the sea for some time, crossing a half-cultivated space, then
reached Loch Creran, a large irregular sea loch, with low sloping banks,
coppice woods, and uncultivated grounds, with a scattering of corn fields;
as it appeared to us, very thinly inhabited: mountains at a distance. We
found only women at home at the ferry-house. I was faint and cold, and
went to sit by the fire, but, though very much needing refreshment, I had
not heart to eat anything there – the house was so dirty, and there were so
many wretchedly dirty women and children; yet perhaps I might have got
over the dirt, though I believe there are few ladies who would not have
been turned sick by it, if there had not been a most disgusting combination
of laziness and coarseness in the countenances and manners of the women,
though two of them were very handsome. It was a small hut, and four
women were living in it: one, the mother of the children and mistress of
the house; the others I supposed to be lodgers, or perhaps servants; but
there was no work amongst them. They had just taken from the fire a great
pan full of potatoes, which they mixed up with milk, all helping themselves

out of the same vessel, and the little children put in their dirty hands to dig out of the mess at their pleasure. I thought to myself, How light the labour of such a house as this! Little sweeping, no washing of floors, and as to scouring the table, I believe it was a thing never thought of.

Recollections of a Tour Made in Scotland

BEATRIX POTTER
1866–1943

All at once he fell head over heels in the dark, down a hole, and landed on a heap of very dirty rags.

When Tom Kitten picked himself up and looked about him – he found himself in a place that he had never seen before, although he had lived all his life in the house.

It was a very small stuffy fusty room, with boards, and rafters, and cobwebs, and lath and plaster.

Opposite to him – as far away as he could sit – was an enormous rat.

'What do you mean by tumbling into my bed all covered with smuts?' said the rat, chattering his teeth.

'Please sir, the chimney wants sweeping,' said poor Tom Kitten.

'Anna Maria! Anna Maria!' squeaked the rat. There was a pattering noise and an old woman rat poked her head round a rafter.

All in a minute she rushed upon Tom Kitten, and before he knew what was happening –

His coat was pulled off, and he was rolled up in a bundle, and tied with string in very hard knots.

Anna Maria did the tying. The old rat watched her and took snuff. When she had finished, they both sat staring at him with their mouths open.

'Anna Maria,' said the old man rat (whose name was Samuel Whiskers), – 'Anna Maria, make me a kitten dumpling roly-poly pudding for my dinner.'

'It requires dough and a pat of butter, and a rolling-pin,' said Anna

Maria, considering Tom Kitten with her head on one side . . .

Presently the rats came back and set to work to make him into a dumpling. First they smeared him with butter, and they rolled him in the dough.

'Will not the string be very indigestible, Anna Maria?' inquired Samuel Whiskers.

Anna Maria said she thought that it was of no consequence; but she wished that Tom Kitten would hold his head still, as it disarranged the pastry. She laid hold of his ears.

Tom Kitten bit and spat, and mewed and wriggled; and the rolling-pin went roly-poly, roly; roly, poly, roly. The rats each held an end.

'His tail is sticking out! You did not fetch enough dough, Anna Maria.'

'I fetched as much as I could carry,' replied Anna Maria.

'I do not think' – said Samuel Whiskers, pausing to take a look at Tom Kitten – 'I do *not* think it will be a good pudding. It smells sooty.'

The Tale of Samuel Whiskers or The Roly-Poly Pudding

ISABELLA BIRD
1831–1904

Though supplies in their cabin were already running low, Bird's companions found it hard to turn away a deserter. His insatiable hunger led them to regret their hospitality.

November 29

Before the boy came I had mistaken some faded cayenne pepper for ginger, and had made a cake with it. Last evening I put half of it into the cupboard and left the door open. During the night we heard a commotion in the kitchen and much choking, coughing, and groaning, and at breakfast the boy was unable to swallow food with his usual ravenousness. After breakfast he came to me whimpering, and asking for something soothing for his throat, admitting that he had seen the 'gingerbread,' and 'felt so starved' in the night that he got up to eat it.

I tried to make him feel that it was 'real mean' to eat so much and be so useless, and he said he would do anything to help me, but the men were so 'down on him.' I never saw men so patient with a lad before. He is a most vexing addition to our party, yet one cannot help laughing at him.

A Lady's Life in the Rocky Mountains

DIANE ACKERMAN

When a vanilla bean lies like a Hindu rope on the counter, or sits in a cup of coffee, its aroma gives the room a kind of stature, the smell of an exotic crossroads where outlandish foods aren't the only mysteries. In Istanbul in the 1970s, my mother and I once ate Turkish pastries redolent with vanilla, glazed in caramel sugar with delicate filaments of syrup on top. It was only later that day, when we strolled through the bazaar with two handsome university students my mother had bumped into, that we realized what we had eaten with such relish. On a long brass platter sat the kind of pastries we had eaten, buzzed over by hundreds of sugar-delirious bees, whose feet stuck in the syrup; desperately, one by one, they flew away, leaving their legs behind. 'Bee legs!' my mother had screamed, as her face curdled. 'We ate *bee legs!*' Our companions spoke little English and we spoke no Turkish, so they probably thought it odd that American women became so excitable in the presence of pastry. They offered to buy us some, which upset my mother even more.

A Natural History of the Senses

GWEN RAVERAT
1885–1957

Pamela was a child with whom I sometimes played, but whom I rather despised . . . She was the sort of person one was always nasty to; because, however hard one tried to be nice to her, she always managed to give you a remorseful feeling that you had not really understood her. It was just a quality she had. Once when I went to tea with her alone, we were given a special little feast; and among the good things were some raspberries. They turned out to be full of maggots, but Pamela ate them all up, both hers and mine. Without saying anything, she implied that she so seldom had anything nice for tea, that she was glad even of maggoty raspberries; while no doubt I, lucky I, had delicious fruit every day of my life (which was very far indeed from being true). I think now, that there was not the faintest reason to believe that her parents were at all unkind to her; but in a patient, tolerant, uncomplaining way, she certainly made me think so then; and all without a word being said on the subject.

Period Piece

MORAG MURRAY ABDULLAH
20th century

'Do you not think my eyes are as the dawn of morning?'

'Yes, indeed.'

No wonder, I thought, this unfortunate woman looked as she did, if for twenty years she had lived in these circumstances. She could not have been more than forty, if the story were true, and yet she might have been seventy, so wrinkled was her face. It was perhaps lucky there appeared to be no looking-glasses anywhere.

The servant brought food, and I was afraid not to eat, lest this might make her return to her idea of my being an *afrit*.

The tin plates were clean and were placed beside us on the floor, where I sat. It was difficult to see what was served out of the cauldrons carried in by two maidservants. The food was dished up in tin cups and looked like chopped straw, though soft, and it contained fat thick pieces of meat resembling eels.

My thoughts went back to the old days at home when we used to catch those squirming 'snake fish,' and to gain time I began to put my hair straight.

'Is this a delicacy of your hills?' I asked pointing to the food.

She gave a laugh. It sounded like a frog's croak.

'We of this clan have eaten naught else. These are rare fishes brought from Hindustan. We keep them and have many in a well in the courtyard. This is a barren land.'

I had to manoeuvre carefully.

'Yes, it is a strange land. In our hills we do not eat fish, as it is against our religion.'

'Then will you partake of bread and of cheese made by our servants from the finest goat's milk?'

'Yes.' Anything to escape those fatty pieces lying so near!

The old woman finished her meal and took up a tin bowl of milk, calling the while softly. She now reached behind her bed and brought a snake up on to the clothes, putting the bowl beside it. Its coils unwound slowly. It raised its head and finally put its mouth into the milk.

'This,' said the woman, 'is one of the Hindustan fishes I saved from the pot.'

My Khyber Marriage

PATRIZIA CHEN

*Two styles of cooking prevailed in Patrizia Chen's household in
Livorno after the Second World War. Upstairs was a vanilla world
of safe white food, while downstairs was the secret realm of garlic,
herbs and spices. It was here that Chen learned kitchen secrets at the
elbow of the beloved family cook, Emilia. Like most children,
Patrizia loved hearing frightening and repulsive stories.*

My absolutely favorite horror story concerned the revolting habits of
Papà's Sicilian cook from his childhood. '*Dai, Papà!* Please tell me again
about Donna Micia and her celebrated *polpette!*' The story's lurid details
would flow freely from his lips, almost at my first plea. My reaction
never disappointed him.

'When I was a child, maybe six or seven,' my father would start, 'I
used to sneak out of the house into the garden to peep through the
kitchen windows. In those days, children were not allowed to spend
time with the help, but I was fascinated by what I had discovered and
never reported to my parents.'

At this point, I would settle even more comfortably in my chair,
sinking with pleasure into a delicious quiver of anticipated disgust,
knowing that the stomach-turning details were about to be delivered.

Nonno Federico, well known for his bizarre habits, wanted his dinners served in the garden without exception at six-thirty, electing to eat
certain dishes and only certain dishes. Eating in the bright, hot, early
evening hours was a disaster in quasi-tropical Sicily, especially in the
summer, but my goodnatured grandmother obliged, fanning herself in
her formal evening gowns under the sweltering sun. Donna Micia's
meatballs were Nonno's favorite recipe, and he raved about them to his
family and friends.

These *polpette* indeed had a special taste. Was the cook using some
secret ingredients? Rare herbs, a special spice? They had a salty tangi-
ness he had never encountered before. One day, my father happened to
pass in front of the kitchen windows and witnessed the unthinkable,

unmentionable truth. 'I happened to observe the most horrifying sight. I stood frozen, hypnotized like a mouse in front of a python!' After a clever pause, knowing perfectly well that I knew the story and just wanted to hear it again and again to delight in the euphoria of being shocked, he would ask, 'What do you think I saw?'

'Please, Papà, please continue!' I begged.

'I saw big, dark, hairy Donna Micia, wearing her usual ample black skirt and a sleeveless top. It was summer and as usual Sicily was scorchingly hot, not a *filo d'aria* was circulating in the huge kitchen. Donna Micia sweated profusely while rolling the little *polpettine* in her thick hands, shaping them with her expert fingers. After shaping each *polpetta* into a perfect roll, before coating it in flour and dropping it into the frying pan, she would quickly pass it under her hairy armpits, where it picked up the pearls of her summer labor.'

Rosemary and Bitter Oranges

HOLLIS CLAYSON

Art historian Hollis Clayson writes about the food crisis in Paris during the Prussian siege.

To the degree that the Prussian siege of Paris is remembered at all today, it is recalled as a crisis of food. The event survives as a cluster of food legends, as the mythic and repellent moment in the life of a world-class gourmet culture when hungry Parisians were reduced to eating rats, cats, dogs, and even animals from the city zoo. The large number of visual images that address this theme speaks to the unprecedented emphasis that fell upon the everyday realms of eating and grocery shopping. Indeed, the lion's share of representations of the siege address the hunt for food or the availability of strange foods . . .

[T]he famous menus composed entirely from the flesh of animals from the Jardin d'Acclimatation were the results of ingenious exhibitionism rather than necessity. Indeed, the elephants, yaks, and zebras were all sold at high prices to Courtier and DeBoos, elite merchant butchers located on the chic Boulevard Haussmann. The fiction of need disguised and enabled a daring and profitable commerce in slaughtered-to-order exotic animals. Gustave Doré's drawing *Maison Debos [sic] Boulevard Haussmann,* which precedes the elephant picture in his sketchbook, shows that he grasped the discretionary nature of the sale of exotic foods on the Boulevard Haussmann. His drawing shows the gentry ogling slaughtered animals in chic surroundings . . .

People who were able to prepare a rat for the table were well-off enough to purchase other food. The poor preferred cat or dog meat. Cooking a rat, usually prepared as a paté or a *salmis,* required access to the technologies of the highest levels of *haute cuisine.* The rich ate rat not because they had to, but 'because of what they were, and [that] was revealed in the Franco-Prussian war . . . Eating rat was a clever, self-mocking send-up of the French at table that showed the world that they had not forgotten who they were.' Therefore, under the circumstances, a claim to have eaten a rat might have passed as an emblem of patriotism, but the smell of elephant meat on the breath was a less-stable marker of cuisinary nationalism.

Paris in Despair: Art and Everyday Life Under Siege 1870–71

LAURA SHAPIRO

I have only made carrot-and-raisin salad once, the day it was taught to me in seventh grade, but the memory of those bright orange shreds specked with raisins and clotted with mayonnaise has been unaccountably hard to shake. It's easy to understand why the recipe appealed to the teacher – carrots made it nutritious, raisins made it sweet, and mayonnaise made it a salad – but I can't explain why a combination I never hoped to eat again was able to lodge itself so firmly into the apparatus of my adolescence. Perhaps those endless Wednesday-afternoon classes, known by 1958 as 'Homemaking,' had a grip on us that we hardly suspected at the time, codifying as they did a grim and witless set of expectations that loomed across the future like a ten commandments for girls. Eerily enough, this course, which purported to be about the real world, had nothing whatever to do with anything that happened in my home or that I had ever seen happen anywhere else. Why were they claiming life was like this? Who on earth wore pink cotton 'hostess aprons' or, worse yet, had to sew them?

Perfection Salad: Women and Cooking at the Turn of the Century

SUE GRAFTON

When I got back to the Hacienda, I went into the office to check for telephone messages. Arlette had four, but three of them turned out to be from Charlie Scorsoni. She leaned an elbow on the counter, munching on something sticky and dark brown enclosed in cookie dough.

'What is that thing?'

'Trimline Diet Snack Bar,' she said. 'Six calories each.' Some of the filling seemed to be stuck to her teeth like dental putty and she ran a finger along her gums, popping goo into her mouth again. 'Look at this label. I bet there's not one natural ingredient in this entire piece of food. Milk powder, hydrogenated fat, powdered egg, and a whole list of chemicals and additives. But you know what? I've noticed real food doesn't taste as good as fake. Have you noticed that? It's just a fact of life. Real food is bland, watered-down tasting. You take a supermarket tomato. Now it's pathetic what that tastes like,' she said and shuddered. I was trying to sort through my messages but she was making it hard.

'I bet this isn't even real flour in this thing,' she said. 'I mean, I've heard people say junk food just has empty calories, but who needs full ones? I like 'em empty. That way I figure I can't gain any more weight.'

A Is for Alibi

AGATHA CHRISTIE
1890–1976

The following recipe comes from a cookery book published by the Ministry of Food to help women cope with wartime rationing. The other contributors included Joyce Grenfell, Stella Gibbons, Marie Stopes and Rebecca West.

OMELET AGATHA CHRISTIE

(Enough for 5 or 6 people)

½ lb mushrooms
A little margarine
Jar of shrimps
¼ lb cooked ham or tongue

6 eggs
Pepper and salt
Dessertspoonful of olive
   oil or small lump of
   butter or margarine

Method: Peel mushrooms and cook in a closed casserole with a little margarine, either in moderate oven or on a very low gas. When tender, add a jar of shrimps and ham, or tongue, cut up in small pieces. Keep warm and make omelet by breaking eggs into bowl and beating up lightly with fork (not whisk). Add pepper and salt, put olive oil or butter or margarine in large frying-pan. When steaming hot pour in eggs, stir round once or twice and let set. Take off flame, put filling mixture on one-half of omelet and fold other half over. Slip off on to dish. Serve at once.

If liked, small tin of cream of mushroom soup can be thickened with a little cornflour and poured over as sauce.

A Kitchen Goes to War

SUSAN FERRIER
1782–1854

The family group had already assembled round the breakfast table, with the exception of Lady Juliana, who chose to take that meal in bed: but, contrary to her usual custom, no Lady Maclaughlan had yet made her appearance. All was busy speculation and surmise as to the *could-be* cause of this lapse of time on the part of that hitherto most perfect of morning chronometers. Scouts had been sent ever and anon to spy, to peep, to listen; but nothing was brought back but idle guesses and shallow conjectures. It had, however, been clearly ascertained that Sir Sampson had been heard to cough and find fault with Murdoch in the dressing-room, and Lady Maclaughlan to humph! in her sternial tone, as she walked to and fro in her chamber. So far all was well. But for Lady Maclaughlan still to be in her chamber twenty minutes after the breakfast-bell had rung – 'twas strange – 'twas passing strange!

'The scones will be like leather,' said Miss Grizzy, in her most doleful accent, as she wrapped another napkin round them.

'The eggs will be like snow-balls,' cried Miss Jacky, warmly, popping them into the slop-basin.

'The tea will be like brandy,' observed Miss Nicky, sharply, as she poured more water to the three tea spoonfuls she had infused.

Marriage

CHARLOTTE BRONTË
1816–55

The refectory was a great, low-ceilinged, gloomy room; on two long tables smoked basins of something hot, which, however, to my dismay, sent forth an odour far from inviting. I saw a universal manifestation of discontent when the fumes of the repast met the nostrils of those destined to swallow it; from the van of the procession, the tall girls of the first class, rose the whispered words—

'Disgusting! The porridge is burnt again!'

'Silence!' ejaculated a voice; not that of Miss Miller, but one of the upper teachers, a little and dark personage smartly dressed, but of somewhat morose aspect, who installed herself at the top of one table, while a more buxom lady presided at the other. I looked in vain for her I had first seen the night before; she was not visible. Miss Miller occupied the foot of the table where I sat, and a strange, foreign-looking, elderly lady, the French teacher, as I afterwards found, took the corresponding seat at the other board. A long grace was said and a hymn sung; then a servant brought in some tea for the teachers, and the meal began.

Ravenous, and now very faint, I devoured a spoonful or two of my portion without thinking of its taste; but the first edge of hunger blunted, I perceived I had got in hand a nauseous mess: burnt porridge is almost as bad as rotten potatoes; famine itself soon sickens over it. The spoons were moved slowly; I saw each girl taste her food and try to swallow it; but in most cases the effort was soon relinquished. Breakfast was over and none had breakfasted. Thanks being returned for what we had not got, and a second hymn chanted, the refectory was evacuated for the schoolroom. I was one of the last to go out, and in passing the tables, I saw one teacher take a basin of the porridge and taste it; she looked at the others; all their countenances expressed displeasure, and one of them, the stout one, whispered— 'Abominable stuff! How shameful!'

Jane Eyre

ELISABETH RUSSELL TAYLOR

The hero of I Is Another *is an English chef encouraged by his ambitious Swiss wife to reinterpret* la grande cuisine, *following in the
steps of the great French masters*.

During the first flush of Sabine's enthusiasm for her literary luncheons,
I well remember the Jane Austen occasion, for I particularly resented
having to prepare that meal. I was asked for ox-cheek and dumplings
and baked *everything*: apples, custard, biscuits. And a sweetbread fricas-
see and a boiled (*sic*) fowl with oyster sauce. The rest escapes me, as well
it might. So disturbed by these concoctions, I was curious to see the
members of the Jane Austen Society tucking in. They appeared as inel-
egant as the food they specified. The young women were without
make-up, in pleated skirts, twin-sets and sensible shoes. They were
accompanied by rather older men with loud, piping voices, dressed in
heavy tweeds, some with garish waistcoats, all with watch-chains.

I felt more in harmony with Nana's dinner for the Zola Society. Zola
had taken the precaution to include the menu of an actual meal in his
novel, one prepared at Brébant's, a popular restaurant with the
Bohemian society of Paris in the 1880s. The menu was well balanced
and conveyed well-being. Other groups, societies and dining-clubs
attached to other authors involved me in the less rewarding tasks I had
undertaken for the Jane Austen Society. I am reminded, particularly, of
the Trollope Diners, the Walter Scott Table (Bag-pudding, Loch Fyne
herrings and boiled sheep's head), the Virginia Woolf Association and
the Pope and Thackeray Clubs. Then there was the Roman dinner,
dedicated to Hera, taken from the *Chansons de geste*, involving roasted
peacock with pepper sauce and gilded egg yolks . . .

The preparation of the medieval feasts gave me little satisfaction.
The taste of the dishes was repulsive to my palate. Dates do *not* enhance
salmon and eels, figs are *not* improved by being prepared with pepper
and ginger, and I do not like fruit pies to be seasoned with herbs. And
far too much emphasis is placed on the appearance of food in this period

of history. I did as I was asked, none the less. I refeathered the fowl to make them appear alive, but with their claws and beaks gleaming with gold (it was only paper). I served the birds on huge pewter platters with golden apples (meat balls wrapped in more of the same paper) with tinted green pastry leaves. I had spit-roasted the suckling-deer whole. Lying on its bed of watercress, it reminded me of a domestic cat luxuriating in the sun. I felt quite sick.

I Is Another

JENNIFER BRENNAN

Jennifer Brennan was raised in the Punjab and Mysore during the colonial period in India. Her earliest culinary memories are of sensual textures, vivid colours and pungent aromas. Laurie Colwin called Curries and Bugles *'One of the great cookbooks of all time'. In this extract, Brennan's mother is speaking.*

I was a new bride, in fact it was the first dinner party that Daddy and I attended after we were married. It was, of course, the social custom to give the newly married lady precedence over other, more senior women. The dessert was served, and it was the usual large basket of fruit all encased in spun sugar, like Venetian glass. I was in conversation with the man next to me, and the hostess signalled that I should commence helping myself. Still in conversation, I tapped the basket smartly with my spoon, to break off some of the caramel to eat along with my fruit, and it broke . . . but it wasn't caramel, it was the real thing, Venetian glass, and there I was, left with this big chunk of valuable glass in my hand!

Curries and Bugles

LADY JEKYLL
1860–1937

A blue-blooded and conservative marquis may be forgiven his temporary loss of self-control when the newly-engaged cook sent on its gay
career round a decorous dinner-party of county neighbours a transparent and highly decorated pink ice pudding concealing within inmost
recesses a fairy light and a musical box playing the 'Battle of Prague.'
Words were spoken, and, like the chord of self in Locksley Hall, this
over-elaborated creation 'passed in music out of sight.' . . .

Over-elaboration then, even in our kindest cooks, must be discour-
aged: games of dominoes played in truffles over the chicken cream,
birds' nests counterfeited round the poached eggs, jazzing jellies, and
castellated cakes show misdirection of energy. Not that an occasional
exception may not prove the rule – let it be made on behalf of *Gelée
Crème de Menthe*, an emerald-green pool, set in a flat glass bowl, reminiscent of Sabrina fair in her home below translucent waves, or of Capri
caverns, cool and deep; whilst the delicate aroma of peppermint will
recall to Presbyterian minds those Sabbath indulgences practised by
young and old at kirk in far-off Highland glens.

Kitchen Essays

ELISABETH VIGÉE-LE BRUN
1755–1842

During my pregnancy I had painted the Duchess de Mazarin, who was
no longer young, but still beautiful. My daughter had the same kind of
eyes and resembled her amazingly. This Duchess de Mazarin was said to
have been endowed at her birth by three fairies: Riches, Beauty, and
Ill-Luck. It is perfectly true that the poor woman could never under-
take anything, not even giving a party, without some misfortune or
other turning up. Many misfortunes of her life have been related, but
here is one less known: One evening while entertaining sixty persons

to supper, she contrived to have on the table an enormous pie, in which a hundred small birds were shut up alive. At a sign from the Duchess the pie was opened and all the frantic little creatures flew out, dashing into faces and clinging to the hair of the women, who were all carefully attired and hair-dressed. You can imagine the tempers, the shouts! The unfortunate birds could not be got rid of, and were such a nuisance that the guests were obliged to leave the table, cursing such a foolish flight of fancy.

Memoirs
trans. by Gerard Shelley

BARBARA PYM
1913–80

[Jane] was to meet Prudence at a quarter to one and found that when she got to Piccadilly she still had some time to spare. So, in anticipation of lunch or perhaps to tantalise herself by looking at dainties she would most certainly not be eating, she wandered into a large provision store and moved slowly from counter to counter, her feet sinking into the thick carpet, her senses bemused by the semi-darkness and the almost holy atmosphere. She finally stopped in the middle of the floor before a stand which was given over to a display of *foie gras*, packed in terrines of creamy pottery, some of them ornamented with pictures.

A tall man, rather too grandly dressed for his function, Jane thought, came up to her.

'Can I help you, madam?' he asked quietly.

'Well, now, I wonder if you could,' said Jane.

'I shall certainly endeavour to, madam,' said the man gravely.

'The point is this. How can a clergyman's wife afford to buy *foie gras*?'

'It would seem to be difficult,' said the man respectfully. 'Let us see now.' He took down a card from the stand. 'The smallest size is fourteen and ninepence.'

'Yes,' said Jane. 'I saw that. But I shouldn't really want the smallest size. Those large decorated jars have taken my fancy.'

'Ah, madam, those are one hundred and seventeen shillings,' said the salesman, rolling the words round his tongue.

'Well, I'm sorry to have wasted your time like this,' said Jane, moving away. 'I should like to have bought some.'

'To tell you the truth, madam, I don't care for it myself,' said the salesman, bowing Jane out of the door, 'and my wife doesn't either.'

Jane and Prudence

SIGNORA BAROSI
20th century

First published in 1932, The Futurist Cookbook was described by Elizabeth David as a 'publication of preposterous new dishes'. It was the brainchild of the Italian Futurist Filippo Tommaso Marinetti, a manifesto for revitalising Italian culture by changing the way Italians ate, and one of the biggest artistic jokes of the twentieth century. Nourishment and taste were totally unimportant as far as the recipes' ingredients were concerned; what mattered was their colour, shape or tactile qualities. Surprising and bizarre combinations such as the one that follows were intended to shock and reawaken the palate and to drag the diners into a futuristic age. Only two women contributed to the cookbook. Traidue means literally 'between the two' – in this case a sandwich.

SWEET AND STRONG

A *traidue* of two slices of bread and butter, spread with mustard and enclosing bananas and anchovies.

The Futurist Cookbook
trans. by Suzanne Brill

MARGARET ATWOOD

In Atwood's first novel, Marion gets engaged – and loses her appetite.
She finds it again when she bakes a cake in the form of a woman.

Suddenly she was hungry. Extremely hungry. The cake after all was
only a cake. She picked up the platter, carried it to the kitchen table
and located a fork. 'I'll start with the feet,' she decided.

She considered the first mouthful. It seemed odd but most pleasant to
be actually tasting and chewing and swallowing again. Not bad, she
thought critically; needs a touch more lemon though . . .

She was halfway up the legs when she heard footsteps, two sets of
them, coming up the stairs. Then Ainsley appeared in the kitchen
doorway with Fischer Symthe's furry head behind her . . .

'Hi,' said Marian, waving her fork at them. She speared a chunk of
pink thigh and carried it to her mouth.

Fischer had leaned against the wall and closed his eyes as soon as he
reached the top of the stairs, but Ainsley focussed on her. 'Marian,
what have you got there?' She walked over to see. 'It's a woman – a
woman made of cake!' She gave Marian a strange look.

Marian chewed and swallowed. 'Have some,' she said, 'it's really
good. I made it this afternoon.'

Ainsley's mouth opened and closed, fishlike, as though she was trying
to gulp down the full implication of what she saw. 'Marian!' she
exclaimed at last, with horror. 'You're rejecting your femininity!'

Marian stopped chewing and stared at Ainsley, who was regarding
her through the hair that festooned itself over her eyes with wounded
concern, almost with sternness. How did she manage it, that stricken
attitude, that high seriousness? She was almost as morally earnest as the
lady down below.

Marian looked back at her platter. The woman lay there, still smiling
glassily, her legs gone. 'Nonsense,' she said. 'It's only a cake.' She plunged
her fork into the carcass, neatly severing the body from the head.

The Edible Woman

AMUSE-BOUCHES

BARBARA GRIZZUTI HARRISON
1934–2002

I refuse to believe that trading recipes is silly. Tunafish casserole is at least as real as corporate stock.

Visions of Glory

VIRGINIA WOOLF
1882–1941

'One cannot think well, love well, sleep well, if one has not dined well.'

A Room of One's Own

EDITH SITWELL
1887–1964

To Rée Gorer

Renishaw Hall

24 December 1942

Darling Rée,

. . . My beloved parent has succeeded in getting out of Italy, and making his way to Switzerland, accompanied by a nurse. There, he is teaching an unfortunate pair who scarcely knew him, before the war, what life can be. The wife is the daughter of that world-scourge, Inez Chandos-Pole, the husband is a charming, practical, quiet Swiss. The old gentleman simply descended on them like a blight. He inhabits their house, he has changed all their modes of existence. He won't let them go to bed at night, because he wishes them to sit up with him; he insists on having a hot meal of roast chicken at 4 o'clock in the morning, so that the cook has to sit up too; and when he wants anything expensive and they say that they have no money, he makes a clucking sound, puts his head on one side, tossing it irritably, and says, 'I'm afraid I can't help that!'

Letters

HSIANG JU LIN
TSUIFENG LIN
20th century

OPULENT
(suitable for visiting dignitaries, merchant princes and rich relatives)
Shark's Fins with Crab Sauce
  Happy Family
    Stuffed Duck
      Whole Chicken Stuffed with Bird's Nest
        Pastry Peaches

PSEUDO-RUSTIC
(suitable for artists, gourmets, noted authors)
Black Hen Soup, with Black Mushrooms
  Tungpo Pork, with Pinwheels
    Soochow Cabbage Stew
      Duck Steamed in Wine
        Sweet Bird's Nest

RECHERCHÉ
(for entertaining good cooks and distinguished company)
Bêche-de-mer Gourmet
> *Crisp Spiced Duck, with Buns*
>> *Bird's Nest with Bean Sprouts*
>>> *Carp in Lamb Broth*
>>>> *Silver Fungus with Candy Sugar Syrup*

THE BEST
(neither too showy nor mock simple, it is excellent for all occasions)
Velvet Chicken I
> *Prawn (Shrimp) Balls*
>> *Peking Duck*
>>> *Minute Beef*
>>>> *Steamed Fish*
>>>>> *Peking Dust**

*A mound of chestnut purée covered with whipped cream.

Chinese Gastronomy

ALICE WATERS

Thursday May 28 1987

Poached sea bass vinaigrette
with garden vegetables

Pigeon and spring garlic soup

Charcoal-grilled veal chop from
Summerfield farm

Garden salad

Apricot and cherry tart
with vanilla ice cream

Dinner forty-five dollars

Menu from Chez Panisse

KATE BURRIDGE

Recently I was thumbing through various collections hunting for obscure words describing food. I came upon a truly extraordinary lost lexicon of gastronomy. Of course, there were many names of now unknown dishes like *pottage*, *mortrews*, *buknade* and *civet* (all porridge-like substances). The necessity in medieval times to smash, pulp and spice food beyond recognition makes many early dishes appear now quite unappetizing. Small wonder these disappeared. But what happened to the *flurch of flampoints*, I want to know, the *licious lozens*, the *fitchet pies*? The descriptions under these throw flashes of light on past luxurious banquets, gastronomic galas and superb cooks. Among these forgotten terms are *opsophagist* 'frequenter of pastry shops'; *symposiast* 'one of a drinking party, banqueter'; *pabulous* 'abounding in food'; *eubrotic* 'good to eat'; *orectic* 'characterized by appetite or desire'; *esculent* 'good to eat'; *deipnetic* 'fond of eating'; *pamphagous* 'omnivorous'; *coenaculous* 'fond of suppers'; *gulch* 'to swallow hungrily', and *pinguedinize* 'to make fat'. The entries under *pabulous comessations* and *dapatical ebrieties* say it all. Many such valuable and interesting words have vanished. I've grown attached to *smellfeast* 'the uninvited dinner guest' and *shotclog* 'the companion tolerated because he or she pay for drinks'. *Potvaliant* is a wonderful word for someone who's courageous through drink. However, my current favourite would have to be *supernaculum*, a word referring to the act of drinking the very last drop from a glass or bottle. How can we do without it?

Blooming English

KATHERINE MANSFIELD
1888–1923

It grew hot. Everywhere the light quivered green-gold. The white soft road unrolled, with plane-trees casting a trembling shade. There were piles of pumpkins and gourds: outside the house the tomatoes were spread in the sun. Blue flowers and red flowers and tufts of deep purple flared in the roadside hedges. A young boy, carrying a branch, stumbled across a yellow field, followed by a brown high-stepping little goat. We bought figs for breakfast, immense thin-skinned ones. They broke in one's fingers and tasted of wine and honey. Why is the northern fig such a chaste fair-haired virgin, such a soprano? The melting contraltos sing through the ages.

Journal

EDITH SITWELL
1887–1964

To J.R. Ackerley

Montegufoni

18 September 1954

Dear Joe,

[. . .] I hope you will have as wonderful weather as we are having for your holiday. (I hardly dare mention the weather.) With the exception of one day of raging thunder storms we have been able to lunch and dine out every day, and we eat figs that are really almost the size of small melons, and with seas of honey in them.

Yours
Edith

Letters

SYDNEY OWENSON, LADY MORGAN
c. 1783–1859

Everywhere are spread the fantastic stalls of the fruiterer, and the *aqua-jolo*, the iced-water vendor, all flowers and foliage, supported by cupids and angels, surmounted with a Madonna in heaven or sinners in purgatory, and streaming with flags of gilt paper and red stuff. Half-naked beggars stop to *ber fresco*, drink cold, or eat an ice, confidently trusted to them with a silver spoon, by the merchants they habitually deal with . . . the pavement is strewn with mounds of oranges, and the air resounds with that acute Babel-like noise which belongs exclusively to Naples.

Italy

MARINA WARNER

In the 17th century the general opinion of herbalists and botanists and connoisseurs of simples was that the banana was the strongest candidate for the original tree of the knowledge of good and evil.

No Go the Bogeyman

SYLVIA PLATH
1932–63

I should sugar and preserve my days like fruit!

'Last Words'

JANE AUSTEN
1775–1817

FROM HANS PLACE TO CASSANDRA AT CHAWTON

17 October 1815

I am glad the new cook begins so well. Good apple pies are a consider-able part of our domestic happiness.

Letters

HSIANG JU LIN
TSUIFENG LIN
20th century

The luxury-loving Empress [Yang Kweifei] was blamed for the downfall of the Tang dynasty. She loved fresh lichees, which were shipped to her by a kind of pony express from the South to Changan, the capital of Tang in central China. She paid dearly for her extravagances, being forced to hang herself during a revolution. There is also a dish named after her (Kweifei Chicken). The plump, white, voluptuous Empress loved to drink, and the dish consists of a plump white chicken mari-nated in a great deal of alcohol, fried, stewed with wine and then sauced with more wine. What woman wants to be so represented? A subtle insult.

Chinese Gastronomy

ELLA EATON KELLOGG
1853–1920

Peas were introduced into England from Holland in the time of Elizabeth, and were then considered a great delicacy. History tells us that when the queen was released from her confinement in the tower, May 19, 1554, she went to Staining to perform her devotions in the church of Allhallows, after which she dined at a neighboring inn upon a meal of which the principal dish was boiled peas. A dinner of the same kind, commemorative of the event, was for a long time given annually at the same tavern.

Science in the Kitchen

EDITH TEMPLETON

Surely, no right-thinking person would forgo willingly the excitement of deflowering the artichoke. As leaf after leaf is stripped away, the texture becomes more tender and the flavour changes. Slowly, as the innermost leaves are reached, one finds that their fleshy part is creamy and pale, with a melting taste which is exquisite. Eating an artichoke is like watching a dance of the seven veils. When the last wreath is peeled off from its base there is the last obstacle to overcome; the centre full of strawy threads which must be scraped away carefully so as not to injure the tender heart underneath.

Most people eat the heart with a fork. I think this is wrong. In any case, if a fork is used, it must be of silver. But better still is to eat it by hand.

The Surprise of Cremona

MARGARET VISSER

Cannibals themselves often regard the eating of human flesh in general with awe and horror; it is ritually marked off from regular eating. The ancient Fijians, for example, ate everyday meals with their hands; when it came to eating human flesh, and only then, they used a special wooden fork.

*

People have always longed to fling food at each other, and to smash the crockery. Louis XIV (he who ruled over the etiquette of Versailles) is said to have baited his brother, the august Monsieur, by splashing soup at his wig until Monsieur lost his temper and flung his bowl of boiled beef at the king.

*

It is a universal temptation to play with food before eating it. People pick their sandwich cookies open and scrape the filling off with their teeth; they make themselves rules about when and how to prick the yoke [*sic*] of a fried egg; they twirl and squish ice cream on their cones, pushing it down inside with their tongues and then eating the cone from the point up.

The Rituals of Dinner

EMILY BRONTË
1818–48

We always ate our meals with Mr. Heathcliff. I held the mistress's post in making tea and carving; so I was indispensable at table. Catherine usually sat by me; but to-day she stole nearer to Hareton, and I presently saw she would have no more discretion in her friendship, than she had in her hostility.

'Now, mind you don't talk with and notice your cousin too much,' were my whispered instructions as we entered the room. 'It will certainly annoy Mr. Heathcliff, and he'll be mad at you both.'

'I'm not going to,' she answered.

The minute after, she had sidled to him, and was sticking primroses in his plate of porridge.

Wuthering Heights

DARRA GOLDSTEIN

Gathered around the feast table, Georgians like to retell the tales of how their land was made. One of their favorite creation myths finds the first Georgians seated under a pergola at a table laden with wine and food. So engrossed are they in feasting on grilled lamb with plum sauce and garlicky roasted eggplant that they miss God's deadline for choosing a country, and the world is divided up without them. His task complete, God sets off for home, only to find the Georgians still merrily toasting and singing. God stops to reproach them for their negligence, but the *tamada*, the toastmaster, is not worried that the Georgians have no place to live. They have spent their time well, he explains, thanking God in lavish toasts for having created such a magnificent world. Pleased that the Georgians have not forgotten Him, God rewards them with the very last spot on earth, the one He had been saving for Himself. And so it was that the Georgians came to live in paradise.

Another myth is slightly less reverent. While creating the world, God wisely took a break for supper. But He became so involved in His meal that He inadvertently tripped over the high peaks of the Caucasus range, spilling a little of everything from His plate onto the land below. So it was that Georgia came to be blessed with such riches, table scraps from Heaven.

The Georgian Feast

LAURA SCHENONE

This idea that a woman's very body brings forth edible plants to the world was quite popular among agricultural tribes of the eastern woodlands of North America. Here, women were the chief farmers of their tribes, presiding over the seeds, the fields, and the crops. According to the Seneca, the first potatoes of the world sprang from a woman's feet; beans came from her fingers, squash from her abdomen, tobacco from her head, maize from her breasts. The Creek say that a woman created the first corn by rubbing her feet. The Cherokee tell us of Selu, who rubbed her stomach to fill her basket half with corn, and then her armpits to fill it to the top with beans.

Selu, whose name in Cherokee means 'corn,' offers an archetype for Corn Mother, one of the greatest deities of North America whose legacy exists, in one form or another, from present-day Maine to the Southwest. In all these sacred stories, it is women who bring the most sacred food – corn – to the world and its people.

A Thousand Years Over a Hot Stove

FLORENCE WHITE
1863–1940

One of the most interesting results of research into English Folk Cookery is the revelation of the number of great commercial enterprises that have originated in the good cooking in the kitchen, still-room or dairy of some one woman.

The following are a few examples:

1. *Stilton cheese*. Lady Beaumont's cheese, the receipt for which was taken by Elizabeth Scarbrow, the housekeeper when she married from Quenby Hall, seven miles from Leicester, to Little Dalby . . .

2. *Huntley and Palmer's Biscuits*. Mrs. Huntley was the wife of a Quaker schoolmaster, who had a boys' school at Burford, early in the nineteenth century . . .

3. *Everton Toffee*. This was made by Molly Bush, at Everton, a suburb of Liverpool . . .
4. *Romary's Wafer Biscuits*. Tunbridge Wells.
5. *Harvey's Sauce*.

  Good Things in England: A Practical Cookery Book for Everyday Use

PIERETTE BRILLAT-SAVARIN
1755–1826

'Bring on the dessert . . . I think I am about to die.'

  Great-aunt of Brillat-Savarin, shortly before her 100th birthday

FURTHER READING

Aresty, Esther B., *The Delectable Past: The Joys of the Table, from Rome to the Renaissance, from Queen Elizabeth I to Mrs Beeton: The Menus, the Manners and the Most Delectable Recipes of the Past, Masterfully Recreated for Cooking and Enjoying Today*, Simon and Schuster, New York 1964

Bober, Phyllis Pray, *Art, Culture and Cuisine: Ancient and Medieval Gastronomy*, University of Chicago Press, Chicago 2001

Bynum, Caroline Walker, *Holy Feast and Holy Fast: The Religious Significance of Food to Mediaeval Women*, University of California Press, Berkeley 1987

Davidson, Alan (ed.), *The Wilder Shores of Gastronomy: Twenty Years of Food Writing from the Journal 'Petits Propos Culinaires'*, Ten Speed Press, Berkeley 2002

Feeding America: The Historic American Cookbook Project, Michigan State University Library http://digital.lib.msu.edu/projects/cookbooks/index.html.

McGee, Diane, *Writing the Meal: Dinner in the Fiction of Early Twentieth-Century Women Writers*, University of Toronto Press, Toronto 2001

Sceats, Sarah, *Food, Consumption and the Body in Contemporary Women's Fiction*, Cambridge University Press, Cambridge 2000

Schenone, Laura, *A Thousand Years Over a Hot Stove: A History of American Women Told Through Food, Recipes and Remembrances*, W.W. Norton & Co, Inc, New York 2003

Shapiro, Laura, *Perfection Salad: Women and Cooking at the Turn of the Century*, Farrar Straus Giroux, New York 1986

——, *Something From the Oven: Reinventing Dinner in 1950s America*, Viking, New York 2004

Tannahill, Reay, *Food in History*, Headline Review, London 2002

Theophano, Janet, *Eat My Words: Reading Women's Lives through the Cookbooks They Wrote*, Palgrave, New York and Houndmills, 2002

Visser, Margaret, *The Rituals of Dinner: The Origins, Evolution, Eccentricities and Meaning of Table Manners*, Penguin Books, Harmondsworth 1992

Blogs
banlieusardises.com
chocolateandzucchini.com
domesticgoddess.ca
eGullet.org
saucymag.com
thefoodsection.com
theory of the daily at http://web.utk.edu/~hwallac2/weblog

INDEX OF AUTHORS

ACKNOWLEDGEMENTS

I would like to thank the following individuals for their intriguing suggestions, support and, in one case, permission to use previously unpublished material: Tamsyn Berryman, Kristina Blagojevitch, Malcolm Bull, Jill Dupleix, Jean Foulston, Victoria Granof, Andy Hine, Sesyle Joslin, Tami Koenig, Michelle Lovric, Kathleen Mapel, Micki Mapel, Mark Meadow, Sheelagh Neuling, Jill Norman, Susanna Pinney, Marcia Reed, Elisabeth Russell Taylor, Imogen Taylor, Charles Thompson, Junnaa Wroblewski, Ornella Tarantola, Tatiana Senkevitch, Andrew Wille.

I would also like to express my gratitude to the Getty Research Institute. The staff of the Interlibrary Loan department, who exhibited exemplary patience and efficiency in tracking down a variety of sources, deserve special mention.

How to Cook and Eat in Chinese by Buwei Yang Chao, reprinted courtesy of Random House, Inc. Copyright Buwei Yang Chao 1945, 1949, © 1963, 1970.

Rosemary and Bitter Oranges: Growing Up in a Tuscan Kitchen by Patrizia Chen, reprinted courtesy of Virago Press and Scribner, an imprint of Simon & Schuster Adult Publishing Group. Copyright © Patrizia Chen 2003.

Mastering the Art of French Cooking, vol. I, by Julia Child, Louisette Bertholle and Simone Beck, reprinted courtesy of Alfred A. Knopf, a division of Random House, Inc. Copyright © Alfred A. Knopf, a division of Random House, Inc 1961.

'Omelet Agatha Christie' from *A Kitchen Goes to War: A Ration-Time Cookery Book with 150 Recipes by Famous People*, published by John Miles, Ltd in 1940, reprinted courtesy of Agatha Christie Estate.

Sally Clarke's Book: Recipes from a Restaurant, Shop & Bakery, reprinted courtesy of Macmillan Publishers Ltd. Copyright © Sally Clarke 1999.

Paris in Despair: Art and Everyday Life under Siege (1870–71) by Hollis Clayson, reprinted courtesy of the University of Chicago Press. Copyright © The University of Chicago 2002.

My Mother's House and Sido by Colette, translated by Una Vincenzo Troubridge and Enid McLeod, reprinted courtesy of Farrar, Straus and Giroux, LLC and Secker & Warburg, an imprint of The Random House Group Ltd. Translation copyright © Farrar, Straus & Young 1953, renewed © Farrar, Straus & Giroux, Inc 1981.

Letters from Colette selected and translated by Robert Phelps, reprinted courtesy of Farrar Straus & Giroux, LLC. Translation copyright © Farrar Straus & Giroux 1980.

Home Cooking: A Writer in the Kitchen by Laurie Colwin, reprinted courtesy of Donadio & Olson, Inc and Alfred A. Knopf, a division of Random House, Inc. Copyright © Laurie Colwin 1988.

Sisters by a River by Barbara Comyns, reprinted courtesy of Virago Press and Johnson & Alcock Ltd. Copyright © The Estate of Barbara Comyns 1947.

Handbook of Cookery for a Small House by Jessie Conrad, published by William Heinemann Ltd in 1923.

In Love and War by Maria Corelli, reprinted courtesy of Short Books. Copyright © Maria Corelli 2001.

Four Seasons Cookery Book by Margaret Costa, reprinted courtesy of Grub Street Publishing. Copyright © Margaret Costa 1970.

Holiday in Barcelona and the Balearics by Bon Viveur, reprinted courtesy of Rosemary Bromley Literary Agency. Copyright © John and Phyllis Cradock 1954.

'The Missing Piece' from *Krik? Krak!* by Edwidge Danticat, reprinted courtesy of Soho Press Inc. Copyright © Edwidge Danticat 1991, 1992, 1993, 1994 and 1995.

Is There a Nutmeg in the House? by Elizabeth David, compiled by Jill Norman and reprinted courtesy of Jill Norman. Copyright © The Estate of Elizabeth David 2000.

Dying for Chocolate by Diane Mott Davidson, reprinted courtesy of Allison & Busby Ltd and Bantam Books, a division of Random House, Inc. Copyright © Diane Mott Davidson 1992.

The Mistress of Spices by Chitra Banerjee Divakaruni, reprinted courtesy of Anchor Books, a division of Random House, Inc. Copyright © Chitra Banerjee Divakaruni 1997.

Honey from a Weed by Patience Gray, reprinted courtesy of Prospect Books. Copyright © The Estate of Patience Gray 1986.

Jane Grigson's Fruit Book, by Jane Grigson, reprinted courtesy of David Higham Associates Ltd. Copyright © The Estate of Jane Grigson 1982.

Chocolat by Joanne Harris, reprinted courtesy of Doubleday, an imprint of Transworld Publishers, a division of The Random House Group Ltd and Viking Penguin, a division of Penguin Group (USA) Inc. Copyright © Joanne Harris 1999.

Food in England by Dorothy Hartley, reprinted courtesy of Virago Press and Sheil Land Associates Ltd on behalf of the Estate of Dorothy Hartley. Copyright © The Estate of Dorothy Hartley 1954.

The Little Madeleine by Mrs Robert Henrey, reprinted courtesy of J.M. Dent, a division of The Orion Publishing Group. Copyright © The Estate of Mrs Robert Henrey 1951.

Cooking for Mr Latte: A Food Lover's Courtship, with Recipes by Amanda Hesser, reprinted courtesy of the Doe Coover Agency and W.W. Norton & Company. Copyright © Amanda Hesser 2003.

Selected Writings by Hildegard of Bingen, translated by Mark Atherton, reprinted courtesy of Penguin Books Ltd. Translation and editorial matter copyright © Mark Atherton 2001.

Minnie, Lady Hindlip's Cookery Book, reprinted courtesy of Lord Hindlip.

The English Housewife in the Seventeenth Century by Christina Hole, reprinted courtesy of Johnson & Alcock Ltd. Copyright © Christina Hole 1953.

A Very Private Eye: An Autobiography in Diaries and Letters edited by Hazel Holt and Hilary Pym, reprinted courtesy of Macmillan Publishers Ltd. Copyright © Hazel Holt 1984.

'Making Jelly' from *Everything Begins with the Skin* by Sue Hubbard, reprinted courtesy of Enitharmon and Sue Hubbard. Copyright © Sue Hubbard 1994.

Indian Cooking by Madhur Jaffrey, reprinted courtesy of BBC Worldwide Ltd. Copyright © Madhur Jaffrey 1982.

Kitchen Essays: with Recipes and Their Occasions by Lady Agnes Jekyll, reprinted courtesy of Persephone Books.

Chinese Gastronomy by Hsiang Ju Lin and Tsuifeng Lin, reprinted courtesy of Hastings House/Daytrips Publishers. Copyright © Hsiang Ju Lin and Tsuifeng Lin 1969.

Simply British by Sybil Kapoor, reprinted courtesy of Sybil Kapoor. Copyright © Sybil Kapoor 1998.

The Moosewood Cookbook by Mollie Katzen, reprinted courtesy of Ten Speed Press, Berkeley, CA. www.tenspeed.com. Copyright © Mollie Katzen 1977, 1992.

The Sun in the Morning by M.M. Kaye, reprinted courtesy of David Higham Associates Ltd. Copyright © The Estate of M.M. Kaye 1990.

The Nancy Drew® Cookbook: Clues to Good Cooking by Carolyn Keene, reprinted courtesy of Simon & Schuster Children's Publishing Division. Copyright © Simon & Schuster 1973, renewed © 2001 by Simon & Schuster. NANCY DREW is a registered trademark of Simon & Schuster, Inc.

Bombers and Mash: The Domestic Front 1939–45 by Raynes Minns, reprinted courtesy of Virago Press and Johnson & Alcock Ltd. Copyright © Raynes Minns 1980.

'Banquet' by Joni Mitchell, reprinted courtesy of Sony/ATV Music Publishing Ltd. Copyright © Crazy Crow Music. Sony/ATV Music Publishing (UK) Ltd.

Beloved by Toni Morrison, reprinted courtesy of International Creative Management, Inc. Copyright © Toni Morrison 1987.

Monsoon Diary: A Memoir with Recipes by Shoba Narayan, reprinted courtesy of Villard Books, a division of Random House, Inc. Copyright © Shoba Narayan 2003.

'Sugarcake Bubble' by Grace Nichols from www.guyana.gwebooks.com.

'Like a Beacon' from *The Fat Black Woman's Poems* by Grace Nichols, reprinted courtesy of Virago Press. Copyright © Grace Nichols 1984.

The Merchant of Prato by Iris Origo, reprinted courtesy of Penguin Books Ltd and the Estate of Iris Origo. Copyright © The Estate of Iris Origo 1957, 1963.

'Mole Poblano and Turkey' by Elisabeth Lambert Ortiz, first published in *Petits Propos Culinaires* 3. Copyright © The Estate of Elisabeth Lambert Ortiz 1979.

How America Eats by Clementine Paddleford, reprinted courtesy of Scribner, an imprint of Simon & Schuster Adult Publishing Group, Inc. Copyright © The Estate of Clementine Paddleford 1960.

A Flower for My Mother by Clementine Paddleford, reprinted courtesy of Henry Holt & Company, LLC. Copyright © The Estate of Clementine Paddleford 1958.

Marguerite Patten's Post-War Kitchen: Nostalgic Food and Facts from 1945–1954, reprinted courtesy of Hamlyn, an imprint of the Octopus Publishing Group on behalf of Marguerite Patten. Copyright © Marguerite Patten 1998.

Guide for the Greedy by a Greedy Woman by Elizabeth Robins Pennell, published by John Lane the Bodley Head, Ltd in 1923.

'Last Words' from *Crossing the Water* by Sylvia Plath, reprinted courtesy of Faber & Faber Ltd and HarperCollins Publishers, Inc. Copyright © Ted Hughes 1971.

The Tale of Samuel Whiskers by Beatrix Potter, reprinted courtesy of Frederick Warne & Co. Copyright © Frederick Warne & Co 1908.

La Cucina by Lily Prior, reprinted courtesy of Black Swan, an imprint of Transworld Publishers, a division of The Random House Group Ltd and HarperCollins Publishers, Inc. Copyright © Lily Prior 2000.

Recipe for 'Honeymoon Special' sandwich by Alice Adams Proctor from *Wonder Sandwich Suggestions*, 1930, reprinted courtesy of Wonder Bread/Interstate Bakeries Corporation.

The Witch in History: Early Modern and Twentieth-Century Representations by Diane Purkiss, reprinted courtesy of Routledge, an imprint of the Taylor Francis Group. Copyright © Diane Purkiss 1996.

Excellent Women by Barbara Pym, reprinted courtesy of Jonathan Cape, an imprint of The Random House Group Ltd. Copyright © The Estate of Barbara Pym 1952.

A Glass of Blessings by Barbara Pym, reprinted courtesy of Jonathan Cape, an imprint of The Random House Group Ltd. Copyright © The Estate of Barbara Pym 1958.

News, 50 (summer 1985), reprinted courtesy of Leo Baeck Institute, New York.

A Thousand Years Over a Hot Stove: A History of American Women Told Through Food, Recipes and Remembrances by Laura Schenone, reprinted courtesy of Levine Greenberg Literary Agency, Inc and W.W. Norton & Company, Inc. Copyright © Laura Schenone 2003.

Women of Theresienstadt: Voices from a Concentration Camp by Ruth Schwertfeger, reprinted courtesy of Berg Publishers Limited. Translations copyright © Berg Publishers Limited 1988.

'Conclusion: A Leaf or Two of Lettuce' from *Perfection Salad: Women and Cooking at the Turn of the Century* by Laura Shapiro, reprinted courtesy of International Creative Management, Inc and Farrar, Straus and Giroux, LLC. Copyright © Laura Shapiro 1986.

In Memory's Kitchen: A Legacy from the Women of Terezin edited by Cara De Silva, translated by Bianca Steiner Brown, reprinted courtesy of Jason Aronson Inc, an imprint of Rowman & Littlefield Publishes, Inc. Copyright © Anny Stern, Cara De Silva and Bianca Steiner Brown 1996.

On Persephone's Island: A Sicilian Journal by Mary Taylor Simeti with drawings by Maria Vica Costarelli, reprinted courtesy of and Bantam Books, an imprint of Transworld Publishers, a division of The Random House Group Ltd and Alfred A. Knopf, a division of Random House, Inc. Copyright © Mary Taylor Simeti 1986.

Bitter Almonds: Recollections and Recipes from a Sicilian Girlhood by Mary Taylor Simeti and Maria Grammatico, reprinted courtesy of Bantam Books, an imprint of Transworld Publishers, a division of The Random House Group Ltd and Robert Cornfield Literary Agency. Copyright © Mary Taylor Simeti and Maria Grammatico 1994.

Selected Letters of Edith Sitwell edited by Richard Greene, reprinted courtesy of David Higham Associates Ltd. Copyright © F.T.S. Sitwell and Richard Greene.

A Sor Juana Anthology translated by Alan S. Trueblood, reprinted courtesy of Harvard University Press, Cambridge, Mass. Copyright © The President and Fellows of Harvard College 1988.

'The Roving Feast' by Marlena Spieler, first published in the *San Francisco Chronicle*, December 10th, 2003, reprinted courtesy of Marlena Spieler (www.marlenaspieler.com). Copyright © Marlena Spieler 2003.

The Constance Spry Cookery Book by Constance Spry and Rosemary Hume, reprinted courtesy of Grub Street Publishing. Copyright © Campana Holdings Ltd 2004.

Tender Buttons by Gertrude Stein, reprinted courtesy of David Higham Associates Ltd and Stanford G. Gann, Jr, Literary Executor of the Estate of Gertrude Stein.

'God as Pâtissier' by Patricia Storace, first published in *Condé Nast Traveler*, April 1995, reprinted courtesy of Patricia Storace. Copyright © Patricia Storace 1995.

Mrs Miniver by Jan Struther, reprinted courtesy of Virago Press and Curtis Brown Ltd, London. Copyright © The Estate of Jan Struther 1939.

The Joy Luck Club by Amy Tan, reprinted courtesy of Abner Stein and G.P. Putnam's Sons, a division of Penguin Putnam, Inc. Copyright © Amy Tan 1989.

Acknowledgements 405

Opal: Journal of an Understanding Heart by Opal Whiteley, arranged and adapted by Jane Boulton, published by Three Rivers Press, a division of Random House, Inc. Copyright © Jane Boulton. International copyright (outside the US) for all works of Opal Whiteley held by the University of London. Musical, literary and dramatic rights to *Opal: Journal of an Understanding Heart* held by Robert Lindsey Nassif.

Little House in the Big Woods by Laura Ingalls Wilder, reprinted courtesy of HarperCollins Publishers, Inc. Copyright Little House Heritage Trust 1932, 1960. Little House® is a registered trademark of HarperCollins Publishers, Inc.

The King of Capri by Jeanette Winterson reprinted courtesy of Bloomsbury Publishing. Copyright © Jeanette Winterson 2003.

The Passion by Jeanette Winterson reprinted courtesy of Bloomsbury Publishing and William Morris Agency, Inc. Copyright © Jeanette Winterson 1987.

A Room of One's Own by Virginia Woolf, reprinted courtesy of The Society of Authors as the Literary Representative of the Estate of Virginia Woolf, and Harcourt, Inc. Copyright 1929 by Harcourt, Inc, renewed 1957 by Leonard Woolf.

Love Lessons: A Wartime Diary by Joan Wyndham, reprinted courtesy of Virago Press and PFD on behalf of Joan Wyndham. Copyright © Joan Wyndham 1985.

Kitchen by Banana Yoshimoto, translated by Megan Backus, reprinted courtesy of Grove/Atlantic, Inc. Copyright © 1988 by Banana Yoshimoto. Translation copyright © Megan Backus 1993.

Every effort has been made to trace the copyright holders of the copyright material in this book and to provide correct details. Virago regrets any oversight and upon written notification will rectify any omission in future reprints or editions.

THE VIRAGO BOOK OF THE JOY OF SHOPPING

Edited by Jill Foulston

Shopping has always been an art, a chore, a pleasure – even a danger. It started at home and at fairs, with written orders for husbands, servants or suppliers to fill. The department stores in the nineteenth century turned shopping into an event, and coincided with a new freedom for women. Independent women travellers wandered through exotic foreign bazaars with a familiar zest for the enchanting, if useless, trinket.

As people began to shop more, novelists imagined them doing it. Jane Eyre cringes at Mr Rochester's pre-wedding excess, while The Girl with a Pearl Earring turns up her nose at some stale meat, and Mrs Dalloway chooses flowers on Bond Street.

The Virago Book of the Joy of Shopping revels in the lists, the etiquette and the thrills of finding just the right thing.